DETROIT RESURRECTED

DETROIT RESURRECTED

TO BANKRUPTCY *and* BACK

Nathan Bomey

W. W. NORTON & COMPANY

INDEPENDENT PUBLISHERS SINCE 1923

NEW YORK | LONDON

For information about permission to reproduce selections from this book,
write to Permissions, W. W. Norton & Company, Inc.,
500 Fifth Avenue, New York, NY 10110

For information about special discounts for bulk purchases, please contact
W. W. Norton Special Sales at specialsales@wwnorton.com or 800-233-4830

Manufacturing by Quad Graphics Fairfield
Book design by Nick Caruso

Production manager: Anna Oler
Library of Congress Cataloging-in-Publication Data

Names: Bomey, Nathan, author.
Title: Detroit resurrected : to bankruptcy and back / Nathan Bomey.
Description: First edition. | New York, N.Y. : W. W. Norton & Company, Inc., 2016. |
Includes bibliographical references and index.
Identifiers: LCCN 2016001681 | ISBN 9780393248913 (hardcover)
Subjects: LCSH: Municipal bankruptcy—Michigan—Detroit—History—21st century.
|Financial crises—Michigan—Detroit—History—21st century. | Detroit (Mich.)—Economic
conditions—21st century. | Detroit (Mich.)—Politics and government—21st century.
Classification: LCC HB3754.D47 B66 2016 | DDC 336.774/34—dc23
LC record available at http://lccn.loc.gov/2016001681

ISBN 978-0-393-35443-0 pbk.

W. W. Norton & Company, Inc.
500 Fifth Avenue, New York, N.Y. 10110
www.wwnorton.com

W. W. Norton & Company Ltd.
15 Carlisle Street, London W1D 3BS

1 2 3 4 5 6 7 8 9 0

To Kathryn

CONTENTS

July 18, 2013, was a bad day for Bill Wertheimer's 2005 Saturn Vue to overheat. The crossover vehicle lumbered westward on Interstate 96 in mid-Michigan, its overworked engine straining to make the ninety-mile trek from the Motor City to the state capital of Lansing.

As Wertheimer eased off the accelerator, United Auto Workers general counsel Mike Nicholson typed furiously on a laptop in the back seat, putting the finishing touches on a legal brief supporting an emergency effort to block the City of Detroit from filing the largest municipal bankruptcy in U.S. history.

The two labor attorneys—longtime friends who had marched in picket lines together and spent their careers fighting for union rights—were determined to undermine any attempt by the city to use a bankruptcy to cut benefits for retirees and active workers.

With two hundred thousand miles on the odometer, Wertheimer's Vue sputtered along the pavement, the urgency of the moment unrecognized.

"We pay you enough—get a new fucking car!" Nicholson screamed.

Even for a city whose descent was half a century in the making, minutes still mattered.

Detroit emergency manager Kevyn Orr—who had been installed four months earlier by Michigan governor Rick Snyder as the all-powerful de facto CEO of the city's government—was poised to thrust Detroit into Chapter 9 bankruptcy.

Orr, a Democrat, reported to the technocratic Republican governor. Not the City Council. Not the mayor. Elected officials had been rendered powerless under a controversial state law that allowed

x PROLOGUE: 4:06 P.M.

the governor to seize control of cities in fiscal chaos. The emergency manager had the authority to sever union contracts, dramatically overhaul city government, dispense of city assets, and control the budgeting process.

The son and grandson of African Methodist Episcopal ministers, Orr, a bankruptcy attorney before becoming emergency manager, spent the first several months of his appointment preaching the same sermon over and over: Detroit's financial position is not sustainable, the government is broken, and the city's neglected residents deserve better.

By now the strategy was set. Earlier in the week, Orr had requested the governor's permission to file for bankruptcy and mapped out a plan to file the official documents with the court at 10:00 a.m. on Friday, July 19. Bill Nowling, Orr's mustachioed senior advisor and spokesman, had even sketched a blueprint for a media blitz involving Orr and the governor immediately after the filing. They would barnstorm Michigan news media and the national press in an effort to define the bankruptcy filing as a fresh start for the city, rather than a dead end.

Attorneys for Jones Day, the city's lead restructuring law firm, teed up the appropriate legal documents.

"Not uncommonly, when you're preparing for a bankruptcy you circle a target date for a filing, and we did that here," said Jones Day lawyer David Heiman, the city's lead attorney in the case. "In Chapter 11, we call it a soft landing, so that you continue the operation of a corporation on the day you file as though there was no filing and everything continues to operate smoothly. That's what you strive for."

Wertheimer, Nicholson, and attorneys for the city's two pension plans were hell-bent on injecting chaos into the equation by outmaneuvering the city's legion of restructuring lawyers, consultants, and bankers before the case could begin. They seized the chance to blast a hole in Orr's orderly plans around mid-day Thursday, July 18, when the *Detroit Free Press* reported on its website that a Chapter 9 bankruptcy filing could come at any time. They figured, correctly, that they had a limited window for a surprise attack. Fearing the prospect of unprecedented pension cuts—which Orr had already threatened to help balance Detroit's books—the attorneys immediately devised plans to seek a temporary restraining order, or TRO, preventing the city from filing for bankruptcy.

Nicholson and Wertheimer jumped into the ramshackle Saturn Vue and set out from the UAW's Solidarity House headquarters in Detroit—the same complex where, four years earlier, labor leaders had navigated the historic bankruptcies of General Motors and Chrysler—on a course to the Ingham County Circuit Court in Lansing.

When Nowling discovered that the *Free Press* was set to post a story, he alerted Orr. They headed to Cadillac Place, a palatial state government complex in Detroit that at one time had served as the headquarters of GM, to revise their game plan. They feared that after the *Free Press* story hit the Internet, it would prompt creditors to pursue a TRO to block the case.

"We were very nervous about it," Heiman said. And for good reason. That's exactly what the city's opponents had set out to do.

With no knowledge of the efforts to block the filing, Orr and Nowling called Snyder and urged him to sign a letter immediately authorizing the filing on the assumption that creditors would act after reading about the city's plans for Friday. But the governor resisted accelerating his timeline, embracing a methodical approach to the historic process despite a natural proclivity for expediency. "I'm committed to my process, and this is what we're going to do," Snyder, who had already been reviewing Orr's request for about two days, said on the call.

Nicholson, who once directed the UAW's efforts to protect workers in auto-supplier bankruptcies, knew that a bankruptcy could devastate vulnerable Detroit retirees and union members. Although the union's direct involvement in Detroit city labor negotiations was minimal, UAW president Bob King had taken a special interest in the city's plight and personally directed Nicholson to help fight pension cuts.

On their way to the courthouse, Wertheimer and Nicholson bounced ideas off each other, tweaking their emergency request and strategizing for their appearance before Ingham County Circuit Court judge Rosemarie Aquilina.

An ethical quandary quickly presented itself. They had no legal obligation to alert the City of Detroit or the governor's Republican allies in the Michigan attorney general's office to their sneak attack.

"Mike, do you think we should notify the state?" Wertheimer said.

Reluctant to relinquish the element of surprise, Nicholson nonetheless believed they had an ethical responsibility to say something.

"Yeah, Bill," he told his friend. "It's not in our interest, but I think we have to do that. That's the right thing to do."

They figured that as soon as they placed the call, Orr's team of bankruptcy lawyers would devise a counterattack.

"We knew damn well what would happen," Wertheimer said. "But we didn't feel like we could be in front of Aquilina without giving them notice. We didn't think we could do that ethically."

The pair waited until about 3:35 p.m. before placing a call to alert the attorney general's office that Aquilina would hold a hearing at 4:00 p.m.

Back in Detroit, Orr was initially unaware of the emergency hearing. He had spent the last several days fending off a steady barrage of lawsuits challenging his appointment, the potential bankruptcy, and the city's decision to stop paying its unsecured debts.

Orr had concluded that rehabilitating Detroit without bankruptcy was impossible. He needed a U.S. Bankruptcy Court's protection from the onslaught of lawsuits and creditors. Orr's team had grown impatient at his efforts to entice retirees and financial creditors to reach settlements in lieu of bankruptcy.

"Their view was: 'It's nice you're trying to do this Kumbaya thing and get everybody to work together. But it ain't workin', they ain't listening, and you're starting to lose momentum and the initiative,'" Orr said.

Even so, cities are creatures of state government. Federal bankruptcy law still requires cities to obtain state approval to file for Chapter 9.

Still unaware of the attempt to undermine his plans, Orr joined a preplanned conference call with Snyder in the three o'clock hour to discuss the course of events for the next day's bankruptcy filing, even though the governor had not yet signed the authorization letter.

Suddenly, the door to the governor's meeting room in Lansing burst open. Snyder's lawyer, Mike Gadola, was panting. He caught his breath and spilled the news: Aquilina was poised to hold a hearing that could culminate in an order prohibiting Detroit from filing for bankruptcy.

"As your legal counsel," Gadola told the governor, "I advise you to sign the authorization letter."

Snyder, realizing he may have only had minutes to spare, decided he had thought about it enough. He grabbed a pen and signed the already drafted authorization letter approving the bankruptcy filing.

"We'll fax it," the governor's advisors told Orr's team over the phone.

Nowling sprinted from the emergency manager's suite in the Cadillac Place building to the other side of the sprawling complex to wait by the fax machine. A minute went by. Another minute went by. The emergency hearing was fast approaching.

He dashed off a frantic text message to Greg Tedder, the governor's liaison to the emergency manager's office: "I'm standing right by the fax machine."

The liaison called. "They were concerned the fax machine didn't have the right time stamp on it," Tedder told Nowling.

Tedder scanned the document onto the governor's computer and emailed it to Orr's team with a verifiable digital time stamp of 3:47 p.m.

Nowling hurried back to Orr's office and printed out the authorization letter. Orr signed it in a rush and called Heiman.

"Let's file," the emergency manager instructed.

With the pre-prepared bankruptcy filing in hand, Jones Day attorneys rushed to log onto the web filing system called Public Access to Court Electronic Records, commonly referred to as PACER. As they uploaded the digital documents, the antiquated recordkeeping system crashed.

"Unable to upload file," PACER blared.

"We only filed sixteen pages, but something happened," Heiman said.

Desperate for a solution, associates based at city hall stuffed hard copies into their briefcases and took off on foot for the federal courthouse, a few blocks away in downtown Detroit. At the Cadillac Place complex, attorneys furiously scrambled to reboot the system to take a second crack at an electronic filing.

Meanwhile, the attorney general's office stalled, making a request for extra time to get to the hastily convened hearing in Lansing.

Several minutes passed. The judge and the attorneys waited.

Wertheimer and Nicholson had arrived with minutes to spare—no thanks to the Vue—having left Detroit so fast that Wertheimer had no time to change out of the jeans he was wearing.

"Excuse me, your honor," Wertheimer said. "I apologize for my dress."

"I don't care how people are dressed," Aquilina responded. "It's more important that you are here."

But 4:00 p.m. passed, and the state's attorneys were nowhere to be found.

Minutes later, Thomas Quasarano, an assistant attorney general, entered the courthouse, and the hearing officially began at around 4:10 p.m.

It was too late for the objectors. Detroit's bankruptcy filing had dribbled into PACER while the attorney general's office stalled.

The official time of the filing: 4:06 p.m.

A law clerk dashed off a note to Aquilina, notifying her that the bankruptcy was official.

"Aquilina, of course, was pissed," said Clark Hill lawyer Robert Gordon, lead attorney for the two pension funds that joined Nicholson and Wertheimer in the attempt to block the filing.

Federal bankruptcy law provides debtors a shield against lawsuits. The filing had rendered Aquilina powerless to stop the city's Chapter 9 petition. "It was my intention to grant your request," she told the objecting attorneys.

Heiman, the city's attorney, was relieved. "I think our heart skipped a beat for a while there," he recalled later.

At 4:06 p.m., July 18, 2013, Detroit hit rock bottom.

At 4:06 p.m., Detroit finally had hope.

On the city's bankruptcy petition, moments before the filing was scanned and digitally submitted, someone had crossed out the "9" in "July 19" with a pen.

Orr had quickly scrawled "8," bumping up the bankruptcy filing by a day and changing the course of Detroit's future.

DETROIT RESURRECTED

INTRODUCTION

Everyone has an explanation for how Detroit went broke.

The contraction of the U.S. auto industry. White flight and the exodus of wealth that began in the 1950s. Discriminatory real estate practices. The 1967 riots. Regional political discord. Pervasive gov ernment corruption. A lack of corporate social responsibility. The destruction of black neighborhoods to make room for highways.

Former mayor Coleman Young. Former mayor Kwame Kilpatrick. Former president George W. Bush. Wall Street bankers. A dysfunctional mass transportation system. Shattered public schools. The disintegration of the job market.

Predatory lenders. The Great Recession. A collapse in home prices. Greedy unions. Democrats who were in bed with unions. Republicans who tried to kill unions. Republicans who were in bed with big business. Skyrocketing taxes. A failure to collect those taxes. Crime-ridden neighborhoods. Police brutality. Police lethargy. Drugs. Blight.

Neglectful City Council members. Hapless bureaucrats. Generous pensions. Gold-plated health care benefits. Overspending. An explosion of debt. A culture of denial.

There's truth in all of these, and in their complex interplay. By 2013, Detroit was broke—and broken. The city government had morphed from a municipal services provider into a retiree benefits supplier, distributing about four out of every ten dollars from its budget to fund pensions, pay for retiree health care insurance, and service debt, most of which had been issued to pay retirees. Without drastic action, that figure would balloon to more than seven out of every ten dollars by 2020 and continue rising.

For decades, local politicians had tried quick fixes. In 1962, they enacted an income tax—and proceeded to raise it several times during the next half century. In 1971, they started taxing utility bills. In 1999, they passed a casino gambling tax. On numerous occasions, they hiked property tax rates until they reached the State of Michigan's legal limits. But tax increases—which pummeled businesses, residents, and commuters alike—didn't stave off the city's financial collapse.

Coleman Young, who served from 1974 through 1994, slashed spending in the 1980s in an effort to stabilize the budget. Contrary to conventional wisdom, he had a conservative fiscal streak, spurning debt in favor of fiscal austerity. He laid off police officers and firefighters. He shuttered swimming pools, skating rinks, and even swim-mobiles, metal tanks filled with water that traveled from neighborhood to neighborhood giving kids a place to take a dip. Kwame Kilpatrick, who is now serving a decades-long sentence in a federal prison for racketeering, cut several thousand jobs to balance the city's budget from 2002 through 2008.

Those job cuts, which had devastated basic services, provided temporary relief to the budget but ignored the fundamental source of Detroit's debt crisis. With a severely contracting revenue base caused by population decline and industry disinvestment, the city could no longer afford benefits that so many other communities take for granted. The city allowed pension costs and retiree health care obligations to balloon. Instead of negotiating deals that Detroit could afford, unions repeatedly scored contracts that ignored the city's fiscal reality: retiree benefits consumed the city's budget, redirecting money away from public safety. At city hall, a cascading series of ineffective politicians—who lacked the will, foresight, or ability to make drastic changes—turned to Wall Street to foot the bill for their fiscal recklessness, choosing debt over the hard choices necessary to protect the people of Detroit and ensure the financial security of the city's retirees.

By 2013, Detroit's 688,000 residents—down from nearly two million at the city's peak in the 1950s—faced a humanitarian crisis. Its retirees encountered an insolvent city that could no longer afford to meet its obligations. Most Detroit neighborhoods had devolved into a state of chaos that appeared bizarrely acceptable to the political establishment.

Shirley Lightsey, a 1951 graduate of Cass Tech High School in Detroit, worked for the city for three decades, retiring as a human resources manager in the Detroit Water and Sewerage Department. She was an eyewitness to the monumental collapse in the city's finances and basic services and then, as president of the Detroit Retired City Employees Association, became an eyewitness to the fallout enveloping vulnerable pensioners.

"To have lived through the vibrant Detroit that I lived through and to see what has happened to it and to see the city come to this point without somebody stopping it before now," she said, her voice trailing off. "People don't realize. They've never seen a grand city. And we were a grand city. I was right in the middle of it. It was something to be proud of."

The grim scene in Detroit was cause for panic. The city had more murders in the year before its bankruptcy than Milwaukee, Cleveland, Pittsburgh, and St. Louis combined—386 to 329. That year, the average police response time to emergency calls was half an hour.

By 2013, about 40 percent of the city's streetlights did not work. Tens of thousands of properties were abandoned and dangerous. Rickety buses didn't arrive on time—if at all. The city's information technology systems were so dilapidated that workers would hit "send" on emails that never reached their destination.

About half of the city's residents weren't paying their property taxes—many because they couldn't afford it or refused to pay in protest of the abysmal services they were provided. Few people will pay bills for services they don't receive.

For Detroit's city government, Chapter 9 bankruptcy was a consequence not only of sixty years of social and financial decline— but also of bureaucratic mismanagement, a refusal by unions to acknowledge reality, a failure of Washington to extend a helping hand, a complicit lending atmosphere on Wall Street, and a global economic collapse. But bankruptcy was also a fresh start.

"Every case is about people—people who have made mistakes, had bad luck, did bad things," said U.S. bankruptcy judge Steven Rhodes, who spent nearly three decades handling personal and corporate bankruptcies before overseeing Detroit's case. "And it's about how they tried to get out of it and the mistakes they make when they try to get out of it and the denial they're in."

For Detroit, bankruptcy offered help.

"We Americans believe in the obligation of the community to promote the dignity of its residents and visitors. We Americans believe in the obligation of the community to promote the welfare of its residents and visitors," Rhodes said. "We Americans believe in the mission of the City of Detroit."

If there's any region of America that knows a thing or two about bankruptcy, it's the Motor City. The Chapter 11 bankruptcies and federal bailouts of automakers General Motors and Chrysler in 2009 had saved Michigan from plunging into an economic depression. But the auto industry bankruptcies were considerably different from the bankruptcy of Detroit.

"Relatively speaking, the car companies was a way easier deal," said Ron Bloom, a former member of President Barack Obama's task force assigned to overhaul the auto companies, who later represented Detroit retirees in the city's bankruptcy. "You had a private corporation, you had a clear judicial process, you had the government with a lot of money. So it was pretty easy to figure out how to fix it."

Fixing the City of Detroit was more vexing. "Detroit had the misfortune to go bankrupt about two years too late. If Detroit had failed as part of the failure of the car companies, I'm not so sure that Washington, through TARP, couldn't have found a way to help," Bloom said, referring to the Troubled Asset Relief Program, which had provided bailouts to financial giants and auto companies. "But Detroit had the misfortune to fail when bailouts were passé. We were sort of done with our bailout phase as a government. There was no chance Congress would do this."

For Detroit, help instead came in the form of a technocratic, white Republican governor who called himself "one tough nerd" and a black bankruptcy attorney who identified as a "yellow-dog Democrat."

Their decision to plunge Detroit into the hopeful, but profoundly uncertain, territory of bankruptcy set off a clash in the courtroom and at the negotiating table between the city and its creditors over prospective cuts to pensions, health care benefits, and bond payments. The surprising centerpiece of the showdown was the potential liquidation of the Detroit Institute of Arts, a world-class, city-owned museum with treasured works from artists including Van Gogh, Picasso, Monet, Rodin, and Matisse.

It has become something of a cliché to cite the city's well-worn motto—coined by Father Gabriel Richard in the wake of the 1805 fire that leveled the town to describe Detroit's future: *Speramus meliora; resurget cineribus.*

We hope for better things; it will arise from the ashes.

By any measure, Detroit is still trying to rise. Despite tremendous progress in the downtown and Midtown districts—where business executives Dan Gilbert and Mike Ilitch are plunging money into neglected real estate, and new apartments are bustling with young professionals—Detroit's neighborhoods are still coursing with violent crime, blight, joblessness, and poor schools. It remains exceedingly rare to hear of a family with kids moving into Detroit.

The city may never again be the source of innovation that it was in the early twentieth century, when the auto industry delivered advancements appropriately likened only to today's Silicon Valley. It may never again be a world power as it was during World War II, when Detroit transformed into the Arsenal of Democracy, and manufacturing plants converted into weapons factories built warplanes, tanks, and guns and shipped them off to the Allies.

It may never again lift the soul of American music as it did when Motown produced legendary artists in the 1960s.

But Detroit deserves a chance to rise. It deserves a chance to prove its doubters wrong.

Most of all, the people of Detroit deserve a more responsive city government—a city that prioritizes the health and welfare of its citizens above the health and welfare of union interests and financial creditors.

"As I look at the landscape of cities, there is no city more important to America today than Detroit," said Darren Walker, CEO of the New York–based Ford Foundation, which traces its beginnings to Detroit's industrial boom. "It's because of what Detroit represents in the American narrative. In the American narrative, the idea of cities equaling opportunities, cities equaling jobs and economic opportunity, and cities also regrettably meaning decay and decline—Detroit manifests all of that. So it is symbolically, metaphorically, America's most important city. If we don't solve the challenges of Detroit, we won't solve the challenges of America."

To map out a hopeful future, Detroit first had to wipe out the mistakes of its past.

This is the story of what happens when a great American city goes broke.

CHAPTER 1

The Nerd

Rick Snyder was an academic whiz by the time he met Rich Baird in the early 1980s on the leafy campus of the University of Michigan Law School in Ann Arbor. But he knew little about Detroit.

Born in 1958 in Battle Creek, Michigan, to Dale and Helen Snyder, he lived in a nine-hundred-square-foot home on North 22nd Street as a kid, surrounded by neighbors who worked for the town's cereal giants, Kellogg and Post. He collected cereal box prizes and accompanied his family on summer trips to Gun Lake, a vacation spot between Kalamazoo and Grand Rapids, where he gained a love for outdoor sports.

At age sixteen, he made his first foray into politics, volunteering to help with the gubernatorial campaign of moderate Republican William Milliken.

But academics were his passion. After earning community college credits while still attending Lakeview High School, he convinced an admissions counselor at the University of Michigan to allow him to enroll early as an undergraduate. He sped through college, earning a bachelor's degree and a master of business administration degree by age twenty. Then he enrolled in the University of Michigan Law School and graduated in May 1982 at age twenty-three.

As law school was ending, Baird and Jerry Wolfe, leaders of the Detroit branch of accounting firm Coopers & Lybrand, visited the law campus to interview Snyder. Baird pressed the graduate to outline his long-term career path.

"The vast majority of people would basically say, 'Well, you know, I haven't really thought that far ahead. I'd like to become a partner in your firm.' Or they might say, 'I want to learn about business and tax, I'd like to become a CPA, and we'll see what happens next,'" Baird said.

Snyder had already mapped out a three-part career: business first, politics second, teaching third.

"I sat there kind of blown away," Baird recalled. "I'm not that much older than he is. But it wasn't bullshit. It was clear he had given this a lot of thought."

After the interview, Baird leaned over to Wolfe. "Jerry," he said, "if we only hire one guy this year, we should hire this guy."

Coopers, which would become PricewaterhouseCoopers years later, offered Snyder a salary of about forty-two thousand dollars to join the firm's office in downtown Detroit.

"That doesn't sound like a king's ransom now, but that was an awful lot of money in 1982," Baird said. "We made him the highest offer we had ever made up to that point for any new, inexperienced person coming into the tax practice."

Coopers had competition. After receiving several job offers, Snyder narrowed them down to two: the Coopers job in Detroit and one with oil giant Exxon's tax law department in Houston, Texas. Exxon offered him about 50 percent more.

"I thought, 'We've lost this guy. How can I compete with that?'" Baird said.

But Snyder was torn between the job in Houston and the one in Detroit, which would allow him to stay in Michigan.

"Frankly, I believe that if I went to work at Exxon, I'd end up being a really good corporate attorney, but I wouldn't learn anywhere near as much about business as I would if I came to work for you guys," Snyder told Baird. He accepted the Coopers job.

Snyder's experience at Coopers—where he would meet his wife, Sue—fostered a deeply held belief in the importance of mentorship in the workplace. It also led to lifelong friends and professional colleagues in Baird and fellow Coopers professional Chris Rizik.

"He came into the Detroit office as a superstar already with a reputation of being a really bright guy," Rizik said. "It was a really rough time to be here. But he ended up becoming partner in four years, which was the fastest anybody had ever become a partner in the Detroit office."

THE SCARS OF DEINDUSTRIALIZATION, racial strife, and white flight were still raw in Detroit when Snyder arrived for his job. The twenty-three-year-old transitioned from the comfortable confines of a prestigious educational institution to the rapidly contracting metropolis of the Motor City.

Michigan's economy was in tatters—and Detroit's was worse. The oil crisis of the 1970s and the emergence of Japanese automakers in the U.S. market had exposed the Big Three car companies—General Motors, Ford, and Chrysler—as ill-prepared to adjust their offerings to appeal to consumers who were demanding intelligently designed, fuel-efficient small cars. The fall of the Big Three exacerbated the economic crisis in Detroit, whose population had already plummeted from its 1950 peak of 1.85 million to 1.2 million in 1980. A few months after Snyder arrived in Detroit, Michigan's unemployment rate hit a post-Depression high of 16.8 percent. At city hall, Mayor Coleman Young was aggressively chopping Detroit's budget to help the city remain solvent.

Snyder immersed himself in his work at the Renaissance Center, an insular office complex in downtown Detroit that today houses the headquarters of GM and the offices of many other companies.

"When I moved to Detroit to take a job with Coopers, I knew two people in metro Detroit," he said later. "I'd been to, like, one Tiger ballgame. The riverfront was a disaster. The Renaissance Center was like a fortress."

At Coopers, Snyder met Sue Kerr, a Dearborn resident who was working there as an executive assistant. They married in 1987. Rick and Sue Snyder moved to Chicago to join Baird, who had offered Snyder a promotion to lead Coopers' Midwest mergers-and-acquisitions business. One of Coopers' customers was an obscure and rapidly growing South Dakota–based computer company named Gateway, co-founded by entrepreneur Ted Waitt.

Snyder and Waitt were opposites. Waitt was a ponytailed dreamer. The son of a fourth-generation cattle rancher, he cultivated a free-wheeling culture at Gateway. He famously allowed employees to drink beer in the office, raced his car to work with other employees, and envisioned big things for the company that eventually became famous for slapping cow logos on computer boxes.

Snyder was a straight-laced, no-nonsense midwestern workaholic. He drove the speed limit, followed the rules, obsessed over the numbers. Waitt recruited Snyder to become the top operating executive for his company, which was then on a fast track to an initial public offering.

"Ted Waitt was a visionary, an entrepreneur, a paint-the-sky-blue thinker," Baird said. "That was like a yin and a yang coming together."

In 1991, the Snyders moved to the region straddling the southeast corner of South Dakota and the northwest corner of Iowa. At

Gateway, Snyder absorbed Waitt's penchant for grandiose thinking, and Waitt leaned on Snyder to operate the company. "Ted was really a marketing genius and a visionary. Rick made the trains run on time," said Rizik. "Rick was able to create order in this really fast-growing company. On the other hand, Ted was helpful in Rick developing as a big visionary. They were really good for each other."

Though he did not receive the title of president until 1996, Snyder was effectively the No. 2 executive in the company, helping it grow from 700 employees in 1991 to 10,600 U.S. workers when he left in 1997. "He was kind of the adult supervision," Waitt once said.

The rise of Gateway transformed Snyder into a multimillionaire. He moved back to Michigan, eventually settling in Ann Arbor, where he became a venture capitalist in partnership with his friend, Rizik, and others. Through firms called Avalon Investments and Ardesta, they invested in a wide range of tech companies, including health-care information technology start-ups and medical-device makers. Snyder cut personal checks to pay the salaries of the workers at one of his companies, Ann Arbor–based software firm HealthMedia, when the business turned sour. Years later, he cashed in when the company recovered and soared to a sale for about $200 million to Johnson & Johnson. As a successful venture capitalist and co-founder of an influential economic development group, Ann Arbor SPARK, Snyder was arguably the preeminent business leader in Ann Arbor. But aside from an effort to promote U.S. visas for immigrants who held advanced degrees or who worked at local start-up companies, he was barely known outside of the area and had no meaningful political ties.

His nasally voice, distaste for ideology and negativity, and aversion to neckties did not constitute a good recipe for a political career, despite the plan he had articulated years before to Wolfe and Baird. But in early 2009, Rick and Sue were on a dinner date at the

West End Grill in downtown Ann Arbor. Snyder was uncharacteristically grouchy about the state of affairs in Michigan. That's when Sue suggested that he should stop whining and run for governor.

"The moment that happened, he became single-minded and focused on trying to figure out how to make that work," said Rizik, an ardent supporter. "As his close friend, I was trying to lower his expectations."

Rizik had good reason to temper his friend's hopes. Snyder's gubernatorial prospects were slim. Polls would soon show his support in the low single digits among Republican voters, putting him within the margin of error of zero support. But Snyder committed several million dollars of his personal fortune to build name recognition, portraying himself as the consummate outsider with the business sensibility necessary to rehabilitate Michigan's economy after the GM and Chrysler bankruptcies.

During the Super Bowl in February 2010, voters were introduced to Snyder as "one tough nerd" in a TV commercial that aired in several Michigan markets. He pledged to employ a businesslike approach to uproot the political paralysis in the state capital. With a bizarre slogan—"relentless positive action"—and a campaign bus nicknamed the "Nerdmobile," Snyder appealed to moderates and independents.

At rallies, aides handed out boxes of Nerds candy to emphasize the governor's academic credentials, techie roots, and obsession with spreadsheets. Pledging to overhaul the state's business tax code and calling himself a "job creator," he won the Republican nomination by several percentage points and cruised to a blowout in the general election.

BEFORE SNYDER TOOK OFFICE on January 1, 2011, signs of Detroit's looming financial disaster were painfully evident.

Detroit was facing booming expenses and imploding revenue. It didn't help that the state's own budget crisis reduced the number of dollars that lawmakers were devoting to city budgets in the wake of the auto industry's collapse. The flow of cash from Lansing to municipal governments fell 31 percent from 2000 to 2010, diverting about $4 billion away from cash-strapped cities and townships. Even after he took office, Snyder slashed municipal funding further, part of a comprehensive plan to plug a massive budget deficit that was lingering from the previous administration.

For Detroit, the loss of state revenue-sharing was dramatic. A handshake deal in 1998 between Republican governor John Engler and Democratic Detroit mayor Dennis Archer had turned rotten for the city. In that accord, the city had agreed to reduce its income tax rate in exchange for a steady stream of state revenue-sharing dollars. But state lawmakers backtracked on their end of the deal as Michigan's budget encountered chronic deficits in the 2000s, draining the city of badly needed cash.

Michigan's fiscal crisis nudged the snowball of Detroit's financial collapse a little farther down the hill. As Snyder pondered how to prevent an avalanche, he selected the Democratic Michigan Speaker of the House, a financial specialist named Andy Dillon, to serve as the treasurer in his administration. In their search for solutions, they met an investment banker from New York who was born in Detroit and had his sights set on helping to fix his hometown.

Ken Buckfire lived on Frisbee Street in northwest Detroit as a young boy, a few blocks south of Eight Mile Road, which divides the city from its northern suburbs. His parents moved to the suburb of Southfield when he was five years old, and he grew up sailing on the Great Lakes. After earning his bachelor's degree from the University of Michigan in 1980 and an MBA from Columbia Business School in 1987, he went into investment banking. In 2002, he co-founded New York–based Miller Buckfire & Co., now a subsidiary of Stifel Financial.

Buckfire lives a comfortable life on Park Avenue in New York. But the soft-spoken banker, whom CNBC once called "the turnaround king," delivers uncomfortable truths at the bargaining table, earning him a reputation as an aggressive negotiator interested in getting a good deal for his clients, not making friends. He openly shared a disdain for the ambivalence of suburban, mostly white communities that had profited from Detroit's contraction—namely, towns in Oakland County and Macomb County to the city's north—by building their tax base at the expense of the city's decline. And he blamed community institutions for chronic neglect.

"When the city had problems, no one cared enough to figure out how to solve them. And it had nothing to do with the mayors," Buckfire said. "Look at what happened in New York. New York had a string of terrible mayors. It had terrible problems. But the city came back. Why? Because there were institutions—investors, businesses, universities, hospitals, churches, synagogues—that were dug in and weren't going to abandon the city. The same thing happened in Boston, Chicago, Philadelphia. Name the city. You had a core group of civic institutions. They became the center of gravity. There was no comparable group in Detroit."

What about the Detroit Institute of Arts, a world-class museum that anchors the Midtown neighborhood?

"That's the hobby of a group of rich people who moved to Bloomfield Hills," Buckfire said, referring to a wealthy suburban enclave north of Detroit.

Buckfire believed he could be helpful in Detroit and figured there could eventually be a business opportunity as well. He wrote a letter to Dillon in December 2010 offering to "provide our insights on how Chapter 9 of the Bankruptcy Code can and should be used optimally to managing municipal balance sheets."

"There have been very few examples of Chapter 9s," Buckfire wrote, "and fewer still successful uses. Like its Chapter 11 corporate counterpart, we believe it should only be used on a strategic basis."

Dillon began discussing Detroit's financial crisis with Buckfire. Snyder had by now concluded that to successfully address municipal crises in Michigan, he had to give more powers to emergency city managers. Appointed by governors under a two-decade-old law to take over the financial operations of struggling Michigan cities, emergency managers at the time had minimal powers to force change.

After a battle with public-sector unions, which wanted to prevent emergency managers from obtaining the power to rewrite contracts, the Republican-controlled state Legislature enacted a new law giving emergency managers the ability to usurp the authority of locally elected officials, revoke labor contracts, suspend collective bargaining rights, control budgets, and sell assets.

The strengthened law's concept was simple: when municipal governments—which are subdivisions of the state government—are facing a fiscal crisis, the state can appoint an emergency manager.

In the wake of the Great Recession, which eviscerated property taxes and jobs, Detroit was hurtling toward insolvency, making the city a prime candidate for an emergency manager. Despite the revenue implosion, liabilities continued to climb. Faced with a financial meltdown, the new mayor of Detroit—former NBA star Dave Bing, who was elected in 2009—fired off the financial equivalent of an air ball months into his tenure. He convinced the City Council to authorize $250 million in "deficit elimination bonds," sold primarily to investors on Wall Street to help resolve the city's financial crunch.

Bing laid off a few thousand employees too, but that had no effect on the fundamental source of the city's insolvency: debt service, pension payments, and retiree health care costs had seized control of Detroit's budget. Meanwhile, basic services such as police and fire protection spiraled downward amid massive budget shortfalls, chronic mismanagement, and a disaffected workforce.

Envisioning a financial day of reckoning for Detroit, Dillon gave Buckfire an audience with Snyder in mid-2011. Buckfire proffered that the best way to restructure a flailing municipality is to appoint a single executive who takes charge of the situation, just as a chief restructuring officer does in a corporate context. In Detroit, that would manifest itself as an emergency manager—someone who retains responsibility for the key decisions.

"That's good business," Buckfire said. "That's the way it's supposed to work."

The governor was determined not to allow Detroit to flounder without a sensible plan to restore fiscal order and viable city services. In April 2012, the City Council signed a consent agreement pledging to boost its finances and overhaul its bureaucracy by consolidating departments, modernizing its budgeting system, improving public safety, rehabilitating streetlights, and upgrading public transit, among numerous other steps.

But sharp political divisions and bureaucratic incompetence prevented the city from implementing those changes on its own.

"It could have worked. The problem was that Bing and the Council didn't get along," Dillon said. "They couldn't govern themselves."

The City Council's maneuvering only allowed elected officials to maintain political control of the city for a little longer.

"It became clear Detroit could not fix its problems," Buckfire said. "The condition of the city was so dire that it was likely they would run out of money sometime in 2013."

———

ON ELECTION DAY in November 2012, Michigan voters dealt a blow to the governor's strategy for rehabilitating the state's distressed cities, overturning the strengthened emergency manager law by a margin of 53 percent to 47 percent.

The referendum reflected a brief triumph for unions. But the governor and his Republican allies in the Legislature had anticipated the defeat. Within weeks, GOP lawmakers passed a new emergency manager bill and shrewdly attached a minor spending provision that inoculated the law from public referendums.

The new measure, bulletproof at the ballot box, engendered indignation among some voters. But on the day after Christmas 2012, Snyder signed it into law.

CHAPTER 2

Deal of the Year

In Ernest Hemingway's classic *The Sun Also Rises*, a character named Bill famously asks his friend, "How did you go bankrupt?"

"Two ways," the friend, Mike, responds. "Gradually and then suddenly."

The astonishing deterioration in Detroit's revenue base throughout the second half of the twentieth century was the fundamental source of the city's financial crisis, obliterating Detroit's ability to pay for basic services. But it was a slow bleed, gradually draining more and more of the city's finances over several decades. Toward the end, however, the pace of decline accelerated rapidly, primarily because of the Great Recession and a debt deal that ultimately wrecked the city's budget. Political corruption—often cited as a major contributor to Detroit's financial demise—played only a small role.

According to an exhaustive review of a half century of the city's financial records, the total value (in inflation-adjusted dollars) of private property in Detroit—a good measure of the vibrancy of the economy—plummeted from $45.2 billion in 1958 to $9.6 billion in 2012. But the collapse in Detroit's population and economy, which destroyed tax collections and thus undercut the city's ability to care for its citizens, did not follow a purely linear path.

Some critics believe that the first African American mayor of Detroit, Coleman Young, a charismatic and polarizing Democrat who served from 1974 to 1994, is chiefly to blame for the city's economic collapse. Even today it's not uncommon to hear residents of metro Detroit blame Detroit's demise squarely on Young. While his sharp rhetoric contributed to regional political tension (he once infamously told "pushers," "rip-off artists," and "muggers" to "leave Detroit" in a speech later misrepresented as a proclamation that white people should move out), a close look at Young's mayoralty reveals a surprisingly frugal reign defined by balanced budgets, an aversion to debt, and wars with unions over legacy costs.

Amid Michigan's early 1980s economic mayhem, when the state's unemployment rate hit a post-Depression high triggered by the global oil crisis and the Big Three automakers' crisis, Young was forced to slash the city budget. His tough, but necessary emphasis on fiscal austerity—which included substantial layoffs and cuts to areas such as recreation—stabilized Detroit's books. In fact, for several years during his reign, the city's annual revenue topped its debt load. Young kept insolvency at bay despite the city's population decline of about a half-million residents under his watch, plunging to about one million by the time he left office.

During the post-Young, two-term reign of Mayor Dennis Archer, whose tenure coincided with the booming economy of the Clinton era, the city enjoyed a period of relative stability. Tax revenue was sufficient to pay the bills—and although Archer, facing union opposition, missed an opportunity to reduce steadily increasing retiree costs, Detroit was still solvent when he left office. In fact, the city's pension funds reported a collective surplus as of June 30, 2002.

The city's finances took a sharply negative turn soon after Kwame Kilpatrick became mayor in 2002. Elected at the age of thirty-one after a stint as a representative in the Michigan Legislature, Kilpatrick quickly earned the nickname "hip-hop mayor." He oozed charisma—and the persuasive force of his personality captivated voters. With the physique of an offensive lineman and an electrifying rhetorical touch, the charismatic Kilpatrick inspired Detroit for a time.

But lurking underneath the shimmering surface was a stew of incompetence and corruption. After a sexting scandal exposed by the *Detroit Free Press* in 2008 showed that Kilpatrick had lied under oath during a whistle-blower lawsuit about an affair with a staffer, he agreed to resign and serve several months in prison.

"I want to tell you, Detroit, that you done set me up for a comeback," Kilpatrick proclaimed in a farewell address.

While the sexting scandal occupied the headlines, the Federal Bureau of Investigation was probing a criminal ring headquartered in the mayor's office. The FBI discovered that Kilpatrick had coerced city contractors into diverting at least $73 million in subcontracts over several years to companies owned by co-conspirator and contractor Bobby Ferguson. As a trustee responsible for directing Detroit's independently controlled pension funds, Kilpatrick also leveraged his powerful position to seize more than $1 million in contributions from people who wanted deals with the city or its pension funds. Together, the two friends siphoned cash from the city for luxury vacations, spa trips, exercise lessons, and golf equipment. The investigation snared several-dozen other people, and Kilpatrick was convicted of twenty-four counts of racketeering, extortion, mail fraud, and tax violations. In October 2013 he would be sentenced to twenty-eight years in a federal prison.

Although a criminal conspiracy sent him to prison, Kilpatrick's financial failures sealed Detroit's fiscal fate. To be sure, global forces played a key role in gutting Detroit's economy. A toxic mix of predatory subprime loans, foreclosures, and the collapse of the credit markets during the Great Recession conspired to demolish the city's property tax base. The city's unemployment rate hit about 25 percent by the end of the decade, reducing income tax revenue.

However, despite cuts to the city's operating budget, the underlying driver of Detroit's skyrocketing costs—pensions and retiree health care benefits—remained largely unchanged. Facing a pension shortfall a few years into his administration, Kilpatrick's administration committed its biggest fiscal blunder—a wildly sophisticated borrowing scheme that temporarily improved the city's finances while dealing a deathblow to the budget in the long run. Regarded at the time as creatively structured to preserve jobs and shore up pensions, the transaction later helped plunge Detroit into insolvency.

ON DECEMBER 6, 2005, long before Kilpatrick's ring of corruption was exposed, the physically imposing mayor strode onto the stage of a New York City ballroom to applause. He was soon cradling a trophy that honored his administration for engineering a $1.44 billion borrowing deal unique in Michigan history. Kilpatrick's former finance chief, Sean Werdlow, who had helped devise the terms, stood behind him on the stage, applauding and guffawing.

Detroit had discovered a new way to borrow money. It was the *Bond Buyer*'s Midwest Regional Deal of the Year, a gleaming example of an inventive debt structure hatched during the financial bubble to enrich Wall Street and enable Main Street.

The city had tried cockeyed ideas before. For example, shortly after Kilpatrick took office, the city issued $61 million in "fiscal stabilization bonds"—otherwise known as putting your monthly bills on a credit card. That ill-advised deal involved piling up fresh debt simply to cover the ordinary cost of doing business, such as keeping the city safe.

But this? This was like a subprime loan on steroids.

By law, the city was required to distribute payments to its pension funds to ensure that retirees' monthly benefits could be paid. In mid-2004, the pension funds had accumulated a shortfall of $1.7 billion after poor investments and mismanagement led to a stunning $852 million decline in value in the first two fiscal years under Kilpatrick's reign. The city had to find a way to pay up or accrue interest on the amount it owed. There's no indication that city politicians or union leaders considered devising a plan to pursue reductions in retiree costs to give the city a chance at paying its bills.

Detroit's political leaders had, instead, issued a series of empty promises to workers and retirees, bowing to union pressure instead of embracing sustainable compensation and benefits. Detroit, facing rapidly declining revenue from property and income taxes, could not afford to continue traditional defined-benefit pension plans and costly retiree health care insurance. As retiree promises accumulated unaddressed, the price tag increased at a compounding rate. But no one was willing to admit that reality.

Kilpatrick instead cooked up a scheme to convince the City Council to green-light new debt to pay for pensions. He threatened to lay off at least two thousand city workers—about one-ninth of the city's workforce at the time—to free up enough funds in the city budget to pay pensions.

That was political anathema for City Council members.

"I remember Council members saying, 'These people need jobs,'" said Joseph Harris, the city's auditor general from 1995 through 2005. "The fact that the city had deficits was not even a part of the conversation."

In a shrewd stroke, Kilpatrick conveniently provided an out for City Council members who feared union retribution in the event of massive job cuts. His team had devised a complex borrowing scheme in partnership with the world's blue-chip banks, including UBS and Merrill Lynch. The plan: borrow $1.44 billion in so-called pension obligation certificates of participation, or COPs, to virtually eliminate the city's unfunded pension liabilities. The certificates worked like bonds, promising a steady flow of interest to investors in exchange for upfront capital.

Kilpatrick's strategy simply mirrored business as usual in politics. Let future generations pay the bill while you glean a short-term political boost. But he also had the political sense to concoct a complex structure to disguise his motive: avoiding tough decisions.

With variable-rate, no-down-payment mortgages being distributed to homeowners at a frothy pace, it is not surprising that Wall Street rushed to lend money to what was arguably the nation's most financially distressed city. Detroit was like a homeowner who couldn't afford to pay. But that was irrelevant to the dealmakers. Their principal concern was not whether Detroit could afford the debt payments. Their concern was Detroit's legal capacity to borrow.

Detroit was tapped out.

Under Michigan law, cities cannot carry bond debt totaling more than 10 percent of the assessed value of private property within their borders. In 2005, that meant Detroit was only legally allowed to hold $1.3 billion in bond debt. It was already carrying more than $700 million in general obligation bonds on its balance sheet—traditional municipal debt primarily issued to fund city infrastructure projects—so borrowing another $1.44 billion was untenable. It would cause the city to exceed the state limit. This fiscal reality spawned a legion of lawyers and financial advisors who collaborated to create a byzantine new structure that would make the deal possible.

With the city unable to issue any more traditional bonds, Kilpatrick in November 2004 officially proposed creating two shell corporations to do the deal. The entities—officially called "service corporations"—were fashioned as legally independent of, but financially intertwined with, the city government. The service corporations, which were controlled by Kilpatrick appointees, would contract with a newly created entity called the Detroit Retirement Systems Funding Trust. The trust would sell $1.44 billion in COPs to the banks, which would then sell them to their investment customers.

Two bond insurers—Financial Guaranty Insurance Company (FGIC) and a company that later became known as Syncora Holdings—would wrap the certificates in insurance that would pay out to bondholders in the event of default.

Despite its apparent sophistication, the concept was actually quite simple. Kilpatrick and the City Council took out a jumbo mortgage, gave the sparkling mansion—in this case, a pile of cash—to their politically connected friends, and kept the debt obligation. It was a classic pass-through structure. The city would create new legal entities to issue the debt, making it appear like the shell corporations actually owed the payments. But in reality, the city would always be on the hook for the payments. The shell corporations would simply pass along the city's money to the funding trust, which would then direct the cash to the debt holders.

If it smells like debt and looks like debt, it is debt. But the State of Michigan looked the other way, arguably allowing the city to violate the state's legal debt limits.

In a rare moment of political lucidity, the Detroit City Council was reluctant to agree to Kilpatrick's plan, fearing the long-term fiscal consequences. For months four Council members refused to pass the necessary amendments to city law. They warned that stock market volatility could transform the can't-miss proposal into a budget-buster—and they accused Kilpatrick of political gamesmanship. "Throughout all my research," Council member Barbara-Rose Collins said at the time, "everyone concurs that this type of venture is risky, and it should be implemented as the very last option. I believe we should clean our house first and begin the task of eliminating waste and restructure government. The Kilpatrick administration has known of the problems that we face today for three years. The only solutions that were proposed are one-time fixes."

Residents streamed out of Council hearings in tears, fearing job cuts as Council members repeatedly deadlocked on the deal. The deal's supporters lambasted its opponents. Obstructionists "have decided to gamble the city's future, its reputation, its ability to deliver services, and lastly its credibility by opposing this measure for the sake of political gain, rather than making a decision based on good public policy or in the interest of the city's residents," City Council member Ken Cockrel Jr. said.

The political opposition eventually fizzled after the local chapter of the American Federation of State, County and Municipal Employees union applied pressure to convince the Council to embrace the deal. The city's leaders adopted Kilpatrick's proposal in February 2005.

By any measure, it was an inventive transaction. The cash raised through the deal was split between the city's two pension funds. The COPs effectively promised debt holders a piece of Detroit's cash flow—with fixed interest rates ranging from about 4 to 5 percent on $640 million of the certificates and a variable rate on the other $800 million.

Variable-rate mortgages are typically viewed as a bad bet for a long-term deal because interest rates can rise over time. To address this uncertainty the city decided to lock in a steady interest rate on the $800 million in variable-rate certificates. To do so, it purchased interest-rate swaps, also insured by FGIC and Syncora, effectively obtaining a fixed rate on the transaction and creating more predictability for the city budget. The city figured it was better off paying 6 percent annually on the COPs instead of giving its pension funds the statutorily required 8 percent interest on overdue pension contributions.

Aside from the fact that it was probably illegal, the transaction "made no financial sense," said Ken Buckfire, who became the city's investment banker years later during bankruptcy. The city, Buckfire said, should have acknowledged its pension crisis and realized that borrowing cash would not solve the fundamental issue: the city could not afford the benefits it had promised.

"This didn't have to happen. It's like you're trying to deflect a comet. If you get to it a billion miles away, you don't have to do much to get it to miss the earth. If you get to it 500,000 miles away, it's too late," Buckfire said.

Recognizing the legal sensitivity of the matter in 2005, the city shopped around for a law firm that would review the structure of the transaction. Detroit-based Lewis & Munday wrote an endorsement letter that was included in a prospectus advertising the debt to potential investors. The letter—the kind of document that would generally be considered a formality in a municipal bond offering—sought to justify the deal.

"The obligation of the city . . . does not constitute indebtedness," Lewis & Munday wrote, since Detroit was not pledging its taxing power, revenues, or faith and credit to make the COPs payments.

All three major ratings agencies loved the deal too. The insured certificates, in their estimation, were bulletproof. Fitch, Standard & Poor's, and Moody's all set their initial ratings on the insured COPs at a pristine AAA. The rating on the underlying debt—that is, if the debt didn't come with insurance—was a few notches lower.

On Wall Street the deal earned plaudits and elicited pronouncements from its engineers. Investment firm Robert W. Baird & Co.'s public finance division practically saluted the dubious foundation for the deal in a press release: "The challenge for Baird and the City of Detroit was to demonstrate the city's clear authority to do the transaction, even though there is no single law that authorizes the transaction and there was no precedent in the state of Michigan for this kind of deal."

Over the next several years, the city's budget continued to deteriorate, and job cuts ironically became impossible to avoid. But Kilpatrick's COPs and swaps deal helped put off much of the pain. The city made interest-only payments on the debt for several years, allowing lawmakers to temporarily escape the financial realities of the debt they had embraced. But in January 2009, the city's eroding finances prompted Standard & Poor's to downgrade Detroit's credit rating to junk status, triggering a default in the city's swaps contracts. The default meant the city owed a termination payment to Merrill Lynch and UBS of anywhere from $300 million to $400 million. For a broken city with a general-fund budget of about $1 billion at the time, the termination payment was enough to bankrupt Detroit.

Ken Cockrel Jr., who had assumed the role of interim mayor in the wake of Kilpatrick's resignation, sought an alternative resolution. Cockrel, whose quiet manner exuded a measure of thoughtfulness and sincerity Kilpatrick lacked, understood that the swaps implosion threatened a chain reaction that would force Detroit into insolvency. His administration moved to diffuse the bomb.

Unlike General Motors and Chrysler—which secured bailouts from Washington in late 2008 by drawing on their deep political connections and suggesting that their liquidation would trigger a depression—there was little recognition on Capitol Hill of the city's brush with insolvency. And Michigan was dealing with its worst unemployment crisis in a quarter century and chronic budget shortfalls, making a bailout from the state implausible.

"What we told UBS was, 'Listen, if you take us to court and require us to pay $400 million, we're just going to have to ask the government to allow us to go bankrupt.' The city could declare bankruptcy and they would get maybe pennies on the dollar," said Joseph Harris, who served as chief financial officer under Cockrel.

The city searched for a revenue stream that might make the problem go away. About a decade earlier, officials had welcomed three casinos into the city: the MGM Grand, Greektown Casino, and MotorCity Casino. A reliable, high-quality source of cash, gambling taxes quickly became a crucial source of income for the city government, topping property taxes. Eventually the banks agreed not to demand the termination payment from Detroit— cash they knew the city didn't have. Instead, they accepted the city's pledge of its casino taxes as collateral on the swaps.

Through an arcane new addition to the already byzantine legal structure of the broader transaction, the casinos were instructed to send the gambling taxes every month to a lockbox controlled by U.S. Bank before the money could be passed along to the city government. If the city ever defaulted, the banks would be able to seize the casino money, jeopardizing the most vital source of income for Detroit's government.

Since pledging future taxes as collateral was an altogether novel idea in Michigan, the city cleared the deal with its advisors and a state gaming oversight board.

"I remember the discussions. Our attorneys said, 'Yeah, the law does not prevent this. There's no provision against using that revenue as security,'" Harris said.

The tweak would later haunt the city.

The interest-rate swaps were also rehashed in the 2009 transaction and structured to benefit the banks that held them: UBS and Merrill Lynch. Under the new agreement, the banks could cancel the swaps contracts if interest rates rose above 6 percent, but the city could not cancel the deal if rates fell below 6 percent. A few years later, with U.S. interest rates near zero amid the global financial crisis, the city was stuck with swaps contracts at a 6 percent interest rate. It was the equivalent of a toxic mortgage that could not be refinanced.

The deal transformed the unsecured swaps into secured debt, thus jeopardizing the city's most important source of cash, the casino taxes. (This reflected a devastating change for the city because unsecured debt can be slashed in bankruptcy, while secured debt is typically untouchable. To be sure, federal law gives swaps preferential treatment in some bankruptcies, but Detroit's swaps carried the dubious distinction of a connection to underlying debt that—because the state had limited municipal borrowing capacity—was probably illegal to begin with.)

When assessing the city's budget for Governor Rick Snyder in 2012, Buckfire quickly recognized the potential threat the casino collateral pledge posed. The city was paying 5 percent of its operating budget for the swaps, delivering nearly $50 million in annual revenue to UBS and Bank of America (which had acquired Merrill Lynch during the global financial crisis) and the bond insurers on the deal, FGIC and Syncora. Even more troubling, the banks could move to trap the city's casino cash after the city slipped into a financial emergency, which was considered an event of default on the swaps contracts. This endangered the lives and livelihoods of ordinary Detroiters by jeopardizing a substantial source of revenue used to bolster public safety.

"This is what really got the city in trouble," Buckfire said about the city signing over its casino taxes. "Banks always behave the same way. They always ask for the sun, moon, and stars, hoping to get, like, a little bit of earth. In this case, they got the sun, moon, and stars. They didn't in their wildest dreams expect to get everything they asked for."

For more than half a decade Detroit had been a dream-maker for financial creditors. Until Governor Snyder decided Wall Street had profited enough.

CHAPTER 3

Kevyn Orr

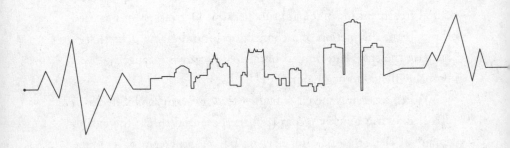

Kevyn Orr's path to the legal profession started on November 22, 1963, at age five. The son of the late Allen Eugene Orr, an Army veteran who later became a minister in the African Methodist Episcopal Church, and Dorothy Jackson, a teacher who earned a doctorate and became a school administrator, Orr grew up near Fort Lauderdale, Florida.

"My dad came and picked me up from nursery school. He was crying. All the adults were crying. I'll never forget it," Orr recalled.

"What happened?" he asked his father.

"They shot the president," his dad replied.

"That's the first time I saw my dad cry. And my one question to him was, 'Why did they kill that little boy's daddy?'" Orr remembered. "So that night, I slept there with him to protect him."

Soon after the assassination of President John F. Kennedy, Kevyn told his teachers that he wanted to be a lawyer, a profession through which he figured he could protect people.

As a schoolboy, Kevyn often traveled to the leafy, 1960s campus of the University of Michigan in Ann Arbor, where his mom was earning her master's degree during the summer. Kevyn and his brother galloped about the beautiful campus, skipping along the Diag, a crossroad of pedestrian pathways fit for pep rallies and student protests, and popping into shops on South University Avenue, where strangers would buy them candy.

"People were really nice. This was in the '60s. Michigan is a progressive institution. So two young little black boys were probably being protected by virtually everyone," Orr said.

But in southern Florida, Orr could not escape the reality of racism. In those days, Fort Lauderdale was largely segregated, Orr recalled, with blacks, working-class whites, and affluent whites separated into three areas by two sets of railroad tracks.

One day during his senior year in high school, Kevyn found his way down to a beach along the Atlantic Ocean.

"Some white surfer boys came up and started calling us the 'n' word. We didn't react. We could've thumped 'em, but we didn't. Some cops came around the corner, and we told the police. We were trying to do the right thing," Orr said.

"We told the cops, 'These guys called us names and assaulted us—why don't you do something?' They said, 'OK, don't worry, we'll take care of it.' So we left, got in our cars, and drove back. We saw the cops sitting out there on the beach laughing with those kids. They thought it was funny."

Orr mapped out plans to escape Florida and run track at the University of Southern California, but his mother vetoed the plan. California was too far away. So he enrolled at the University of Michigan, where he earned his bachelor's degree, followed by his law degree in 1983.

After a stint as a private lawyer in Miami in the 1980s—where he jokingly acknowledges that he was the first black member of the local yacht club—he became an attorney in the early 1990s for the Resolution Trust Corporation, which mopped up the U.S. savings and loan crisis by disposing of distressed financial assets. There, he helped lead the agency's role in the Whitewater investigation.

After a stint monitoring bankruptcy cases for the Justice Department's U.S. Trustee Program, Orr reentered the private sector in 2001 as an attorney and partner for the law firm Jones Day. In 2009, he joined a large team of Jones Day lawyers who helped Detroit-area automaker Chrysler regain profitability and avoid liquidation by slashing dealerships, cutting jobs, and leveraging a government bailout to restructure in bankruptcy.

Although politically powerful dealers were incensed by Chrysler's actions, the episode didn't faze Orr—little does. His cool demeanor and gleaming smile contrast with the disruptive nature of his expertise as a restructuring advisor who must often uproot businesses to save them. He rattles off legalese like it's a second language, but he can speak to regular people with the ease of an experienced politician, peppering public speeches with rhetorical flourishes and private conversations with sharp humor.

He walks with a slight limp that he attributes to a lifetime of pickup basketball, but it appears to unsuspecting observers as something more like swagger. It's an appropriate gait for a powerful bankruptcy lawyer who was headed back to the comforts of southern Florida in early 2013, when the governor of Michigan changed his life.

Jones Day, some of whose partners can earn millions a year, had recently selected Orr to lead its new Miami practice. He had picked out an office for the firm on sparkling Brickell Avenue, which is lined with ultra-luxury condominiums steps away from the ocean. Orr had visions of cruising down to South Beach in a convertible, enjoying the fruits of his labor at age fifty-four. At the time, he was working at Jones Day's Washington, D.C., office and living in affluent Chevy Chase, Maryland, with his wife, Donna Neale, a Johns Hopkins doctor, and their two young children.

When Jones Day submitted an application to serve as the restructuring law firm for the City of Detroit, Orr viewed the Motor City's financial troubles as simply another opportunity for his employer to land a high-profile legal deal. Jones Day's competitors for the job included other top bankruptcy law firms, such as Weil, Gotshal & Manges and Skadden, Arps, Slate, Meagher & Flom. A team of several Jones Day attorneys, including managing partner Steve Brogan and Orr, traveled to Detroit in January 2013 to meet with city advisors, politicians, and several state leaders, including Ken Buckfire, Andy Dillon, and Rich Baird, now a senior advisor to Governor Rick Snyder.

In preparation for the meeting, the Jones Day attorneys conducted extensive research on Detroit's financial disaster and concluded that a deal with creditors to negotiate debt cuts without resorting to bankruptcy was "preferred" for the city but "extremely difficult to achieve in practice." The prospective appointment of an emergency manager to take over the city would "create negotiating leverage" with Detroit's creditors, especially if the leader threatened to file for Chapter 9 bankruptcy, Jones Day attorneys told the governor's advisors in the meeting.

Buckfire had combed his company's internal database for potential emergency manager candidates and delivered names to Baird, who was compiling his own list of candidates. They included recently retired CEOs, executives with experience transforming troubled companies, and consultants. Baird discussed the job with two candidates, who were extremely reluctant to accept the position for fear of personal ramifications.

"We couldn't find anybody who was interested in taking on the role," Buckfire said. "They had to have substantial executive experience. They needed restructuring experience and the willingness to execute a plan with a very high level of public scrutiny and potential acrimony."

And that person would need to withstand the inevitable whirlwind of controversy.

"They would have to be prepared to lead in a combat environment," Buckfire said. "This is like going to war."

Race was a key consideration too.

"We strongly believed that the emergency manager should be an African American," Buckfire said. "Clearly given the political tensions and history of race relations in the city, if the emergency manager was a white person, and even if they were the most qualified candidate, people would characterize the choice as, 'Whitey's taking over the city again.'"

Baird's criteria were similar. He wanted the emergency manager to have an extensive turnaround track record, strong operational experience, deep ties to Detroit or at least to Michigan, and conviction.

"I think I used the term 'titanium backbone'—somebody who had a strong track record of not being intimidated by the various factions that would view this as the most terrible thing in the world," Baird said.

The Reverend Malik Shabazz, a civil rights activist in Detroit, had already inflamed tensions nearly a year earlier by calling on citizens to "burn down the city of Detroit before letting the state take over," labeling the potential appointment of an emergency manager an act of "white supremacy."

No one wanted the job.

So the January meeting with Jones Day was serendipitous. Though Buckfire had worked with several Jones Day lawyers on past deals—including David Heiman, Corinne Ball, and Heather Lennox—he had never met Orr. Nor had Baird.

As Jones Day delivered its pitch for the contract, state advisors asked whether the city even needed an emergency manager.

"And I just went off," Orr said.

"You got to be kidding me!" he had blurted out. "This place is so far beyond the need for an emergency manager. You cannot do this in the regular order. That's pretty clear. Elected officials won't get this done. You've been coming this way for sixty years. You just had six and a half years of kleptocracy. Debt ratios to your income are out of whack. This is a dumb question. You're so far beyond needing an emergency manager, it's not funny."

Baird was spellbound.

"Baird's eyes lit up in the meeting and he says, 'Oh, that's really interesting. Who is that guy?'" Buckfire said.

As the Jones Day attorneys were leaving, Baird leaned over to Dillon, the top Snyder administration official assigned to monitor Detroit's financial situation. "Andy, that's our emergency manager right there," Baird whispered.

Orr was oblivious to the fact that his rant had struck a chord. After the meeting, he even second-guessed his approach.

"Did I go too hard on that?" he asked Brogan, his boss and mentor. "I just got tired of this civil discussion."

"You may have dialed it back a little bit," Brogan said. "But you were candid, and that's what they want. Don't worry about it."

The fact that Orr had no recent connections to the area appealed to Baird. It would presumably allow him to handle the restructuring without emotional baggage. "Everybody realized what an incredibly heavy lift it was going to be," Baird said.

He called Brogan to discuss Orr. Baird told Brogan that Orr seemed like a perfect fit to become the emergency manager, but that he'd have to completely sever his financial ties to Jones Day to ensure he would not profit off the law firm's potential contract with the city.

"I don't think you'd be able to talk him into this," Brogan said. But, Brogan told Baird, you can ask him yourself.

Back at Jones Day in Washington, D.C., Brogan called Orr

into his office. Orr figured it was time to provide an update on lease negotiations for the firm's Miami office, so he stuffed the relevant materials under his arm and walked down the hall.

"Well, I just heard from Rich Baird," Brogan said.

Orr assumed the verdict was in. "Did they make a decision?" he inquired.

"No," Brogan corrected his mentee, "they want to hire you."

Orr reacted exactly according to Brogan's prediction. "No, this is not gonna happen," he said. "How do we do this so we still remain in the running for the work but tell them very nicely, 'Thank you, but no thank you'?"

Fine, Brogan said. "But you should, as a courtesy, call Rich," he told Orr.

Orr tried to let Baird down softly, but the governor's longtime friend and advisor prodded him.

"Would you be willing to talk to your wife?" Baird said. "And before you say no, would you at least come out and meet with us?"

Orr agreed to continue the conversation but remained skeptical. By his own admission, he liked his comfortable life at Jones Day and was looking forward to the pristine beaches, bustling urban nightlife, and economic vitality of Miami.

Becoming Detroit's emergency manager would require Orr to move temporarily to the Motor City, leaving his family at home in suburban Washington, D.C., for long stretches at a time and thrusting himself into a politically combustible situation with a significant risk of failure. It would also require a massive pay cut. The governor's advisors cobbled together private donations to help pay for the emergency manager's living expenses, but that was simply a gesture of goodwill.

"I knew there was no amount of money that we could pay," Baird said.

Orr's inclination was to reject the opportunity. He had only recently convinced his wife, Donna, an accomplished professional of her own, to make a life change by moving to Florida.

But Donna presented an alternative case. She helped Kevyn embrace the opportunity by recognizing that it was a call to service, a chance to make a difference instead of grousing and groaning about the nation's political stasis every Sunday morning during *Meet the Press.*

"Here's your call to action," she told her husband. "Put up or shut up. Do it or don't do it. We'll be fine. We'll work through this."

Baird appealed to Orr's religious upbringing by telling him that God wanted him to do it.

"He saw this almost as a calling. And I think his wife had a very big influence," Baird said. "I started referring to her as Saint Donna. I said, 'Well, tell Saint Donna hello and to keep it up.'"

Still, Orr had yet to meet the governor. Politically, the two were far from a match. For starters, Orr calls himself a "yellow-dog Democrat"—he would vote for the Democrat on the ballot even if it were a yellow dog. He had backed Barack Obama in the 2008 and 2012 presidential elections.

Snyder, the technocratic Republican, had already horrified Democrats and their union allies with a series of moves during his first two years in office. In his most provocative decision, he had signed a so-called right-to-work bill making it illegal to require anyone in Michigan to join a union as a condition of employment.

Despite their political differences, Snyder and Orr clicked. In their first meeting on the fourteenth floor of the Cadillac Place state government building in Detroit, they discovered that they had nearly met three decades earlier as students at the University of Michigan. They realized that as undergrads they had probably been on opposite sides of an epic snowball fight between two dormitories.

Snyder didn't sugarcoat Detroit's crisis. A blistering controversy was inevitable upon the appointment of an emergency manager. And he knew that bankruptcy was a serious possibility.

"There's probably a thousand reasons not to take this job," Snyder told Orr. "But the one reason there is to take it is that you can make one incredible difference in an iconic city. And we are committed to doing the right thing with Detroit."

ACTIVISTS WERE GEARED UP for a battle. "The governor is sending an emergency manager to take care of the corporate interests and the banks and Wall Street," declared the Reverend Charles Williams II, president of the Michigan chapter of the civil rights group National Action Network, as Orr's appointment was rumored in March 2013. Williams said he wanted to tell Snyder to "go to hell."

But on March 14, 2013, Snyder introduced Orr as his pick to become emergency manager for the City of Detroit. His appointment rendered Mayor Dave Bing and the City Council powerless.

At his introductory press conference, Orr sent a message to unions and Wall Street creditors: It was time to stop denying Detroit's fiscal fiasco—and if bankruptcy was the only way to deliver a reality check, so be it. "I don't want to pull that cudgel out unless I have to," Orr told reporters. The threat lingered in the air, an unmistakable forewarning to the city's creditors.

Despite the political enormity of the moment, Orr was clearly cognizant of the job's potential effect on his career, saying it could be "one of the greatest turnarounds in the history of this country."

"It's the Olympics of restructuring," he said.

Presciently, Orr's arrival in Detroit came the same month that a federal jury closed the book on the reign of former mayor Kwame Kilpatrick. In a remarkable twist, the announcement of Orr's appointment as emergency manager occurred only three days after Kilpatrick was convicted in his criminal conspiracy case.

Detroiters were relieved to finally witness the end of the Kilpatrick era, which left behind a trail of financial wreckage, soured ties between voters and city hall, and ravaged the city's global reputation.

In Kilpatrick's wake, Bing had failed to plug the city's chronic budget deficits, though it was almost surely too late to do so. He at least restored integrity to the office. And even in his opposition to the appointment of an unelected emergency manager, he was gracious in acknowledging the need for drastic change. Bing's decision to stand behind Orr at the emergency manager's introductory press conference ensured as peaceful a transition as could be expected, though the now-hamstrung mayor would later grow frustrated with his lack of involvement in the emergency manager's daily decision-making process.

Still, Orr's appointment engendered outrage among activists who despised the governor for displacing Detroit's elected officials and decried the emergency manager for supposedly betraying his racial heritage.

Protestors swarmed city hall. The Reverend Shabazz, who had called on Detroiters to burn the city down, brought Oreo cookies for Orr, a racial insult insinuating that the target is black on the outside but white on the inside. Opponents accused the white Republican governor of trampling the democratic rights of the majority black city.

"As opposed to having a city council that's democratically elected and a mayor, you'll have a plantocracy—a plantation-ocracy—replacing a democracy," the Reverend Jesse Jackson proclaimed a week after Orr's appointment was revealed.

By his own admission, Orr had underestimated the inevitability of racial tension over his arrival. From an academic perspective, he understood it. He had read the preeminent historian Thomas Sugrue's *The Origins of the Urban Crisis*, the defining book illuminating how pervasive racial discrimination contributed to Detroit's urban decay, and remembered hearing stories about racial strife in Detroit when he was younger.

"I didn't realize people would be showing up every day for the first couple of months hanging me in effigy," Orr said.

In one of his first weeks in town, a delivery guy knocked on the door of his condo at the Westin Book Cadillac in downtown Detroit with room service.

"What do people think about this?" Orr asked him.

"Oh, they think you're an Uncle Tom," the African American delivery man responded without hesitation.

That the governor's appointment of the unelected Orr could ignite civil unrest was a serious concern in a city with a history of violent confrontations inflamed by racial inequality, a lack of economic opportunity for low-income residents, and distrust between city hall and the community. As Sugrue had documented, discriminatory federal regulations, racist local real estate brokers, white oppressors in Detroit neighborhoods, and biased employers collectively conspired to marginalize blacks in Detroit for much of the twentieth century.

The clash of simmering racial discontent and a tyrannical police force gave rise to deadly riots in 1967 that laid waste to the city economically, socially, and politically. The violence was by no means the singular cause of Detroit's population decline, which had been under way for about a decade. Many people left Detroit simply seeking a garage, a spacious yard, and better schools. But the 1967 riots helped accelerate the exodus from the city. The departure of whites for suburbs in Oakland, Macomb, and Wayne counties only deepened the racial divide in metro Detroit.

When Snyder portrayed his appointment of Orr as the sensible thing to do for the city's long-neglected residents, racially charged rhetoric was bound to follow, however altruistic the governor's motives. Orr's background as a world-class bankruptcy lawyer made it easy for the city's union leaders and liberal activists to paint him as an elitist outsider.

Detroit's financial crisis was immeasurably more political than the typical corporate restructuring gig to which Orr was accustomed. Facing accusations that he was trampling democracy and crushing union rights, he would need help navigating the thicket from an experienced political operative. So he hired Bill Nowling, who had served as Snyder's campaign spokesman in 2010 and later became a corporate communications consultant, to fend off the swarm of media and public hysteria that enveloped the city.

"Bill, I need your help because I'm not a politician," Orr told Nowling.

Nowling corrected him. "You're a politician," he told Orr. "You're just not elected."

As the months went on, Orr's team quietly seized an opportunity to diffuse the political tension. The governor's chief urban policy advisor, Harvey Hollins, arranged regular, private meetings between Orr and the city's influential black pastors, unbeknownst to the press. The gatherings, which continued throughout Orr's appointment, gave him an opportunity to explain his purpose and his motives.

"My great-granddaddy, my granddaddy, my daddy were all ministers. My daddy was a stump-thumper. He'd go out and build churches. So I'd grown up in a church," Orr said. "So I said, 'Let me speak to the community activists and even my detractors. Let me speak to the ministers in the community because they're the ones who need to see me. And they will make an assessment as to whether or not I'm sincere, or whether or not I'm the evil, sellout Uncle Tom that they think I am. They will get that sense very quickly.'"

The pastors had the people's support.

"Everyone was terrified that the city would burn," Buckfire said. "Because we had every so-called black activist known to man show up in Detroit attempting to stir up trouble. Louis Farrakhan, Al Sharpton, Jesse Jackson, they all visited Detroit. All came trying to characterize the situation as the white man stealing Detroit again. And they got absolutely nowhere because of Kevyn's relationships with the ministers."

Against the backdrop of swirling political outrage, Orr's team was sketching out a plan to rehabilitate Detroit and restructure its overwhelming debt load. To instill confidence in his leadership, it was critical for Orr to deliver a show of force to the city's numerous creditors, including the financial giants blamed by many Detroiters for crushing the city's economy. One of his first creditor meetings was with representatives for one of the bond insurers that had helped Kwame Kilpatrick's administration borrow $1.4 billion. Orr sent an unmistakable message that he had a job to perform—and it would require sacrifices.

As negotiations intensified in early July 2013, Orr told Steve Spencer, a financial advisor for investment bank Houlihan Lokey, which was advising bond insurer Financial Guaranty Insurance Company, that expediency was paramount. Detroit could not wallow in financial despair for an indefinite period, exacerbating the already entrenched sense of hopelessness and preventing the city from acquiring the debt relief it needed to restore basic services to its neighborhoods. Everyone knew that without major concessions, bankruptcy was the city's destiny.

Orr made it clear that the bond insurers would be asked to pay a steep price in exchange for helping the city return to solvency. He offered them ten cents on the dollar for their debt.

"Look, if all you're going to do is fuck the creditors instead of executing a real restructuring, then just tell us," Spencer told Orr.

"Steve, let me be real clear on this," Orr responded. "I'm going to fuck you. The only question is how bad."

CHAPTER 4

Project Debtwa

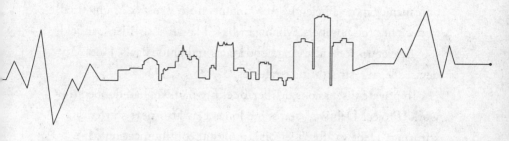

Much of Kevyn Orr's team of consultants, lawyers, bankers, accountants, and bureaucrats was already in place before he arrived. Hired by Mayor Dave Bing and the Detroit City Council while Detroit was trying to avoid the appointment of an emergency manager, the restructuring specialists swarmed the Coleman A. Young Municipal Center, conducting an exhaustive assessment of the city's financial condition and basic services.

Examining the financial books in most municipalities is a standard task. Not so in Detroit. For one thing, some 85 percent of the city's computers were still operating on Windows XP—or even older operating systems—which is not even supported by Microsoft anymore.

About 70 percent of the city's accounting entries were still booked manually. The U.S. Internal Revenue Service in 2012 had declared the city's income tax collection systems "catastrophic"—in part because of ancient software. The city had no way of knowing how much cash it was taking in every month.

Basic services that residents of most U.S. cities take for

granted—tax collection, payroll, and human resources, for example—consistently faltered because of a lack of adequate information technology. Confronted with chaos, investment bank Miller Buckfire designed a general restructuring strategy and began exploring deals to monetize the city's assets and reach debt settlements. A local firm, Conway MacKenzie, dispatched restructuring consultants to identify ways to operate the city government's sprawling bureaucracy more efficiently. Accountants from Ernst & Young tried to decipher the numbers. Michigan-based law firm Miller Canfield sought avenues for addressing bond issues and union deals. Jones Day devised legal restructuring strategies.

In private discussions, Miller Buckfire bankers had dubbed the work "Project Debtwa," and some Jones Day attorneys started substituting "Debtwa" for "Detroit" in digital communications. It was a play on Detroit's French roots, through which the city gets its phonetic French pronunciation: "Day-twa."

In Debtwa, payments to bondholders, banks, and pensioners were prioritized over investments in public protection and government services. By the time Orr's team arrived, the city found itself confined to a twenty-first-century version of debtor's prison, unable to escape the compounding sting of past promises it could no longer afford. To return the city to solvency and restore basic services, Orr embraced an unorthodox strategy. Guided by a municipal theology dictating that citizens are holier than creditors, he prioritized a massive reinvestment push to restore basic services.

Chuck Moore, the lead Conway MacKenzie restructuring advisor for the city, was charged with designing a plan to provide hope to the city's neglected residents. With carefully coiffed red hair, boy-next-door looks, and a steadfast commitment to ethics, Moore eschews harsh rhetoric in favor of facts. But he quickly became appalled at the dilapidated state of city services.

"The lack of reinvestment and the state of operations was so poor, we started to raise the issue that without massive reinvestment and hiring we weren't sure how the city would continue to provide services," Moore said. "It was already to the point where even basic things weren't getting done."

Detroit was an exceedingly violent place, with crime concentrated in impoverished and blighted neighborhoods—not downtown, where most of the city's economic activity was concentrated and visitors clustered. The city's violent-crime rate in 2012 was five times greater than the national average, but police response times were nearly three times worse than the national rate. On average, it took about thirty minutes in 2012 for the Detroit police to arrive on the scene of a high-priority call, compared with eleven minutes nationally. (Widespread reports of one-hour response times were based on an unusual spike in the first half of 2013 that was skewed based in part on the dismal performance of one precinct.) In 2012, the crimes reported included 386 murders, 441 rapes, 4,843 robberies, 9,341 aggravated assaults, 40,956 property crimes, 13,488 burglaries, 15,986 larcenies, and 11,500 motor-vehicle thefts, according to the FBI's Uniform Crime Reporting Statistics database.

Many incidents languished unreported because the Detroit Police Department couldn't or didn't do anything about them. The police solved only 39 of the 344 murders in the city in 2011, reflecting an abysmal 11 percent clearance rate. That compared with clearance rates of 35 percent in Cleveland, 50 percent in Pittsburgh, 66 percent in St. Louis, and 67 percent in Milwaukee—all of which, like Detroit, are Rust Belt cities with several hundred thousand residents.

The city government had slashed 40 percent of its police workforce over the previous decade. Those officers who remained experienced low morale, leadership instability, dilapidated emergency equipment, and insufficient information technology to identify crime hotspots and communicate with colleagues.

Meanwhile, about 40 percent of the city's streetlights were not working—in many cases because thieves had stripped copper wire out of the infrastructure to sell on the underground market. Cleveland, Pittsburgh, St. Louis, and Milwaukee all had at least twice as many working streetlights per square mile.

Blight festered. A groundbreaking study in 2014 estimated that Detroit neighborhoods had 84,641 blighted structures or vacant lots that would require about $850 million to completely eradicate. That's about one blighted residential property for every eight residents.

More than an eyesore, blight operates like a cancer. It diminishes property values and creates a haven for criminals. But it's also a drain on government. About 60 percent of fires in the city occurred in blighted or abandoned structures, diverting crucial fire and emergency resources away from protecting city residents.

"If you think your neighbor painting their house the wrong color impacts the potential value of the single largest asset most Americans will ever buy, which is their house, imagine what it's like living next door to a house that's burned out with a falling down roof with a tree growing out of it. Why would anyone want to move next door to that? That's not rational behavior," Orr said.

Orr considered asking the governor to declare a state of disaster in Detroit because of rampant blight, which would allow Michigan to request special federal disaster relief funds.

"Certainly we qualify, if there's ever a city in the United States that qualifies," Orr said. "But do we want to do that to the city and have the story be, 'The city's in a state of disaster'?"

The city government was still rife with inefficiency and even corruption in some pockets. For example, more than a third of the city's unemployment compensation applications were "highly questionable," with about 13 percent of the applications coming from people who had never lost their jobs or were never even employed in city government, according to the city's inspector general. In some quarters of the city bureaucracy, customer service languished because of a disaffected workforce. In the Department of Transportation, unsafe conditions on buses, where drivers feared unruly passengers, and complacency among vehicle maintenance workers led to a 35 percent employee absenteeism rate on an average day.

"We all looked at each other and said, 'Oh my god, what do we do with this?'" said Heather Lennox, one of the lead Jones Day attorneys. "Things were bleak. They were probably bleaker than people thought. You couldn't hide it. The only way you could restructure the city was to have an honest conversation with people: 'Here are the facts. We're confident you won't like them.' But if you don't tell people the real story, you can't get anything done."

Orr and Ken Buckfire convinced Governor Rick Snyder to approve their core strategy: pursue reductions to pensions, health care liabilities, and bonds—and use the freed-up cash flow to help revitalize the city.

"Kevyn was a great battlefield general, and I was his strategist, but everything we did was ultimately approved by Governor Snyder," Buckfire said. "The governor totally understood it would be pointless to go into a bankruptcy and focus only on allocating the revenue pie between the retirees and other creditors without taking into account the needs of the city."

Chuck Moore and Ernst & Young advisor Gaurav Malhotra concluded that the city needed about $1.25 billion in reinvestment over the next decade, with a heavy emphasis on blight removal, public safety investments, and information technology upgrades. The reinvestment plan would come first. What was left would go to creditors.

"If you simply assume that you've got a billion in tax revenue and someone's going to get it but you're not providing services, inevitably there will be one person left in Detroit who's supposed to pay a billion dollars in taxes," Buckfire said. "So it's ridiculous to have that discussion with creditors, although that's all they ever wanted to talk about."

Orr called the city's biggest creditors—including banks, bond-holders, and unions—to a meeting on June 14, 2013, at the Westin hotel connected to the Detroit Metropolitan Airport. In a two-hour, closed-door meeting, Orr delivered the harsh reality: Detroit was facing insolvency. About 42.5 percent of the city's meager budget was dedicated to paying for retiree health care benefits, pensions, and other debt, including former mayor Kwame Kilpatrick's disastrous certificates-of-participation and swaps deal. By 2017, if nothing changed, about 64.6 percent would be devoted to those legacy costs. In that doomsday scenario, it was hard to envision anything but a sharp devolution into lawlessness, with dwindling dollars for public safety.

Detroit's pension shortfall and unfunded retiree health care liabilities collectively totaled $9.2 billion, according to the city's estimates. That equaled roughly nine times the city's annual core budget. Imagine directing your entire paycheck for nine consecutive years to pay off your credit card debt, without conserving a dime for anything else.

Orr simply told the sobering truth in the hotel meeting: significant cuts to all of the city's unsecured debts, including pensions and retiree health care benefits, were necessary to rehabilitate services. His opening offer—delivered in the airport hotel meeting—amounted to about ten cents on the dollar for all unsecured creditors, who don't have the benefit of collateral afforded to secured creditors. Orr's plan was to effectively treat all the unsecured creditors the same. This was a controversial approach because financial creditors believed their debt deserved higher priority and pensioners believed their checks could not legally be touched.

"People didn't like it. No one liked it," Buckfire said.

But it wasn't personal.

"Who gets up in the morning and says, 'I think I'll cut pensioners today,' as they're brushing their teeth?" asked Bill Nowling, the emergency manager's senior advisor and spokesman, gesturing with an imaginary toothbrush. "Who does that? Nobody does that."

INSIDE THE COMFORTABLE confines of the air-conditioned Westin, with jet engines whirring outside, Orr delivered another jolt to the few hundred creditors in attendance. The city would not make a $40 million payment due that weekend on the COPs debt engineered by the Kilpatrick administration. Because for years the city made interest-only payments on the debt, it still owed $1.43 billion in principal out of the original $1.44 billion. But the COPs debt was fully unsecured and had dubious legal standing, making it an easy target.

"We were the constituency that people were going to try to destroy," said Steve Spencer, a financial advisor for investment bank Houlihan Lokey, which was representing COPs insurer Financial Guaranty Insurance Company.

The move would put the city in default. But if creditors didn't accept deals, Orr was ready to green-light a bankruptcy. The one-sided nature of the meeting irked labor unions accustomed to long, pound-the-table negotiations. Index cards were distributed to attendees for questions, but creditors weren't allowed to speak. They recoiled in disgust.

"I have never, ever been in negotiations where only one side speaks," said Mike Nicholson, the general counsel for the United Auto Workers union.

After the meeting, Orr instructed creditors to make counteroffers.

Secured creditors—that is, the water and sewer bondholders, for example—would get 100 percent of what they were owed because they bargained for it when they bought the bonds. Their debt was backed by specific revenue streams. Everyone else would get less. The unsecured creditors suddenly recognized their precarious position. Orr wanted to vaporize their holdings and use the leftovers to upgrade city services.

His team's proposal carved out $1.25 billion over ten years to tear down abandoned and blighted homes in Detroit, hire more police officers, invest in crime-fighting equipment, modernize fire-fighting gear and facilities, upgrade transit infrastructure, and install new information-technology systems. The funding would cover urgent needs. For example, because of a lack of simple software systems, police were forced to spend a staggering amount of time on manual paperwork, keeping officers off the streets for long stretches at a time. Police officers lacked simple things such as Tasers, business cards, and modern communication systems.

"There was no sharing of information between precincts," Moore said. "That, to us, was amazing. Bad people don't stay within the confines of a precinct. Police officers were essentially being asked to do a job with one hand tied behind their back."

For the fire department, the situation was similarly dire. An emergency alert system had malfunctioned years earlier, requiring firefighters to find creative substitutes using a mix of doorbells, coins, hinges, and other items. At one station, firefighters had jerry-rigged a fax machine to print out notifications that knocked an aluminum soda can to the ground, alerting the station to emergencies.

"The city has to continue and the residents of the city have a right to minimum services and have their needs met. If you don't have policemen who can respond or firemen who can respond, then the city is not living up to its responsibility," said Jones Day's David Heiman, the city's lead attorney. "You must first provide for your citizens. Otherwise everything's going to fall apart. The decline in population and flight from Detroit would only get worse and worse and worse."

FOR DECADES, Detroit politicians and pension officials had made promises they could not fulfill. The bill for those pension promises came due in 2013. Collectively, the pension shortfall totaled about $3.5 billion, Orr estimated at the creditor meeting.

The sheer number of pensioners was staggering. Altogether, 32,427 people were entitled to a monthly pension check from Detroit, more than three times the size of the city's current workforce. Of those, 21,172 were retirees, 8,930 were active employees who were already vested in a pension, and 2,325 had inherited a retiree's pension in some capacity. Four people were still receiving pension checks on the account of someone who retired in the 1950s, including one person living in Glennie, Michigan, who left Detroit's workforce in 1952, an astonishing sixty-one years before the city toppled into bankruptcy.

While the total number of pensioners was unsustainable for Detroit's budget, individually few pensioners were raking generous benefits. The average annual pension for a general city retiree or beneficiary was $19,213. The average annual pension for police officers and firefighters—who don't receive Social Security because they didn't pay into the system—was $30,607.

Pensioners had relied entirely on city leaders and the goodwill of their board members—usually union activists or sympathizers—to ensure the health of their pensions. For years, the city had allowed those pension boards to manage their own investments and set their own fund distribution policies. It was a recipe for mismanagement, secrecy, corruption, and incompetence.

Corruption dogged the pension boards—called the General Retirement System (GRS) and the Police and Fire Retirement System (PFRS)—as part of former mayor Kwame Kilpatrick's criminal conspiracy. In December 2014, Jeffrey Beasley—an ex-fraternity brother of Kilpatrick, former city treasurer, and a member of the city's two pension boards—as well as former pension fund lawyer Ronald Zajac and PFRS board member Paul Stewart were convicted of conspiring to defraud the pension systems by soliciting bribes and kickbacks from investors. Their conspiracy, which they coordinated with Kilpatrick, cost the city's pension funds more than $97 million, according to Federal Bureau of Investigation estimates.

The FBI and federal prosecutors alleged that Beasley had accepted cash, trips, meals, concert tickets, massages, private flights, and other gifts in exchange for steering more than $200 million to certain investments. Stewart pocketed similar gifts, including a $5,000 casino chip and a Christmas gift basket stuffed with cash.

But corruption was not the primary reason for the underfunding of Detroit's pensions. Plain old mismanagement was principally to blame. A substantial portion of the city's pension shortfall was attributable to long-running practices that had only recently stopped: a diversion of city pension funds to workers' annuity accounts, and the so-called 13th check. This was not a function of corrupt officials or secrecy. The city, in fact, had known about it for years, and only a few people had tried to stop it.

As an extra benefit, the pension boards had long allowed active union members to voluntarily contribute to annuity accounts. All the annuity funds were comingled with the city government's pension contributions and invested together, meaning the annuity accounts enjoyed the overall gains of the pension funds. This, on its own, was not controversial. However, in some years general pensioners were credited with more interest in their annuity accounts than the city earned in its traditional pension investments. This practice bilked the city's own retirement investments, exacerbating the pension shortfall and increasing the beleaguered city's bill. In 2009, for example, the city's pension funds lost 24.1 percent of their value, but pension board members credited annuity accounts with 7.9 percent in interest, effectively swiping cash from the city and stuffing it in the pockets of active union members. In some years retirees would get a 13th check, one more than their usual yearly twelve, when investments exceeded expectations.

Combined, the annuity credits and 13th checks severely compromised the health of the pension funds because in years when the investments lost money, the besieged city budget was the only source of new funding for the pension systems. All told, pension board officials diverted more than $1 billion in pension payments to retirees and active employees from the mid-1980s through the early 2010s.

When Chuck Moore discovered the severity of the practice, he was taken aback. One pensioner, for example, had contributed about $100,000 of his own money to his annuity fund. With standard investment practices, his annuity investment should have equaled about $400,000 by the time he retired. But after years of excess annuity interests, the pensioner received a lump sum of $1.4 million when he retired.

"There were many, many hundreds of instances like this where plan assets were just streaming out the door," Moore said. This "had been going on for a very long time and created hundreds of millions, if not billions, of dollars going out the door that never should have."

In the 1990s, Mayor Dennis Archer had tried and failed to stop the practice with a ballot initiative. One of his budget officials, Ed Rago, was disgusted by the practice, which, he recognized, put additional pressure on the city's budget. By law the city was required to eliminate shortfalls in the pension funds. But pension board officials distributed bonuses to pensioners instead of putting all the cash back into the pension systems to ensure that future retirees would not face a shortfall. The pension officials favored a short-term boost over long-term gains.

"It's always been a bug in my ass. Always angry about that," said Rago, who was also a budget official in the administration of former mayor Coleman Young.

If those funds had been reinvested over time instead of being doled out to pensioners, the city would have had an estimated $1.9 billion in additional pension funds as of 2011, according to an actuarial consultant's estimate. With stock market gains, that figure would have almost certainly topped $2 billion by 2013, thus limiting the impact of Detroit's troubles on pensioners.

"It would have been a much, much different situation," Moore said.

By 2011, the City Council and Mayor Dave Bing recognized that these pension practices had siphoned huge amounts of cash from the city's meager budget. They adopted an amendment to the city charter that outlawed the bonuses. But the damage had been done.

By the time Orr had arrived, the composition of the Detroit pension boards had almost completely changed. The trustees who authorized sour investments, approved the distribution of excess earnings to pensioners, and accepted bribes were gone.

The new trustees had taken steps to improve their investment practices and prevent corruption. But politically the pension boards were still tainted, giving Orr a rhetorical advantage in the press. Days after his airport hotel meeting with creditors, Orr ordered an internal probe into the pension boards to root out corruption and threatened to use his powers as emergency manager to remove some board members. Media coverage put the pension boards under a microscope.

The thoughtful but hard-fighting bankruptcy attorney for the pension boards, Clark Hill lawyer Robert Gordon, was exasperated as Orr took aim at board leaders.

"I was begging the Jones Day guys to rein in Kevyn," Gordon said. "I said to them, 'What is going on here? You're fomenting something. You're getting my constituents all upset and angry and we haven't even sat down and talked with you yet. How is that helpful?'"

Still, Gordon advised the new pension board members to keep their mouths shut, despite Orr's media blitz.

"You're never going to win in the court of public opinion right now," Gordon said he told the board members. "No one thinks you guys are a wonderful and empathetic character here. So forget it. Let's not go there."

SIMPLY TRYING TO ESTIMATE the size of Detroit's pension shortfall illustrated the depth of the city's financial two-step. In the corporate world, generally accepted accounting principles govern pension bookkeeping, making it difficult to skew the impact of legacy benefits. But government accounting standards historically allowed cities to disguise the full effect of these costs on their budgets.

"The problem is government pensions aren't regulated, so they can do whatever they want," said Lennox.

What's more, actuarial assessments for pension funds are part mathematical science, part fortune-telling. Actuaries try to predict the future by applying formulas to project investment returns and mortality rates among pension holders. This allows employers to estimate their pension costs. But actuarial methods involve a surprising amount of guesswork, sprinkled with a heavy dose of worldview.

What is a reasonable rate of return to expect on your investments? Anyone with an online investment account knows that past performance isn't an indicator of future results. Responsible families, businesses, and governmental entities project conservative rates of return to avoid unexpected shortfalls when the stock market doesn't perform well. In 2014, the top 100 publicly traded U.S. companies with pension plans projected annual rates of return of 7.3 percent, according to actuarial firm Milliman.

In Detroit, Orr's team concluded that by projecting average annual investment-return rates of 7.9 percent and 8 percent, the two pension funds had made their collective shortfall look a lot smaller than it really was. Why? The higher the assumed rate of return, the less money governments have to contribute to keep their pension funds healthy. With an expectation of high rates, there's an assumption that investment increases will be sufficient to meet future pension obligations. This offers governments little incentive to accurately report the health of their pension funds. By simply maintaining an artificially high projected rate of return, they can lower their annual costs and spend money on other priorities.

Although Detroit's investment expectations are typical of government pension funds, many of these funds, such as Chicago's, are mired in funding crises. Government pension plans projected average return rates of 7.68 percent in 2014, according to the National Association of State Retirement Administrators. That contributed to what Moody's Investors Service concluded was a $1.4 trillion unfunded pension liability for government pension plans in 2013.

Like many other pension funds, Detroit's pension boards also used a polarizing actuarial technique called "smoothing" to spread out investment losses over a long period of time, instead of recognizing the losses immediately. The smoothing process—an actuarial form of lessening the impact of underperforming investments—further masked the seriousness of the pension shortfall in Detroit and allowed the pension boards to obscure the consequences of irresponsible investments.

The shortfall was far greater than the city could afford. A city that was taking in only about $1 billion in total annual revenue through its general fund owed more than three times its entire budget to pensioners. With Orr offering to pay pennies on the dollar to unsecured creditors, retirees feared the cuts could translate into pension reductions of more than 50 percent.

Furious pension officials suggested the city had skewed the numbers to justify pension cuts, pointing out that most government pension plans had similar investment-return assumptions. But Buckfire, the city's investment banker, said the shortfall was a reality the city could no longer deny. As the city neared bankruptcy, the end result of decades of questionable pension practices and economic decline was becoming clear.

"They had grossly underestimated their liabilities and overestimated their assets," Buckfire said. "It's the way they ran these things. No one had bothered to tell them before. We told them the truth."

CHAPTER 5

Chapter 9

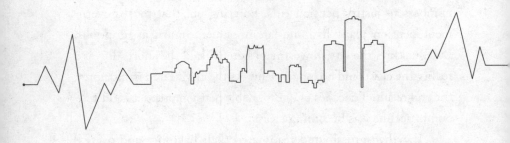

If bankruptcy is a stormy sea, bankruptcy attorneys are pirates who roam the waters. They implacably navigate waves, occasionally plundering their unsuspecting targets and defending their own turf against threats. They pop up suddenly when an opportunity presents itself, identifying hidden weaknesses in their opponents.

They adhere to their own shared honor code—federal bankruptcy law—and speak with a peculiar lingo. They are strangers to all lands, parachuting from spot to spot and spending long stretches away from home. Their alliances are constantly shifting, and they don't typically take things personally because, after all, it's just business and engagements rarely last long. Yet in some quarters, legendary rivalries flourish. Occasionally, bankruptcy attorneys try to demolish their opponent's client in relentless pursuit of a victory. And they're well acquainted with life-and-death scenarios. Sometimes heroes morph into villains, and villains become saviors.

It's a small sea too. Many professionals in the restructuring world interact with each other constantly, sometimes collaborating on cases and sometimes warring. From an outsider's perspective, it's often hard to tell which ones are friends and which ones are enemies. They say things they don't mean and mean things they don't say.

The city's lead law firm in Detroit's bankruptcy was Orr's former employer, Jones Day. At rates of approximately $1,000 per hour for the highest-level lawyers, Jones Day attorneys get paid handsomely to handle the most challenging legal situations. (Attorneys representing the city's biggest financial creditors earn similar rates, though bankruptcy lawyers for the city's labor creditors generally earn hundreds of dollars per hour less.)

The top attorneys assigned to lead Detroit's restructuring included David Heiman, Bruce Bennett, Heather Lennox, and Corinne Ball, but they drew on a support system of dozens of other Jones Day litigators, negotiators, associates, and strategists.

As one of the founding members of Jones Day's restructuring practice, Cleveland-based Heiman had a breadth of bankruptcy experience that made him the leader. He devised strategy and delegated authority to address the countless spokes of the complex case. His calm demeanor fits comfortably within tailored dark blue suits that balance against stately gray hair.

Bennett, a denizen of southern California, had recently represented the Los Angeles Dodgers in the club's bankruptcy sale after the baseball team filed for court protection in 2011. But it was Bennett's role in the 1994 Chapter 9 bankruptcy of Orange County, California, that established him as arguably the nation's leading municipal bankruptcy litigant. He had joined Jones Day in 2012, exiting Dewey & LeBoeuf amid the law firm's financial implosion.

Cleveland-based Lennox was fresh off a sizzling battle in the bankruptcy of Hostess, which she represented. After the junk-food manufacturer failed to reach a deal with its employees, its unions were obliterated, though the company's Twinkies were eventually revived under new ownership. New York–based Ball had spent considerable time in Michigan as the lead Jones Day lawyer on auto-maker Chrysler's 2009 bankruptcy case, working on a team that included Heiman and Kevyn Orr.

When Orr instructed the City of Detroit to stop paying its unsecured debts and liabilities, it was like waving a red flag to the pirates of the bankruptcy world to descend upon Detroit for battle.

To a Chicago attorney named Stephen Hackney, Orr's move was a clear sign that it was time to act. Hackney, a partner for the esteemed global law firm Kirkland & Ellis, is a trial lawyer special-izing in litigation in restructuring and private equity cases. After graduating from high school in East Lansing, Michigan, Hackney earned a bachelor's degree from Rice University in 1994 and a law degree from the University of Chicago in 1997. His short-cut black hair, oft-furrowed brow, and athletically slender build give him the look of Agent Smith, the super-villain of *The Matrix* trilogy whose commitment to his cause would be deserving of scorn if it weren't admirable for its pure relentlessness.

Hackney's voluminous vocabulary stretches from Latin legalese to street-sensible dialect, making it easy for him to converse with the world's top corporate attorneys or connect with ordinary peo-ple. But it's his unwavering gaze in court hearings and in everyday conversation that reveals his ability to, simply, listen to whoever is speaking.

After Orr's proposal to creditors, Hackney jumped to defend his obscure client, a bond insurer called Syncora. Orr's pronounce-ment meant the city would not make a $40 million payment owed to investors holding its pension obligation certificates of partici-pation, or COPs. That was crushing, albeit not unexpected, news for Hackney's client, which had years earlier insured then-mayor Kwame Kilpatrick's COPs and swaps deal. The Bermuda-based Syncora insured or owned about $400 million in Detroit's COPs debt and insured the underlying swaps on the COPs debt. Fellow bond insurer Financial Guaranty Insurance Company, or FGIC, had insured most of the rest of the COPs and swaps.

When Detroit stopped sending payments on the COPs, thus defaulting on the debt, Syncora and FGIC were on the hook to make up the difference by compensating investors. That awoke the street fighters at Kirkland & Ellis, whose rivalry with Jones Day is nearing legendary status in the legal profession. Kirkland's lead restructuring attorney, James H. M. Sprayregen, who was known in the insolvency industry as the "godfather of restructuring" for his outsized role in many major bankruptcies, dispatched Hackney to battle the city.

"He's a very smart, capable, aggressive guy who doesn't wilt under pressure," Sprayregen said. "And that's what we needed because we knew he was going to be the bad boy in the courtroom—the Darth Vader or whatever you want to call it. It wasn't just Hackney. It was the war machine. But Hackney was the general."

He was the general for a cause with little public support in Detroit. But Syncora had its own problems. A smaller insurer than FGIC, Syncora was believed to be facing potential insolvency if Detroit crushed the COPs. Its stock plunged to forty-eight cents per share as Orr made it clear to the markets that the city had no plan to treat Syncora with a soft touch.

Meanwhile, the city continued to make payments on the interest-rate swaps connected to the COPs. The swaps required the payment of more than $4 million per month to Bank of America Merrill Lynch and UBS. The city was quietly negotiating a settlement with those banks—legally called swap counterparties—to rid itself of the swaps.

Syncora's reaction was swift. Hackney concluded that the city's failure to make a payment on the COPs also triggered a default on the swaps. He immediately identified the city's weak spot: it had pledged its steadiest source of revenue—gambling taxes—as collateral on the interest-rate swaps insured by Syncora and FGIC. Three days after Orr's June 14 proposal to creditors, Hackney sent a letter ordering U.S. Bank—keepers of the city's casino-tax collateral—to trap the taxes indefinitely and not release them to Detroit.

"No one is talking to us," Hackney said. "We just don't know what the heck is going on, so we trap the cash. That's the next step to get someone to talk to you."

Like pirates loading projectiles into a cannon, Syncora immediately drew the gaze of the enemy ship across the water.

"We offered an olive branch on June 14 and asked for peace," Orr said. "They fired the first shot. And we said, 'We ain't gonna be your bitch. We aren't gonna be punked by anybody. So let's lawyer up. You want a fight? Let's have at it. Let's have a fight.'"

After a round of negotiations in New York over the COPs debt failed to deliver a settlement, Hackney left for an Independence Day vacation in Whitehall, a sleepy tourist town on the eastern edge of Lake Michigan.

But on the day after the Fourth of July, the city popped a surprise lawsuit on Syncora in a Michigan court, accusing the insurer of improperly attempting to seize the gambling taxes and requesting a temporary restraining order, or TRO, that would force U.S. Bank to release the gambling taxes to the city. The move was explicitly designed to catch Syncora off guard and regain immediate access to the casino cash. It worked.

"I'm hanging out all day with my little girls and my iPhone just completely blows up," Hackney said. "I don't have any Wi-Fi, so I go to this McDonald's, which has unbelievably slow downloads. And I'm just downloading stuff and I'm like, 'These cheaters just ran into court and got a TRO!'"

The city convinced the state court judge to restrict Syncora from taking further action.

"They basically are telling the court it is a matter of life and death that they get the trap lifted, even though they're now at a

point where, by the way, they don't have to pay any of the creditors. They've already not paid us," Hackney said. "When you can
do that, you no longer have a cash-flow problem. If you need cash,
don't pay your pensioners, don't pay health care. You can do whatever you want. You have tons of cash."

But Syncora's attorneys weren't present to argue that point.

"No one says, 'Where is Syncora? Why aren't they here? Did
you even try and give them notice?'" Hackney said.

They hadn't. Jones Day filed the lawsuit without notifying
the insurer's attorneys and convinced the state judge to release the
casino money on the day after the Fourth of July.

"That's the worst form of cheating," Hackney said. "I got back
to my house and I'm reading the *Wall Street Journal*, and it's Orr
saying that he won't let Syncora take the city hostage. I was like,
'This is bullshit.' I was so angry."

Orr, who later called Hackney's boss, Sprayregen, "a good
friend of mine," expressed little sympathy for Kirkland's plight.

"Fuck 'em if they can't take it," Orr recalled, leaning back in his
chair and smiling. "They wanted a fight."

The stage had been set for a bitter conflict between Syncora and
the City of Detroit.

"This really set the tone for the bankruptcy because you've got
to understand how this impacts lawyers. I know everybody thinks
lawyers are sharky, and nobody likes lawyers," Hackney said. "But
the fact of the matter is it's an honorable profession that has a code of
ethics, and we really conduct ourselves in a way that we think we're
supposed to. This was really, really bad cheating that went on."

He prepared a scathing response to Jones Day's actions. "It
basically said, 'You guys are cheaters, and your lawsuit is invalid,'"
Hackney said.

Orr, flashing a wide smile, dubbed Syncora's retaliation a
"nastygram."

"Fuck you very much, have a nice day" was the essence of Syncora's message, Orr said, chuckling. "Yeah, yeah, yeah. Bite me."

AMONG RESTRUCTURING PROFESSIONALS, labeling one side as a scallywag is part of the piratey way. That doesn't mean it's personal. Bankruptcy lawyers, investment bankers, and restructuring consultants can get passionate, yes, but on the job they're generally logical beings. In a corporate context, their actions are best viewed through the mechanical lens of a restructuring formula. Slash the debt. Monetize the assets. Fix the balance sheet. Acquire new financing. Reach settlements. Identify a business plan. Move on to another deal.

When examining a distressed company they remove their personal feelings from the equation. They're like surgeons. If they get emotionally involved in the lives of their patients, they won't be able to do their jobs.

"We don't care how you got cancer. Our job is to cut it out and give you a good chance of survival after that," explained Bill Nowling, senior advisor and spokesman for Orr, describing restructuring professionals. "You've got to stop smoking, you've got to eat better, you've got to get exercise. Otherwise you'll be back on the table, and we'll cut more out. I can't get caught up on how you got here. It doesn't matter. My job is to fix this problem. I may not like that you made bad lifestyle choices to get here. I may disagree with them philosophically."

Still, the political context of a municipal restructuring introduces an emotional element that's often absent in corporate cases. Citizens who rely on police for protection from criminals, pensioners who rely on good fiscal management to protect their livelihoods, and regional leaders who have varying political agendas—all have a significant emotional stake in a Chapter 9 bankruptcy.

That makes Chapter 9 a mystifying realm for even the most seasoned restructuring pirates. Before Detroit, the most significant Chapter 9 bankruptcy was Orange County, California, which had filed in 1994 after a run of bad investments. The largest municipal bankruptcy of the twenty-first century by total debt, until Detroit, was Jefferson County, Alabama, which had filed after a water and sewer debt deal soured.

Several mid-size cities in California filed for Chapter 9 bankruptcy after the Great Recession, but in general, municipal bankruptcy was unexplored territory. In fact, it was so rare that case law in Chapter 9 bankruptcy was quite limited, leaving many fundamental questions unanswered, such as the treatment of constitutionally protected pensions.

Essentially all of the professionals involved in Chapter 9 bankruptcies are veterans of Chapter 11 bankruptcies, in which corporations seek to reorganize their debts. But for good reason Congress established significant differences between municipal and corporate cases. Cities cannot be liquidated, nor can they be split up and sold for parts. So Congress wrote Chapter 9 bankruptcy law to protect cities from being forced to sell assets to satisfy creditors. After bankruptcy, cities must continue to service their residents indefinitely. Police departments must continue protecting the people. Fire departments must continue responding to fires.

In corporate bankruptcies, federal judges can oust executives, effectively seizing control of a company's operations. But the U.S. Constitution's Tenth Amendment says, "The powers not delegated to the United States by the Constitution, nor prohibited by it to the states, are reserved to the states respectively, or to the people."

That gives substantial power to municipalities in bankruptcy. Judges must often defer to cities, even if they believe the debtor is making imprudent budgeting decisions. They cannot remove elected officials from office. The law also makes it easy for municipalities to wipe out collective bargaining contracts in Chapter 9. It allows cities to spend freely without the court's approval. That means cities can plow snow, pave streets, hire employees, and sign new contracts without a court order.

In bankruptcy, municipalities retain the exclusive right to propose a plan for reorganization, which is called a "plan of adjustment" in a municipal context. Once the plan is proposed, the municipality must put it to a vote of the creditors that will endure the cuts.

Despite the power granted to municipalities, federal judges still hold significant influence in Chapter 9. They decide whether the petitioning city is eligible for bankruptcy, control the pace of the case, and reserve the power to approve or deny the city's restructuring plan. Although creditors get to vote on the plan of adjustment, in a process called a "cram down" the bankruptcy judge can force them to accept deals they have refused.

State governments also circumscribe a city's Chapter 9 power: to file, cities must first secure approval from their state governments. Before Detroit, most municipal governments floundered in bankruptcy far longer than they anticipated, expending taxpayer dollars on an arduous legal process that yielded few tangible benefits for citizens. The City of San Bernardino, California, for example, filed for bankruptcy in August 2012 and was still stuck in Chapter 9 three years later.

At the time of its filing, many industry observers believed that if Detroit asked for the court's protection from creditors, it would take several years to reach a restructuring plan and exit bankruptcy, with attorneys and expensive consultants racking up bills and creditors preventing the city from achieving a restructuring.

Similarly, Bruce Bennett, the lead litigating Jones Day attorney representing Detroit, initially feared a drawn-out case.

"A lot of the other Chapter 9 cases have taken a really long time. I thought that was a real problem. If the case took a long time, it would diminish to a great extent whatever could be accomplished," Bennett said. "There's nothing about Chapter 9 that says cases have to take a long time. That's not the way it's supposed to be. It was very important at the beginning to establish a good pace for the case."

But many of the previous municipal bankruptcies that tarried were under the control of elected officials who, by law, had to reach a consensus to make major decisions. In Detroit, that was not the case. Governor Rick Snyder had given Kevyn Orr the power to make fast decisions that the city's elected officials might have debated indefinitely. Still, there was no guarantee the case would move quickly.

For Snyder, that uncertainty held unknown political ramifications. There were few immediate political benefits for the Republican whose personal obsession with positivity contrasted with the raft of negative press that ensued after the city filed for bankruptcy.

Despite job growth and new development in the city's central business areas, there was little to celebrate in the neighborhoods. At the time of the bankruptcy filing, Detroit was successfully collecting only about 53 percent of the property taxes it was owed on an annual basis. Reasons varied. Some residents refused to pay their property taxes as a form of civil protest against sky-high rates and terrible services. Some could afford to pay and didn't. But in many cases, property owners were simply too poor to pay. In 2013, about 34 percent of Detroit households received less than fifteen thousand dollars in income, according to the U.S. Census Bureau.

Detroiters could not afford to foot the bill for the city's $18 billion in debt.

"This level of debt is simply unsustainable," Orr said in a letter requesting Snyder's authorization to file for bankruptcy. "This situation has been managed to date only by deferring other obligations, cutting services to the bone, and ignoring the substantial and obvious need for reinvestment in the city. Residents have paid for this approach with a diminishing quality of life in a city that, over time, has increasingly struggled to protect the health, safety, and welfare of its citizens."

But Snyder still had a decision to make. Hurling Detroit into bankruptcy would subject the city to the whims of a federal bankruptcy judge who might not have the city's best interests in mind. Even if the city lucked out and landed a judge who was sympathetic to its position, bankruptcy can generate unintended consequences. It offers a blank slate for the debtor, but it also extends an invitation to powerful financial companies, retirees, and unions to pursue their respective visions on how the bankrupt entity should restructure its debts. Rarely are creditors empathetic, and Detroit was no exception.

After Orr asked the governor for permission to thrust Detroit into bankruptcy, Snyder, a man known for speedy decisions, briefly paused to assess his options.

The governor's trusted advisor, Rich Baird, and lawyer, Mike Gadola, advised him to attach conditions to the bankruptcy. Authorize the filing, they told the governor, but require Orr to get your approval before proposing a plan of adjustment. They wanted the governor to retain the authority to reject a restructuring plan that could damage him politically or that he might view as inadequate, misdirected, or unfair.

"The thing you've got to understand about this governor that's different from most politicians is he not only expects conflicting points of view be aired within any deliberation, he sort of demands it," Baird said. "If folks that are pitching him on something don't give him the devil's advocate, he believes he's not well served."

Perhaps the most politically combustible element of Detroit's bankruptcy for the governor was the prospect of pension cuts for vulnerable retirees—most of whom still lived in Michigan and vote in elections.

Bankruptcy law does not specify whether municipal government ments can cut their pension obligations. That gray area has spawned a patchwork of theories in the legal community on the balance of power between pension rights—which are often written into state constitutions—and the U.S. Constitution's allowance for contract cuts in bankruptcy.

Michigan is one of at least thirty-five states that protect pensions as a contract, according to the Center for Retirement Research at Boston College. The pensions clause in the state's constitution— Article IX, Section 24, enshrined a half century before Detroit toppled into bankruptcy—dictated that public pensions are a "contractual obligation" that cannot be "diminished or impaired." The latter phrase offered protection to public pensioners, but the phrase "contractual obligation" seemingly placed pensions in the same boat as other contracts.

Orr believed that boat could be rocked in bankruptcy. And the governor agreed. Although Detroit unions and retirees protested that the state constitution provided rock-solid protection for pensions, Snyder, Orr, and Jones Day placed their bets on middle-school civics: Federal law is supreme to state law. When the two conflict, federal law takes precedent.

"The constitution does not say you have a guaranteed right to a pension," Snyder said later. "It says it's an accrued financial benefit that's a contractual obligation. Bankruptcy is really the ability to abrogate a contractual right."

Snyder refused the advice of his attorney and close advisor, giving Orr the authority to file for bankruptcy without conditions. Orr now had the power to pursue pension cuts.

"I shouldn't be imposing my thought process on Chapter 9," Snyder said later, describing his philosophy. "The bankruptcy law is clear. There's a reason for the way it is. And I didn't deem it appropriate for me to interfere in that process."

The city's attempt to restructure without an emergency manager had flopped—and the emergency manager had been unable to extract concessions from creditors. Snyder believed he had given Detroit sufficient room to rescue itself without bankruptcy.

"We had exhausted all the other options and we needed to provide better services to citizens," Snyder said. "This is the part that always gets lost in Chapter 9. Chapter 9 was really developed to help a community be successful to provide for its citizens. I viewed it as a tough call but as the call that needed to be made."

Still, no municipality had tested the waters in bankruptcy to see whether a federal judge would officially authorize pension cuts—in Michigan or anywhere else.

That made the selection of the bankruptcy judge in charge of Detroit's case of paramount concern. And the man who landed the case turned out to be one of the most important figures in the history of Detroit.

CHAPTER 6

Sacrosanct?

Born in Levittown, Pennsylvania, Steven Rhodes moved with his family to Indianapolis, Indiana, during junior high school. His father, an electrical engineer for RCA, held a crucial patent for color television circuitry. After high school, Rhodes earned a bachelor's degree in mechanical engineering from Purdue University in 1970.

"I loved engineering," he said. "I loved Purdue."

Thin, short, and bespectacled, he looks a decade younger than his age, with soft red hair fastidiously swept across his temple. He speaks carefully and slowly, his facial expressions revealing a methodical thought process.

Known for closely guarding his personal life, Rhodes's principal indulgence is playing rhythm guitar in a band of bankruptcy lawyers and restructuring professionals called the Indubitable Equivalents, which describes itself as "the greatest insolvency rock-and-roll band ever."

After graduating from Purdue, Rhodes earned his law degree from the University of Michigan. He became an assistant U.S. prosecutor, practiced law privately, and then served as a U.S. magistrate in the first tranche of his career. In 1985, he was appointed as a U.S. bankruptcy judge based in Detroit.

Over nearly three decades, Rhodes toiled away in the Eastern District of Michigan, handling personal bankruptcy cases and a smattering of corporate bankruptcies, such as the complex restructuring of auto supplier Collins & Aikman. He gained some attention in legal circles as an expert on Ponzi schemes, co-writing a book on the topic with Los Angeles bankruptcy attorney Kathy Bazoian Phelps.

Rhodes earned the respect of restructuring lawyers in southeastern Michigan for his no-nonsense attitude, emphasis on efficiency, and deep grasp of federal bankruptcy code. While kind in his interactions with ordinary citizens, in the courtroom he does not suffer fools. A sharp tongue meets the ill-prepared, his words chosen with precision and scornful of the incompetent.

"If you have a choice of bankruptcy judge to go in front of—smart guy he always has been—but he could make your life miserable," said Doug Bernstein, a bankruptcy lawyer for the Detroit-area law firm Plunkett Cooney, who has handled numerous cases in front of Rhodes. "He asks tough questions. He doesn't ask them in a pleasant manner if you got him on a bad day."

His political persuasion is a mystery to even his closest professional colleagues. "I'm of the firm belief that Rhodes is apolitical. His role and the outcome is and will be determined by him applying the law as he sees it—and not influenced by any political motivations or ramifications whatsoever," Bernstein said.

In municipal bankruptcy, federal law ascribes to the chief judge of the Circuit Court of Appeals the power to appoint judges to oversee cases. In the Sixth Circuit, which encompasses Michigan, Ohio, Kentucky, and Tennessee, chief judge Alice Batchelder indirectly controlled Detroit's fate.

As Detroit edged closer to Chapter 9 bankruptcy, Gerald

Rosen, the chief judge of the U.S. District Court for the Eastern District of Michigan, decided to make a recommendation to Batchelder, who was traveling in Europe at the time. Rosen called the judges in the Eastern District to solicit opinions on who should handle the case, recognizing that it would take someone with strong case-management skills, a supreme intellect, an appropriate judicial temperament, and an ability to corral the school of world-class lawyers who were already circling Detroit. The unanimous pick was Rhodes, and Batchelder signed off.

"I was pleased and delighted, of course. Flattered," Rhodes said later. "More than a little anxious about what it would mean for me and the weight of responsibility that it would mean for me and that it would require."

Rhodes was set to step down from full-time case management at the end of 2013, but handling Detroit's case alone would require him to delay his retirement indefinitely. Yet for Rhodes—who missed a chance to handle the historic bankruptcies of General Motors and Chrysler when those automakers filed for bankruptcy in New York instead of Detroit—it was the opportunity of a lifetime.

Rhodes told Rosen he would accept the job, but under one condition: Rosen must agree to serve as the chief mediator in the bankruptcy. As lead mediator, Rosen would attempt to resolve the case's most contentious issues, including potential pension cuts, debt reductions, and union contracts. He would negotiate deals between the city and its creditors in private sessions, bridging divides among lawyers, bankers, and political officials. But Rhodes would ultimately have the power to approve or reject those settlements.

Unlike a corporate case, restructuring Detroit would require the judges to navigate uncertain political terrain. By his own admission, Rhodes lacks political savvy. But Rosen, who is fond of quoting his personal hero, Winston Churchill, has a keen political IQ.

"I was convinced of the importance of mediation and a mediated and negotiated settlement to the prompt disposition of the case" and to the city's revitalization, Rhodes said. "So I felt it was necessary to appoint the strongest possible mediator that I could. And I felt that Chief Judge Rosen had all of the necessary qualities. Weight of office. Weight of personality. Commitment to the city. Personal and professional contacts. Political contacts. He was the right person."

Rosen grew up in Oak Park, a suburb a few miles north of Detroit in Oakland County, and worked on Democratic presidential candidate Eugene McCarthy's failed 1968 campaign while studying at Kalamazoo College, where he earned his bachelor's degree. Eventually he converted to conservative politics and joined the congressional staff of Republican U.S. senator Robert Griffin. After earning his law degree at George Washington University in 1979, Rosen returned to Michigan to practice law and launched a congressional campaign as a Republican in 1982 for an open seat representing a district in Oakland County. He lost to Democrat Sander Levin, who still holds the seat today.

His electoral hopes dashed, Rosen practiced law for several years before identifying a new route to power in the federal judiciary. President George H. W. Bush appointed him as a District Court judge in the Eastern District of Michigan in 1990, and he ascended to the role as chief judge in 2009.

When Rhodes asked him to be the lead mediator in the bankruptcy, Rosen hesitated at first. Some colleagues expressed apprehension at the prospect of the District Court's chief judge getting involved in the case. But most endorsed the idea, believing that Rosen had the unique mix of assertiveness, persuasiveness, ego, and stature necessary to bring together unwieldy creditors and the city.

During a golf outing, his teenage son Jake made the decision easier by drawing a historical analogy.

"What do you think Churchill would have done?" Jake asked his dad.

Rosen took the job.

The two judges, who knew each other before the bankruptcy but were not considered good friends, made a deal to push the case along quickly, believing it was crucial to ensure that Detroit didn't languish in court for years. Rhodes agreed to keep the conveyer belt of litigation humming along, putting pressure on the creditors and the city in open court, while Rosen agreed to press both sides for concessions in private mediation talks.

If Rhodes was moving too fast in the courtroom, potentially jeopardizing a brewing settlement in mediation, Rosen would ask him to slow down. If Rosen was encountering intractable resistance in mediation, he would ask Rhodes to speed up litigation to put pressure on the negotiators.

Rhodes told Rosen that his "deliverable" was a restructuring plan that was legal, fair, and feasible.

"Judge Rosen is a political animal in a way that I totally am not, so I had complete faith and trust in his political judgments as to what he felt he needed to do to fulfill his obligations as a mediator," Rhodes said.

IN CRIMINAL PROCEEDINGS, preliminary examinations offer a chance for prosecutors to prove that there's reasonable cause, based on the evidence, to put defendants on trial.

Congress established a similar legal threshold to prevent American cities from rushing into Chapter 9 bankruptcy. To enter bankruptcy, Detroit faced a crucial test to be administered by Rhodes: Did it meet the U.S. Bankruptcy Code's standards for eligibility to file Chapter 9 bankruptcy?

The hurdles are substantial. In addition to the requirement that they secure the authority of their state governments to file for bankruptcy, municipalities must also prove that they are insolvent. This prevents them from leveraging bankruptcy to extract bad debt from their balance sheets when their overall finances are healthy.

In most circumstances, cities must establish that they have made a reasonable attempt to negotiate in good faith with their creditors. But there's an escape hatch: if cities can prove it's "impracticable" to negotiate in good faith, that's good enough. Essentially, cities that cannot possibly satisfy all of their creditors are exempt from the requirement to negotiate in good faith.

After Detroit officially filed for bankruptcy, objections flooded in from unions, retiree groups, pension funds, and activists. Their collective howl was cause for a trial in the fall of 2013 to decide Detroit's eligibility for bankruptcy, giving unions, retirees, and other creditors the chance to present evidence and testify in a bid to prove that the city's bankruptcy petition should be dismissed.

In the weeks after the city's filing, lawyers for unions and retirees filed legal briefs challenging the city's eligibility for bankruptcy on several grounds, asserting that the case was illegal and should be overturned. They filed numerous discovery requests and conducted dozens of depositions with city leaders, seeking evidence to convince the judge that the bankruptcy filing was unnecessary. And they assembled their own witnesses to testify that the city was not eligible for Chapter 9. The assortment of objections to Detroit's historic Chapter 9 bankruptcy reflected the bitterness of the dispute between the city and its pensioners. After a lifetime of service to Detroit, pensioners fearful of broken promises became fierce opponents of the city's restructuring.

As the objections stacked up, Detroit emergency manager Kevyn Orr privately proposed pension benefit cuts of more than 50 percent for general city pensioners and massive reductions in health care benefits for all retirees. His jaw-dropping proposal reflected the consequences of the city's steep pension shortfall. Unlike corporate pensions—which have the backstop of the Pension Benefit Guaranty Corporation, a federal agency that helps pay benefits when a company goes broke—municipal pension funds don't have a backup source of funding.

Rhodes, at the city's request, approved the creation of the Official Committee of Retirees, which would be legally empowered to negotiate on behalf of retirees in the bankruptcy. The panel's nine members—a group of union proponents who applied for the job and were selected by the U.S. Trustee, the government's bankruptcy oversight program—hired the global law firm Dentons and investment bank Lazard to represent their cause. The retiree committee joined a nascent coalition of active-employee unions, the city's two pension fund boards, and several retiree association groups to fight the city in mediation and during the eligibility trial.

For the unions, the leaders included Sharon Levine, a New York–based Lowenstein Sandler attorney for the American Federation of State, County and Municipal Employees (AFSCME), and Babette Ceccotti, a New York–based attorney for Cohen, Weiss and Simon, representing the United Auto Workers.

For the retirees, the top advocates included Robert Gordon and Jennifer Green, Detroit-based Clark Hill attorneys representing the two pension funds, and New York–based Dentons attorneys Claude Montgomery and Carole Neville representing the retiree committee.

Despite a widespread assumption among bankruptcy experts that the city would easily hurdle the eligibility bar, the labor creditors believed they had a chance to convince Rhodes to disallow the bankruptcy on the grounds that the city had not negotiated in good faith and did not have the authority to ignore the Michigan Constitution's protection against public pension cuts.

There was only about one month between the time of Orr's first proposal to creditors and Detroit's bankruptcy filing. The airport hotel meeting on June 14 was designed as an initial presentation—

not a thorough negotiation process, the creditors argued—and a few brief follow-up meetings consisted largely of simple discussions of the facts. It was hardly a collaborative, hard-fought negotiation process.

"We weren't actually 100 percent sure that we were going to lose," Levine said later. "We thought the judge might actually send us back to the drawing board and make the city negotiate with us."

The labor creditors protested the bankruptcy on the grounds that the state's emergency-manager law was unconstitutional because it suspended democracy and improperly allowed the emergency manager to pursue pension cuts.

"We sort of found it surprising, to say the least, that people that were at or pretty close to the poverty level" were facing cuts, Levine said later. "It felt like we were the target out of the box."

Gordon argued in a court filing that the state constitution "forbids" the reduction of pension benefits, and the governor is "duty-bound to uphold" that protective provision.

AFSCME went a step further, attacking the very constitutionality of Chapter 9 bankruptcy. It was the legal equivalent of a moonshot, specifically designed to provide the foundation for a potential appeal to higher courts. The federal government's municipal bankruptcy law improperly allows the U.S. government to interfere in state rights, the union asserted.

Having witnessed their town torn apart by racial injustice, wrecked by globalization, and trampled by crime, families in Detroit—and the city's thirty-two thousand pensioners—finally found a listening ear in Rhodes. Before the official start of the eligibility trial the judge handed the courtroom podium—usually reserved for polished bankruptcy attorneys in tailored suits, neckties, and expensive shoes—over to the real faces of the bankruptcy: the people of Detroit and its retirees.

One by one, citizens aired their grievances in a September court hearing with all the makings of a town hall. By allowing individual citizens to speak up in Bankruptcy Court without a lawyer, Rhodes flashed a populist's edge.

"Everyone gets two minutes to object. I don't think you ever saw that before," said John Pottow, a University of Michigan law professor and national bankruptcy expert who followed the case closely and knows Rhodes personally. "I think he saw it as a social catharsis. People just have to be able to scream. I think he listened to their arguments. He let them literally have their day in court."

Some took umbrage with Orr's presence in Detroit, saying his appointment was illegal—and thus the bankruptcy was illegal. But many of the individual objectors were ordinary folks who simply wanted to tell their stories. They wanted Rhodes to know how the bankruptcy would affect their lives.

Cynthia Blair, a widow of a Detroit police officer who retired as a sergeant with a three-thousand-dollar-a-month pension, reminded the judge that police and fire retirees don't receive Social Security. The possibility of pension cuts was terrifying. "We would be thrown directly to the welfare rolls, and we would just really have to scramble to survive," Blair said.

One pensioner, Paulette Brown, a retired manager in a wastewater treatment plant who began her city career as a junior typist, decried pension cuts for workers who endured grisly conditions in faithful service to their community.

"Many of my coworkers worked in hazardous areas, extreme heat, extreme cold, and unsanitary conditions. We all breathed in air filled with the smell of feces and raw sewage on a daily basis," she said. "We went above and beyond the call of duty. We fulfilled our agreement with the City of Detroit, and for that, upon retirement we receive medical benefits and a pension based on an agreed-upon formula for the rest of our lives. We did our part. We need the City of Detroit to continue to do theirs."

Some speakers appealed to the judge's religious sensibilities.

"We said we don't want an emergency manager," individual objector Sylvester Davis said. "I'm asking you, your Honor, if you got God in you, do the right thing. Disallow this mess that they created."

The words of one tearful objector, Detroiter Jean Vortkamp, left an indelible mark on the case. She painted a sobering picture of real life in the neglected neighborhood streets of Detroit, away from the glimmers of hope downtown and the bustling energy of Midtown. A young man was recently gunned down in her neighborhood, she said. For five hours, his body lay in the street.

"A hundred people came to our street—his family and friends— and they got to see his body lay there for five hours because of the cutbacks to the coroner. This is austerity," Vortkamp said, her voice tinged with sorrow and outrage. "Detroit is already at a point where it is inhumane for the amount of public services that we have. There is no more room for any more austerity in Detroit."

Her despair, coupled with the fears of other residents and retirees, was emblazoned permanently on the heart of the bankruptcy. Rhodes was personally moved.

"I heard many gut-wrenching stories about the harm that residents of the city were suffering because of the city's inability to provide adequate services," Rhodes recalled later. "There was great anger in the city—anger at the appointment of the emergency manager who people felt had taken their democratic rights. And that concern was not unjustified. And there was anger at the bankruptcy filing itself. A lot of people felt it was not necessary."

But the paradoxical nature of these heartfelt protests lay in the fact that they worked to support the city's case for bankruptcy. They simply underscored Detroit's problems—a brokenness that could not be fixed outside of Chapter 9.

"Would we be kicked out of bankruptcy? That was unimaginable," David Heiman, the lead Jones Day attorney on the case, said later. "There was no way in my mind that we would be found to be ineligible."

IN A CASE filled with some of the world's top bankruptcy lawyers, past experience with Chapter 9 was nonetheless in short supply. That gave Jones Day attorney Bruce Bennett, veteran of the most significant previous municipal bankruptcy in U.S. history, a unique advantage.

In the 1994 filing of Orange County, California, at the age of thirty-six, Bennett bludgeoned creditors by wielding the previously unexplored nuances of Chapter 9 that give a sharp home-field advantage to the debtor. He recognized that the law prevented creditors from forcing municipalities to sell assets in bankruptcy, a concept that contrasts sharply with corporate bankruptcies, in which companies are often liquidated for the benefit of creditors.

"You won't find this in the law books explicitly, but I've always thought this was about the ability to provide services at a level that competes with surrounding areas," Bennett said. "I definitely came to the case with that conviction."

The courtroom is where Bennett thrives. His short salt and-pepper hair, interrupted by a small patch of pure white directly above his forehead, his translucent eyeglass frames, and his unexcitable demeanor aren't the hallmarks of a street fighter. But his willingness to brawl was unmistakable. For Detroit to navigate bankruptcy successfully and free up cash to reinvest in basic city services, the city would have to spill the blood of its creditors, he said.

"If you had asked me to predict at the front end, I would have predicted that the judge was going to find Detroit was eligible," Bennett said. "I didn't think it was a close call."

Where the city faced a real hurdle in the eligibility trial was in demonstrating that it had negotiated in good faith with its creditors. The city's closely aligned adversaries said the one-month negotiation process made Detroit's bankruptcy filing a fait accompli and did not provide sufficient time to negotiate in good faith. But Bennett believed that one month of negotiating time was enough for creditors to make reasonable counterproposals.

"Negotiations didn't have to get concluded in the initial period for them to be successful," he said. "They just had to get to a point where you could look at them and say, 'Hey, this is productive, it might lead someplace good.'"

The burden to negotiate in good faith, Bennett asserted, is a two-way street. The Official Committee of Retirees, for example, said negotiations occurred in bad faith simply because the city proposed cuts to pensions.

"Meaning the city wasn't in good faith because we didn't agree with them from day one," Bennett said. "What exactly were [we] supposed to do next in the negotiations that would have helped matters?"

To prove Detroit did not devise a grand scheme to plunge into bankruptcy without regard for the fate of its creditors, Governor Rick Snyder, who appointed Orr and personally authorized the bankruptcy, took the witness stand during the eligibility trial. It put the governor on the defensive for authorizing the largest municipal bankruptcy in U.S. history with no conditions.

After raising his right hand on October 28, 2013, and swearing under oath to testify truthfully, Snyder settled in behind the square-shaped, wooden witness box at the Theodore Levin U.S. Courthouse in downtown Detroit, a space often occupied by hardened federal criminal suspects and their conspirators. As a bevy of national media and local reporters watched on a closed-circuit video feed in a nearby room, attorneys peppered Snyder with questions about prospective pension cuts.

"I believe I'm following Michigan's Constitution and the Constitution of the United States, and the article says accrued financial benefits shall be treated as a contractual obligation," he testified.

Ultimately, settling the question of whether public pensions can be cut in bankruptcy rested not with the governor but with Rhodes.

Robert Gordon, lead attorney for Detroit's two pension fund boards, told Rhodes that the framers of the Michigan Constitution viewed pensions as an "absolute" contract. That is, they had to be paid in full, even in bankruptcy.

But Rhodes flashed a practical side. Are there any absolute rights at all, he asked? Under certain circumstances, even the cherished freedoms enshrined in the Bill of Rights can be abrogated.

"We have laws that limit speech," Rhodes said in court. "Can't threaten the President. Can't yell 'fire' in a crowded theater."

But leaders of Detroit's retiree groups believed the city's legal requirement to pay for pensions took precedent over all other obligations.

"If the City of Detroit were to cease to exist, if there were to be some horrendous natural catastrophe that wiped the city off the state—wiped the city off the map, then we believe the city would still owe that obligation," said Thomas Morris, an attorney for the Detroit Retired City Employees Association and the Retired Detroit Police and Fire Fighter Association.

DURING THE ELIGIBILITY trial, a public appearance Orr made only a few weeks before the bankruptcy came back to haunt him. In a gathering at Wayne State University, Orr had told Detroit residents and retirees that the Michigan Constitution protected pensions as "sacrosanct."

"What I was trying to say was, 'I recognize that you think they're sacrosanct,'" Orr explained long after the trial.

Regardless of his intentions, though, his remarks had given some retirees a false sense of security. He had no plans to spare pensioners. In fact, at the airport hotel meeting with creditors held just a few days after the "sacrosanct" remark, he had proposed significant cuts.

The "sacrosanct" remark served as a core piece of evidence as unions and retirees tried to prove to Rhodes that the emergency manager did not negotiate in good faith. Jones Day rushed to contain the damage, giving Orr a chance to recalibrate as he hit the witness stand during the eligibility trial, just days after Snyder's testimony.

"Were you attempting to mislead that gentleman who asked the question?" Jones Day attorney Greg Shumaker asked Orr.

"No, not at all," Orr offered.

Rhodes interjected. "Excuse me one second," he said. "What would you say to that retiree now?"

Orr, situated in the witness box, turned his head to the right, appearing surprised at the judge's inquiry.

"About what, your honor?" he said.

"What would you say to him?" Rhodes pressed.

Orr, usually eloquent and quick on his feet, stammered for a moment, then found his footing. "I would say that his rights are in bankruptcy now. I would say that his rights are subject to the Supremacy Clause of the U.S. Constitution."

"That's a bit different than sacrosanct, isn't it?" Rhodes said.

Shirley Lightsey, president of the eight-thousand-member Detroit Retired City Employees Association, which was formed in 1960, and a member of the Official Committee of Retirees, couldn't hide her disdain.

"I was speechless to find out they just set aside the state constitution. It was Orr who said the U.S. government trumps the state. I can still see him when he said that on the stand. That just infuriated all of us," Lightsey recalled later. "They didn't realize it was personal. These were stone-cold, hard New York attorneys, and they just took the human element out. We're not corporate America."

Orr's "sacrosanct" remark was a gift for the city's opponents. Claude Montgomery, an attorney for the retiree committee, derided the emergency manager for deceiving.

"'Pensions aren't going to be touched,' is effectively what he said," Montgomery told Rhodes. "A lie. He knew better. I think that that's only one example of the lack of good faith in the process of dealing with creditors."

Jones Day's Bennett tried to walk it back, calling the remark "inappropriately timed."

"This may not be the moment where he used the best words," Bennett acknowledged.

But Orr later came to appreciate the judge's perspective. "I think his view was, 'Were you gaming people at that meeting?' Because he didn't know where I was coming from. So he came at me a little hard, but then I was like, 'He's got to take a shot too. And he's got the gavel. What am I gonna do? I'm gonna live with him for the next year,'" Orr recalled.

JONES DAY'S SPUTTERING effort to prove that it had negotiated in good faith with Detroit's creditors contrasted with an impervious case that the city couldn't function and needed to slash its debts. Bankruptcy defines insolvency through a financial prism. But Detroit was enduring insolvency of another kind. The people's suffering was Exhibit A.

"One of the things that doesn't come across very often is an overriding concern for the citizens of Detroit," Snyder had testified. "While all this is taking place, all we've seen is more blight, more lights going out, challenges on the police force.

These things have to get resolved. It's an unacceptable situation. People are suffering—the 700,000 citizens of Detroit."

If the basic test of a city is its ability to protect its own citizens, Detroit was failing when Orr arrived. Shortly after taking office as emergency manager, Orr had handpicked Cincinnati's chief of police, a charismatic cop named James Craig, to become the new chief of police in Detroit. Craig, who briefly served as a Detroit cop early in his career, immediately began shaking up the Detroit Police Department, which was plagued by poor emergency response times, insufficient equipment, and paperwork that kept too many officers from patrol duties.

The new police chief turned into a star witness for the city.

"Everything is broken," Craig testified during the eligibility trial. "Deplorable conditions."

Morale in the department was the lowest he had ever seen. Officers had taken a 10 percent pay cut before Orr's arrival to help the city pay its bills. In addition, the number of police officers had been reduced by 40 percent during the last decade, as the city's debt gobbled up an increasing share of the budget.

Officers were being forced to work grueling twelve-hour shifts. About five hundred of the department's bulletproof vests had expired, making them unsafe to use. Craig himself brought his own personal vest to use when he arrived in Detroit. About 66 percent of the department's vehicles showed excessive wear. Many were damaged, unsafe, or inoperable.

"There were times when Detroit police officers were called, and no one would ever show up," Craig said, echoing the testimony of resident Jean Vortkamp.

In addition, blighted homes and broken streetlights exacerbated the police department's challenges. Abandoned buildings on unlit streets were hotspots for crime.

"If an area is clean, it's well lit, people take pride in the neighborhood, crime seems to be lower," Craig observed.

Those words resonated with Rhodes. He declared that Detroit had entered a protracted "state of service delivery insolvency" that added heft to the city's case for bankruptcy.

Without cash, the city could not combat the scourge of abandoned buildings, which not only fostered crime but diminished property values of occupied structures. Without cash, the city could not afford to hire new police officers and firefighters. Without cash, the city could not acquire basic information technology to facilitate better communication among emergency responders. Without cash, conditions in the city deteriorated, and population decline accelerated. It was the definition of a bankrupt city.

"I think Steve Rhodes thought that Detroit was broken, and it was broken because of financial disarray," said Pottow, the University of Michigan bankruptcy professor and Rhodes's colleague. "So he's like, 'We owe it to the city to reorganize because people live here.'"

Still, in his ruling Rhodes blasted the city for leaving only a month to negotiate with creditors following Orr's official proposal. It was "far too short," and the offer itself was "vague" and made counterproposals difficult, the judge wrote. The city had failed to negotiate in good faith, he ruled.

But the jab at Orr's team had no effect on the city's eligibility for bankruptcy. Rhodes ruled that it was "impossible" for the city to negotiate in good faith with all of its approximately 170,000 creditors, a list that topped a mind-boggling thirty-five hundred pages.

Rhodes was persuaded to adopt the impracticability standard in part because pensioners openly acknowledged they never would have accepted cuts of any kind—a bargaining position that made it futile for the city to reach a resolution in the absence of bankruptcy.

"It is impracticable to negotiate with a stone wall," Rhodes said, quoting Christopher Klein, the judge handling the contemporaneous Stockton, California, bankruptcy.

Detroit's "financial crisis had been worsening for decades, and it could have and should have filed bankruptcy long before it did, perhaps even years before," Rhodes said.

The City of Detroit, the judge ruled on December 3, 2013, following the conclusion of the eligibility trial, was eligible for Chapter 9 bankruptcy. Despite the warts on the negotiating process, the city had met the legal standard required to officially enter bankruptcy.

"Experience with both individuals and businesses in financial distress establish that they often wait longer to file a bankruptcy than is in their interests," Rhodes said in his ruling. "Detroit was no exception."

That Rhodes dinged the city for failing to negotiate in good faith was a consolation prize for the labor creditors, albeit a nominal one. Rhodes gave some measure of validation to their accusations that Detroit had ignored their concerns.

"He was pretty harsh in rapping the knuckles of the city," Pottow said. "The impracticability thing gave him the ability to call it, to make it clear out of the gates: 'I'm fuckin' watching you.'"

But Bennett maintained, many months later, that the judge got it wrong in that respect.

"I thought I could win under the good-faith negotiation provision, and frankly, to this day I believe we should have," he said.

But he did not lose any sleep over it.

"Frankly, we won!" Bennett said. "I could probably find ways to find little defeats in every single one of my cases. But I try not to do that. I would drive myself crazy."

The second crucial win for Orr and Jones Day came in Rhodes's concurrent ruling that the city could cut pensions. With a swift stroke, Rhodes had dismissed the uncertainty over the legal standing of public pensions.

"We in bankruptcy impair contracts all day, every day," he said later, describing his thought process. "That is what we do."

Simple as that. But if Snyder had tried to impose conditions on the Chapter 9 case—as his own advisors suggested—that "may have rendered the authorization itself invalid," Rhodes ruled.

Although the ruling does not set national legal precedent, Rhodes's decision nonetheless delivered a blow to unions across the country, exposing a serious crack in a financial foundation once believed to be indestructible. Even if they're not legally bound by Rhodes's ruling, judges in future municipal bankruptcies are almost sure to analyze Detroit's case for guidance in their own adjudication. Plus, the ruling had the immediate effect of giving Orr negotiating leverage to demand concessions from pensioners in mediation sessions.

Orr felt vindicated. Earlier in his career, he had successfully convinced judges to subordinate state laws to the federal bankruptcy code, and he figured pensions would not be an exception. While representing Chrysler, for example, Orr and Jones Day had secured authority to steamroll politically untouchable auto-dealership franchise laws.

"We ran them over, so I didn't give that a thought," he said. "It wasn't even a close call."

The judge's opinion also contained an implicit endorsement of the city's plan to use municipal bankruptcy law to reinvest in ailing services—a novel concept in bankruptcy. The ruling gave the city the ammunition it needed to insist that it must divert a substantial portion of its future budget to services instead of creditors.

"He basically said to the creditors, 'You can only fight over what's left over,'" said Ken Buckfire, the city's investment banker.

Still, Rhodes acknowledged "the widespread anguish and distress" that his ruling would trigger for "employees and retirees as well as their families." He pleaded for a thoughtful solution.

"The court, therefore, implores with all urgency those who administer our social safety net, our governor who authorized this case, our state government leaders, our civic and business leaders, our religious and charitable organizations, to focus yet greater attention on the real human needs that will arise because of the city's bankruptcy," he said. "This once-proud and prosperous city can't pay its debts. It's insolvent. It's eligible for bankruptcy. At the same time, it also has an opportunity for a fresh start. I hope that everyone associated with the city will embrace that opportunity."

But the city's retirees and unions were not prepared to give in. They hatched plans for an aggressive appeal of Rhodes's ruling.

"We were ready to go to the Supreme Court," Lightsey said, "because we thought we had the right."

CHAPTER 7

Swaps Saga

The $1.4 billion pension obligation certificates-of-participation (COPs) deal and corresponding interest-rate swaps had incapacitated Detroit. Engineered by former mayor Kwame Kilpatrick's administration in 2005, refinanced in 2006, and collateralized in 2009, the comically intricate deal—Judge Steven Rhodes had called it "complex and confusing" in his eligibility ruling—was a drag on the city. Although the deal delivered substantial benefits to Detroit's two independently operated pension funds—it made them $1.4 billion healthier—it was an albatross on the city's balance sheet.

The swaps, held by UBS and Bank of America Merrill Lynch, were "nothing more than a common bet," Rhodes observed. "If the rate went up, someone would pay the city to help cover the increased interest expense. If the rate went down, the city would have to pay. In 2008 interest rates dropped dramatically. As a result, the city lost on the swaps bet. Actually, it lost catastrophically on the swaps bet."

UBS and Bank of America Merrill Lynch were bookies that

couldn't be ignored. If the swaps had been unsecured debt, they would have been less troubling. The city probably could have vaporized the swaps in bankruptcy. But because the city had pledged its casino taxes as collateral on the swaps in 2009, the deals were fully secured, meaning the banks—at least theoretically—were due a balloon payment of more than $300 million because of the city's cascading series of defaults.

In a city without adequate bulletproof vests for police officers, there was also no shield from financial attacks on the city's meager budget. Detroit had no financial reserves and no reasonable route to make a massive payment. The banks could have seized access to Detroit's casino-tax revenue until they received enough cash to cover the tab.

That scenario is what Ken Buckfire feared: the possibility that the banks would trap the casino cash. (Indeed this is effectively what bond insurer Syncora had tried to do a month before the bankruptcy began, though a state judge issued an temporary restraining order blocking the action and later put the fate of the casino cash in the hands of Rhodes.)

"The city was starting to bounce checks," Buckfire said. "We probably would have had to have laid off thousands of city workers if we had lost access to the casino-tax revenue."

But serious questions about the legality of the swaps gave the city a powerful round of ammunition. During the summer of 2013, Orr had asked the U.S. Securities and Exchange Commission to consider investigating the propriety of the COPs and swaps transactions. The agency told Orr that it had already examined the deals and concluded that no charges or lawsuits were appropriate. Still, the SEC mulled Orr's request further before deciding that the agency's four-year statute of limitations would make it difficult to pursue a case.

The city figured it had no choice. It had to make a deal with the banks to prevent them from seizing the casino cash. Luckily for Detroit, the banks wanted a settlement. Amid a global furor over their respective roles in the global economic crisis, the last thing Bank of America Merrill Lynch and UBS needed was the accusation that they had punched poor old Detroit in the face.

Buckfire set up talks with the banks, represented by Ed Curland and James Nacos of Bank of America Merrill Lynch and Bill Chandler from UBS. He informed them that the city believed the legal position of the swaps was tenuous and offered fifty cents on the dollar to settle the dispute.

Curland laughed in his face. That was comically too low, he said. But after several days of negotiations in the run-up to Detroit's bankruptcy filing, both sides capitulated slightly, and they reached a deal: the city would pay a price ranging from seventy-five to eighty-two cents on the dollar depending on the timing of the payout.

Buckfire figured the deal—a discount of up to 25 percent for Detroit taxpayers on traditionally untouchable secured debt—was good enough. The alternative—waging a public fight against the swaps—would suck the city into a litigation vortex with some of the world's most powerful financial institutions.

"They had financial leverage over the city," Buckfire said. "If we ultimately had won that fight, it would have been a pointless victory because the city would be dead."

Hours after Detroit filed for bankruptcy, Jones Day had slipped details of the settlement into the court's electronic filing system and pleaded for the Bankruptcy Court's permission to finalize the deal.

DETROIT'S SKIRMISH WITH the swap banks appeared as nothing more than a sideshow in a historic bankruptcy that would focus almost entirely on the groundbreaking possibility of municipal pension cuts. With the banks on board for a settlement, it seemed the swaps were a thing of the past—and the judge's approval of the deal a mere formality.

But the city's creditors were incensed by the deal. A team of restructuring lawyers for the Kirkland & Ellis law firm, representing bond insurer Syncora, quietly plotted to pulverize the city's bid to pay off the swaps at a discount.

In the event of a financial catastrophe, bond insurers clean up the mess. When the debtor fails to make payments, the guarantor agrees to cover the losses for insured bondholders. That way, bondholders—whether they're common individual investors or major financial institutions—can limit their risk. Bond insurers take the insurance payments they receive from debt holders and stuff away a large portion in a litigation reserve fund. When something goes wrong, they deploy world-class teams of lawyers to battle bankrupt entities in court in a bid to limit the damage to their own balance sheets.

Because Syncora was smaller than fellow bond insurer Financial Guaranty Insurance Company (FGIC), it had much more to lose, relative to its size. Claude LeBlanc, the chief financial officer and chief restructuring officer for Syncora, recognized that Detroit's debt-cutting plan could be disastrous for his company. He directed the Kirkland lawyers to fight. FGIC became a close ally but allowed Syncora to lead the way.

"Early on I saw that the only way we were ever going to get a hearing was to litigate to the death," said Kirkland's James H. M. Sprayregen.

Stephen Hackney, who was assigned to lead the case on a day-to-day basis for Syncora, spearheaded a strategy designed to undercut the city at any possible moment throughout the case.

He had allies in his fight against the swaps settlement, albeit for different reasons. Detroit's Official Committee of Retirees, two pension funds, unions, and other financial creditors joined his cause. Syncora and FGIC wanted a richer payout. The other creditors wanted the banks to get a smaller settlement. But they were all aligned for one simple reason: they wanted to kill the first swaps settlement Orr and Buckfire had reached with Bank of America Merrill Lynch and UBS.

"Esprit de corps starts to build up, where all the creditors get to know each other," Hackney said. "The city is treating us all like dirt. There's a general amount of anger against the city. And so the creditors just get more and more welded together. As a result, the creditors are working pretty well together. The city is facing this wall of opposition."

In any high-stakes battle, an outmatched general deploys a variety of tactics to unnerve the enemy. As the wall of opposition stiffened, Kirkland attorneys constructed a steady stream of legal barricades aimed at undermining the city's attempt to maintain momentum in resolving the case. Their tactics intensified as the case progressed.

LIGHTING THE STREETS is one of the simplest public services—something most Americans take for granted. But in Detroit, it was an example of dysfunction. An estimated 40 percent of the city's streetlights were out—some because the infrastructure was 120 years old and others because vandals had stripped the old lights of their copper wiring. Drivers couldn't see pedestrians, and darkened streets made it easy for criminals to avoid being seen.

Using a legal structure previously established by Mayor Dave Bing and the state Legislature, Orr in the fall of 2013 asked Rhodes to approve the diversion of a portion of the city's utility-tax stream to pay for a $185 million overhaul of the street-lighting system.

The investment plan would allow the city to replace old bulbs with light-emitting diodes, starting with the city's neglected neighborhoods and finishing with busy thoroughfares.

By 2016, all the lights would be back on. This strategy lined up with the philosophy the city had subscribed to from the beginning of the case: that Chapter 9 bankruptcy is designed to give municipalities a chance to restore a reasonable amount of public services to their residents.

The street-lighting strategy infuriated Syncora.

"The lighting plan seems to exist in a vacuum divorced from the city's needs and any anticipated economic benefit," Syncora's attorneys argued in a court filing. "And it does not answer why, of all things the city can do to protect its citizens and generate revenues, jobs, and investment, upgrading the city's entire lighting infrastructure makes sense for the city at this time."

Syncora had cemented its status as the pugnacious villain in the eyes of the city's supporters.

"They got dealt a shitty hand," said John Pottow, the University of Michigan bankruptcy professor.

But the strategy the Kirkland lawyers deployed on behalf of Syncora appeared straightforward: "We're going to be the junkyard dogs and we're going to swing for the fences and we're going to be the most bastardy bastards ever," Pottow explained. "That's their job. Their job is to make as much money as they can" for their client.

In one sense, though, the city needed a villain, and Syncora served that purpose. By highlighting the seemingly reprehensible nature of Syncora's actions, Detroit could divert attention away from flaws in its own methods. In the case of streetlights, Jones Day's argument was simple: How can any reasonable party protest a plan to turn the lights back on?

"There is no dispute by anybody in this courtroom or anybody in the City of Detroit that the city's lighting system is in a complete state of disarray," argued Robert Hamilton, a Jones Day attorney, in a hearing before Rhodes on November 27, 2013. "There is absolutely no reason not to approve this motion."

Kirkland attorney Bill Arnault argued that the city had not provided adequate information about its plans to overhaul the system. It was a classic delay tactic: attack the process. But he made a blunder.

"We're still very much in the dark as to what exactly is going on with this transaction," Arnault said, without realizing the unfortunate pun.

"Of course, the dark you're in doesn't compare to the dark that the citizens of Detroit suffer day-in and day-out and the crime that results from that," Rhodes asserted.

The judge approved the funding for the lighting upgrades about a week later.

On its face, Syncora's lighting objection appeared ruthless—and the judge's snide remark worthy of applause.

"It was always used as an example of, 'These guys are clearly terrorists because they even oppose fixing the lighting,'" Hackney recalled later, referring to the opinion of Syncora's critics.

But Hackney believed that the need to fix the lighting should have been viewed through a strategic lens that envisioned overhauling the entire city in a holistic fashion. To fix Detroit, in this view, you must acknowledge one of the fundamental issues haunting the city: its size. At 139 square miles, Detroit is geographically larger than Manhattan, San Francisco, and Boston combined. Because of the massive exodus of people from the city in the second half of the twentieth century and continuing into the twenty-first, the census count fell dramatically, but the physical size of the city stayed the same. Police officers and firefighters must still service the entire city. Sometimes it takes extra time to react to emergency calls simply because responders are so far away.

About two months before Orr's appointment as emergency manager, city leaders had released a report called *Detroit Future City*, which was devised using input from thousands of residents and an in-depth assessment of the city's profound challenges. The report urged a rethinking of land usage in the city. Huge swaths of ground should be converted into forest, parks, or storm-water containment areas, the report had concluded. Even if the city's borders didn't shrink, the goal would be to foster a brighter future in which there are fewer neighborhoods but the remaining areas are more densely populated, making it easier for emergency responders to serve the people and enticing businesses to open.

With fewer neighborhoods, there would theoretically be entire areas of the city where streetlights are unnecessary. But Orr had no plans to leverage the powers of bankruptcy to address the city's size. Though Hackney later acknowledged that the lighting system certainly needed massive upgrades, he maintained that the rush to pledge tax revenue as secured collateral on new bonds to pay for lights throughout the entire city was too hasty.

"The speed of the process brushed aside real issues, like the size of the city. That never got addressed," Hackney said later. "There's no philosophical discussion or strategic urban planning— anything—on what I think is one of the most important issues."

He paused to consider the issue further, peering out through an immaculate glass wall onto the Chicago River alongside Kirkland's office on North LaSalle Street.

"I mean, it's not like I just rail about this stuff just because I'm just a firebrand. I actually just objectively think that may have been a real important part of how you fix Detroit," he said. "What if God came down and told you, 'Just so you guys know, you can't fix Detroit unless you fix the size'? Well, that could be the answer— and then we'd all be like, 'Damn, man, I really wish we worked on the size more. We just doomed people to twenty years of trying to fix something that's unfixable.'"

SYNCORA'S BID to torpedo the lighting overhaul had failed, but its effort to stymie the swaps settlement was alive. Retirees and financial creditors were lined up to block the deal too. They prepared an exhaustive legal case designed to disassemble the settlement—a deal worth anywhere from $230 million to $270 million to Bank of America Merrill Lynch and UBS—in a new trial before Rhodes beginning December 17, 2013. Under bankruptcy law, Rhodes had the authority to approve or reject the settlement.

The city's request appeared uncomplicated: give the city the right to pay off the swaps at a discount of up to 25 percent using a new line of credit that the city's investment bank, Miller Buckfire, had procured from global bank Barclays. That would allow Detroit to escape a $4 million monthly bill owed to the swaps banks and eliminate its casino-tax pledge on the swaps.

The city's retiree groups and unions argued that the banks should take a greater hit. Syncora and FGIC believed the settlement was too low and that their legal right to approve the deal as swaps insurers had been brushed aside.

On the witness stand, Orr and Buckfire explained that the city needed to make a deal to escape the collateral pledge that endangered its gambling-tax revenues. "Without it the city cannot operate," Orr said.

Had the city considered the dubious legality of the swaps before offering a settlement to the banks? Yes, Orr testified. Attorneys had prepared legal memos on the pluses and minuses of fighting the banks. For example, they had analyzed the legality of the 2009 casino-tax pledge as collateral on the swaps. (That pledge looked increasingly questionable because the Michigan Gaming Control and Revenue Act lists specific ways in which wagering taxes can be used—and using the money as collateral on debt is not one of those purposes.)

But, Orr testified, the so-called safe-harbor law passed by Congress gave certain assurances to swaps holders, offering them special protection from impairment in bankruptcy. That provision, Orr testified, could give the banks the upper hand if the settlement talks devolved into a legal fight with the city.

So instead of fighting deep-pocketed UBS and Bank of America Merrill Lynch, the city struck a settlement.

"I believe we got the best deal available," Orr said, backing up Buckfire.

Nonetheless, the city had refused to provide legal memos evaluating the swaps to creditors in advance of the trial, citing attorney-client privilege, which allows internal legal communications to remain secret. That frustrated Rhodes, who looked visibly agitated.

"You're claiming the privilege as to those memoranda even though you want to take $270 million from the taxpayers of this city to pay to terminate those swaps?" Rhodes pressed Orr directly.

"I am claiming the privilege, your honor," Orr responded.

Flummoxed, the judge replied, "I don't get it."

The judge's exasperation at the city's defense of its swaps settlement was coming into full view.

"You could feel that Rhodes was like, 'Whoa. What the fuck is going on here?'" Hackney recalled.

The judge interrupted Jones Day's questioning of Orr on the witness stand and aimed a series of his own questions at attorney Greg Shumaker.

"I don't get it," Rhodes said.

Shumaker looked frazzled.

"Why has the city asserted the privilege?" Rhodes pressed.

"I'm asking you," the judge insisted. "You're their lawyer."

Shumaker tried to gather himself. "We were negotiating with large banks who would love to have the . . . memoranda revealed for all the world so it would inform their negotiating position," he said.

Tim Cullen, a senior attorney for Jones Day who had watched the debacle unfold, strode to the podium, placing his hand on Shumaker's back.

"If I may add one thing, your honor," Cullen offered. "One of the reasons we haven't disclosed those memoranda, and we didn't want to disclose those memoranda, is that we may still sue the banks."

The disclosure landed like a bombshell.

"I'm going to say this to you," Rhodes told the city. "Every transaction, including this one, that the city has entered into in connection with these swaps and COPs has been with a gun to its head. That has to stop."

Under that premise, the city had lived the better part of the last decade with a gun to its head. Rhodes was openly signaling his distaste with the settlement with the trial still ongoing.

Orr watched from the witness stand as the swaps settlement imploded in slow motion. During one brief break in the action, he instructed Jones Day attorney Corinne Ball to send an immediate message to the banks: it's time to change the deal.

"It starts to go sideways—clearly go sideways. You're watching this Kabuki theater, and I'm going to Corinne, 'Get your ass over here, get those guys, pull them in. This is about to be a train wreck,'" Orr said, shaking his head in resigned bemusement while recalling the incident.

Attorneys for the banks said they couldn't reach their client to change the deal on the spot.

"I don't care, OK?" Orr said in a message directed at the banks. "Let me tell you what's about to happen. This is not going well for you."

The banks didn't do anything. When the hearing resumed, Rhodes cratered the deal, insisting on a lower price.

"I would encourage that as strongly as I can," he said. "Do you hear what I'm saying?"

The settlement was dead.

FOLLOWING THE STUNNING dissolution of the deal, which imploded before Orr's testimony was even completed, Rhodes held a private conference with several attorneys involved in the case.

"I've always thought the COPs were illegal," the judge blurted out.

The revelation stunned the people in the room. Everyone understood that the COPs deal might be illegal because it allowed the city to circumvent the state's limits on municipal debt.

FGIC attorney Alfredo Perez figured it was an opportunity to score a point.

"If the COPs are illegal, then the pension trusts need to give the money back," Perez told Rhodes.

"No way," the judge retorted.

The attorneys left the room with a new understanding of the judge's position on one of the core issues in the case.

Rhodes had also demanded answers from the city. "Why did you settle at the price you did?" Rhodes pressed Buckfire in his chambers.

Buckfire told the judge he felt the city had few options.

"Your honor, I had no leverage over the creditors and only two weeks to go until the city might have to file for Chapter 9," he told Rhodes. "It was the best I could do to keep the gaming revenues coming to the city."

Shortly thereafter, Rhodes ordered the city and creditors into mediation with Gerald Rosen. In a holiday twist, Rosen set the talks for December 23 and Christmas Eve at his courtroom in downtown Detroit—and he ordered the top leaders from all the respective parties to attend the confidential negotiations, including the European investors that held a substantial portion of the COPs.

"They were all German banks. For them to be there on Christmas Eve was just the worst thing that could happen," said Dentons lawyer Carole Neville, attorney for the Official Committee of Retirees.

Privately, Rhodes told the city that his desired target for a new settlement on the swaps was $150 million—about $80 million less than the original settlement he trashed. That information was relayed to Rosen, who situated representatives of the city, the banks, and the other creditors in separate rooms during the mediation.

It was a legal form of house arrest because negotiators were not allowed to leave while they haggled. Rosen shuttled back and forth between rooms, prodding each side to make concessions.

By this point in the case, Rosen and Orr were already accustomed to rounds of verbal quarreling, like a couple of brothers squabbling.

"Oh, Jerry," Orr said later, flashing a smile while referring to the judge the way most colleagues do privately. "I love him to death. He's a dear, dear friend of mine. But man, we would have fights. 'This is bullshit! I don't think you should do this!' 'I don't care. You guys have got to make a move. You're being unreasonable. I'm gonna report back to Steve Rhodes!' 'I don't care—you don't give a damn about the city, and it's my job and my decision!' Oh my god."

But Rosen reserved an extra dose of scrutiny for UBS and Bank of America Merrill Lynch, threatening to hold the banks in contempt of court for failing to bring the appropriate officials with full settlement authority to the proceeding. With that possibility lingering, he persuaded the banks to improve their offer to $165 million. But the banks wouldn't go lower.

"That's the best number you're going to get today, and I'm going to hold them in contempt if they don't agree to it," Rosen told the city.

Late on the evening of December 23, 2013, the two sides settled on $165 million. But they had yet to finalize the details, so they were forced to return to the courtroom on Christmas Eve.

As the two sides bickered over details, Orr was antsy. His home was in Chevy Chase, Maryland, and he had promised he wouldn't get stuck in Detroit. He pledged to arrive in time to see his son play a shepherd and his daughter an angel in a children's Christmas pageant.

As the clock ticked past noon on Christmas Eve, Orr's wife, Donna, flooded his phone with text messages. He told his colleagues he needed to get the deal done. Orr felt the minutes passing by.

Rosen informed Orr that he was planning to publicly endorse the settlement as soon as they locked down the fine print. "I said, 'Well if you think it will fly, you're the mediator, that's your job. I'm fine. It's a lot less. Works for me. If you're gonna make the proposal, though, please make it by two o'clock so I can make the 3:20 flight to see my kids in the Christmas pageant because my wife is blowing up my phone—'Where are you, we're getting dressed'—and I don't give a shit about you or Judge Rhodes. I'm about to get in trouble.'"

The city and the banks proceeded to seal the deal, even as representatives for retirees and other financial creditors stewed over what they perceived as their lack of influence in the negotiations.

Robert Gordon, the lead attorney for the city's two pension funds, and David Dubrow, an attorney for Ambac Assurance, which had guaranteed payments on some of the city's unsecured general obligation bonds, were sitting in a room together awaiting developments when Rosen walked in.

"He explained the deal, and we looked at each other and we said, 'Judge, that's not a good deal. That's not any better than the old deal,'" Gordon said. "He's like, 'Well, OK, thanks for the input. C'mon into the courtroom.' I'm like, 'I'm glad there's such a robust explanation here.' That was it."

Rosen slipped into his judicial robe and strode into his decadent courtroom, convening a public hearing to announce and personally endorse the new swaps settlement. Coming just moments after the confidential negotiations had concluded, attorneys and bankers in the room were startled to see the deal revealed in open court.

"We were all completely stunned," Gordon said. "We're all thinking the same thing. And yet nobody dared say anything. I think we're all just sitting there and we're all so flabbergasted, and none of us could believe what we're seeing. It was just the most bizarre thing."

THE NEW SWAPS DEAL—the second attempt at a settlement—was less rich for the banks. But the creditors remained displeased. Like the first time, they resolved to try to block the deal in another swaps trial before Rhodes.

Bond insurer Ambac dispatched Caroline Turner English, an attorney from the law firm Arent Fox, to fight the deal. She had spent a considerable share of 2013 examining the legality of Kwame Kilpatrick's deal, identifying a host of potentially fatal flaws in the convoluted structure of the COPs debt and the overlaid interest-rate swaps secured by Detroit's casino-tax revenue.

When the second swaps trial opened on January 3, 2014, the city immediately displayed a sharp shift in strategy. After previously refusing to disclose his reasoning for not suing the banks, Orr hit the witness stand to provide a detailed explanation. The eventual outcome of such a fight, he said, was simply too unclear to risk it.

The emergency manager acknowledged that the casino-tax

revenue pledge might have been illegal. He agreed that the pass-through payment structure the city established to issue the COPs debt—forming two independent "service corporations" and a trust to handle the transaction—may have allowed the city to illegally circumvent the State of Michigan's limit on municipal borrowing. Orr also asserted that the city might have accrued a fraud claim against the banks for leveraging "superior" information about future interest rates. He said that UBS's admitted involvement in a LIBOR rate manipulation scandal might have generated a fraud claim for the city against the bank.

However, the banks and bond insurers had plenty of grounds to argue that the COPs and swaps were entirely legal, Orr insisted. Their evidence included a legal opinion the city had secured years earlier to justify the deal and a letter from the state's gaming board approving the casino-tax revenue pledge.

Fighting the banks would be too risky because it was likely to provoke them to trap the city's casino revenue, thus endangering city services that relied heavily on gamblers to keep gambling, Orr asserted.

"There were strong legal arguments" to sue the banks instead of settling, Orr testified. "But there were also countervailing factual arguments."

The chances of prevailing in a lawsuit were even, he figured.

English pounced. "For every single claim you looked at, you assessed the city's odds as 50-50?" she prodded on cross-examination.

"Yes," Orr admitted.

"Every single claim was just a toss-up in your mind. Correct?" she said.

"Yes," he repeated.

That admission undermined the city's effort to justify embracing the settlement instead of challenging the banks. The probability of succeeding on at least one of the numerous 50-50 legal arguments against the validity of the swaps—and thus proving the deal was bogus—was high.

"We were all emailing each other, saying, 'If it was all 50-50, what is he doing settling at this rate?'" Syncora's Hackney said.

One of the central legal issues was whether the shell corporations the city had established in 2005 to sell the debt constituted a valid method of borrowing. The service corporations issued the debt, allowing the city to technically avoid the state's cap on municipal debt. But the shell corporations were staffed by city appointees even though they functionally had no operations. They existed solely to issue the debt, make the payments, and nothing more.

Although the legality of the service corporations was dubious, for the purposes of the swaps settlement Orr was treating them as if they were legal institutions.

"But you didn't have any negotiations with the service corporations, did you?" English pressed Orr.

"No," he responded. The city had executed the settlement directly with the banks, completely bypassing the service corporations. That added credence to the argument that Detroit had illegally issued the debt.

English was on a roll. She masterfully highlighted how the serious legal questions enveloping the COPs and swaps made an expensive settlement hard to justify.

"That was a knock-the-ball-out-of-the-park performance," retiree committee lawyer Carole Neville said later. "She just packaged it perfectly."

Of course, the idea that the city would make a deal of any kind to pay off a disastrous and possibly illegal debt transaction only served to further enrage Detroit activists who blamed Wall Street for the city's woes.

One of those activists, an attorney named Jerome Goldberg, entered the case as the lawyer for a Detroit retiree named David

Sole. Goldberg's tousled gray hair and congenial style in court contrasts with his bombastic, wield-the-bullhorn persona in rallies outside the courtroom.

His livid client, Sole, exuded contempt for Detroit's political class and the financial giants that lent money to the city. Decades of neglect had left his entire east-side Detroit block with only five occupied homes. The houses on both sides of his home were abandoned and boarded up. One dwelling across the street was believed to be occupied by wild dogs.

"The banks didn't even bother boarding it up after foreclosure," Goldberg said.

For Goldberg, Wall Street was to blame for Detroit's crisis—and Wall Street should not be enriched through the city's bankruptcy, especially not for a deal that destroyed the city's finances. His fierce opposition to the swaps settlement, which acquired a feverish populism, placed him in an unlikely alliance with the group of financial creditors that were also trying to derail the deal.

Of course, bond insurers Syncora and FGIC were fighting the accord because they wanted to be paid more money. On strategy calls with the bond insurers, Goldberg didn't hide his contempt for their cause.

"Jerry would get up and say, 'The Wall Street guys are criminals, and we hate them all!'" Hackney said.

But Goldberg and the bond insurers shared a common interest: kill the second swaps settlement at all costs. "I think he deserves tremendous credit," Hackney allowed.

The creditors knew Goldberg had a role to play. "He was always very nice," Hackney said. "He would say, 'You guys were so fair and friendly to me, I really appreciate it.' We would say, 'Hey, you've got a case to put on like anybody else.'"

Goldberg's case for tanking the settlement was simple: banks hastened the foreclosure crisis in Detroit, thus exacerbating the widespread abandonment of homes, the decline in property values, and the corresponding dilution of the city's property tax base.

"At a time when the people of Detroit are facing terrible services, when we're barely surviving, when our lights aren't on, when services are being cut, when retirees are fearing the loss of pensions, to sit back and make a payment of $165 million to UBS and Bank of America—banks with a history of subprime lending that helped cause this crisis—seems unconscionable," Goldberg railed in court.

Goldberg peppered Orr and Buckfire on the witness stand with questions about foreclosures, subprime lending, and interest-rate fixing. And he slammed the city for settling with UBS despite the Swiss bank's public acknowledgment of its role in the LIBOR scandal.

"He didn't ask questions that were like, 'What color is Mars?' He was a lawyer," Hackney said. "And he was doing a stem-winding cross-examination. And I think in some respects he came to embody the people of the city. I think that actually played a role."

Goldberg methodically built a case that compromised the integrity of the swaps settlement by linking UBS and Bank of America Merrill Lynch—however tenuous the connections may have seemed from a legal perspective—to the city's downfall.

"I'll never forget him thundering away at Buckfire, 'Did you think about all the ruined homes in the city? Did you think about all the shit the swap banks did to destroy the city?'" Hackney said. "It's not like he was saying things that were absurd. He was saying things like, 'What about the culpability of the banks?'"

Nonetheless, at $165 million, the settlement was within range of Rhodes's privately announced target of $150 million. The city had little reason to believe the judge would abruptly change his mind. Orr, Jones Day attorneys, and Miller Buckfire bankers—and even the creditors who hated the settlement—thought the deal was in the bag.

"I thought, 'OK, hopefully Judge Rosen has some idea about what will fly with Judge Rhodes. He's worked with the guy his entire life. He's the chief judge of the district,'" Orr said.

Rhodes convened a hearing on January 16, 2014, to deliver his ruling, and the city's attorneys along with lawyers for the creditors settled in to hear how he would justify authorizing the deal.

"The court stated earlier and states again that it will not participate in or permit the city to perpetuate the very kinds of hasty and imprudent financial decision-making that led to the disastrous swaps and COPs transactions," Rhodes said. "Those practices have already caused great harm to the city's creditors and to its citizens. In the court's view, one goal of this Chapter 9 case is to end these practices so that the city can truly recover from its past mistakes and move forward, and the court intends to conduct itself accordingly."

"The court concludes that the motion," he ruled, "should be denied."

An audible gasp swept the courtroom. For a second consecutive time, Rhodes had smoked the city's effort to eliminate the swaps.

The city, he opined, "is reasonably likely" to succeed if it opted to wage a legal battle against the validity of the COPs and swaps, making it very difficult to justify approving a settlement worth $165 million for Bank of America Merrill Lynch and UBS. The collateral pledge, he said, was probably illegal. And the swaps themselves were likely illegal, he ruled, noting that the city could argue that the shell corporations it established to do the transaction were "a sham."

It's "just too much money," Rhodes said, and the city must stop making bad deals. If the city won't stop, "the court must be the one to stop it," he declared.

At that moment, on a side street by his home near Chicago, Hackney was sitting in his parked car, having celebrated the birth of his third daughter three days earlier. He had dialed in to the court's phone line to listen live to the ruling.

"I take my daughters to preschool, and I almost didn't listen to the hearing because I thought, 'I don't even know what the point of listening to this is,'" he said.

Hackney had assumed the city would win.

"Then Judge Rhodes says, 'It's just too much money and I'm not going to approve it,'" Hackney said. "I kid you not—I almost fell out of my car."

The creditors were equally as stunned as the city, particularly because Rosen had personally recommended the deal.

"There was a flurry of emails that was just like, 'What the fuck just happened?! What does this mean?!'" Hackney said.

Jones Day attorney David Heiman, the city's lead bankruptcy lawyer, was similarly stunned. "That shocked everybody. No one more than Rosen. That was his first settlement," Heiman said. "I think it set him back a little bit and set us back a little bit. Like, what are we supposed to do now?"

Following the hearing, Rhodes called attorneys for the creditors into his chambers for a private conference. "What's your number? What's your number? What's your number?" he pressed each of the attorneys, trying to ascertain what figure would dissolve objections over a settlement.

"Don't ever do that to me again with Rosen," Rhodes told the creditors. "That really puts me in a horrible position."

The death of the swaps settlement amounted to a public repudiation of Rosen's deal and the city's judgment. People involved in the bankruptcy came to call the episode the Christmas Eve Massacre.

"Rhodes shocked everyone by saying, 'I don't like it,'" Buckfire said later. "He kind of slapped Rosen around, saying, 'You settled for too high a price.'"

But Rhodes didn't enjoy embarrassing the chief mediator.

"It was very hard for me to disapprove the swaps settlement because Judge Rosen had publicly recommended it to me," Rhodes recalled later. "I didn't like having to do that."

Regardless, it would later work to his advantage.

"It turned out incidentally—I didn't foresee this—that that decision probably did more to enhance my legitimacy as a fair and neutral judge in the case than anything else I did," Rhodes observed later. "Like I say, I was not expecting that or thinking about it at the time. But it did happen."

In a sense, the death of the swaps settlement was both an embarrassing loss for Orr and a categorical win for the city's retirees, many of its financial creditors, and residents. By torching the transaction, Rhodes gave the city leverage to get an even better deal from the banks, which now understood that the judge viewed the legality of their claims as highly questionable.

"He was in a position to make sure that the casino revenues continued to flow. We were never in a position to ensure that," Heiman said. "Was that too high? Yeah, of course. But compared to what? It's not too high compared to shutting down the city, which was more than theoretically possible. So he took the position, 'I'm not going to let this happen to the Detroit residents again.'"

Even as the swaps saga lingered, the creditors had set their sights on a different prize. A trove of masterpieces on display at the city-owned Detroit Institute of Arts offered a tantalizing source of value that could enrich bondholders, bond insurers, and retirees alike at the risk of compromising the future of one of the city's finest assets.

CHAPTER 8

Pills Over Picasso

Founded in 1885 by art lovers in Detroit as a private institution, the Detroit Museum of Art enjoyed a brief period of prosperity in the late nineteenth century. Backed by donations from its founders, the museum raised $100,000 to construct a building in what was then a mostly residential neighborhood at the corner of Jefferson Avenue and Hastings Street. The castle-like structure, designed in the Richardsonian-Romanesque style by Canadian James Balfour, opened on September 1, 1888.

About five years later, the Detroit Museum of Art encountered financial difficulties and soon began accepting subsidies from the city government. In the midst of World War I, the institution faced an existential crisis. The Michigan Supreme Court ruled in 1915 that the City of Detroit must stop subsidizing the museum because the organization was not a municipal agency.

Fearing the dissolution of the institution—an outcome that would surely endanger its treasured artwork—trustees concluded that the Detroit Museum of Art would be in safer hands under city ownership. They set out to negotiate a deal to transfer ownership of the entire collection and the museum's property to the City of Detroit. But they tried to attach conditions to the transfer.

First, the city must always operate the institution as an art museum. Second, it must agree to erect a new building to replace the previous facility. And third, "if the city should at any time fail to provide for and continue the proper care, maintenance, and exhibition of the art collection," the deed for the collection and the building would revert to the trustees, the museum's William Gray explained later in a January 27, 1920, report cataloged by Clyde Burroughs, secretary of the Detroit Museum of Art. The trustees wanted to ensure the museum would survive indefinitely with its collection intact.

But with the war raging on, Ralph Booth, president of the museum, wrote to his fellow trustees in a 1918 report with a patriotic plea.

"In no sense should we appear to demand a consideration that would in the slightest degree divert attention or detract so much as a featherweight of support from the successful prosecution of the war, and all that it means to our country and to civilization," Booth said, warning against making demands that could be perceived as insensitive amid weightier times.

But, he noted, art is crucial to the community's vibrancy.

"We feel the necessity of uplifting the spiritual side of life at such a time as this especially, that the best in civilization may always be secured to the world," he wrote.

Saving the Detroit Museum of Art was a shared concern for the city's leaders. But the city held all the leverage. With the museum teetering on the brink of collapse, the city offered the security of a financial lifeboat and the apparent permanency of municipal ownership.

"All of the councilmen," Gray wrote, "were of the opinion that no deed would be accepted except one without conditions."

Thus, the city accepted the art in 1919, no strings attached, although the state government enacted a law authorizing the transaction and stating that the donated property must be used for art purposes. The museum was renamed the Detroit Institute of Arts.

"They really, truly believed that it was safer to give the museum to the city," said Annmarie Erickson, current chief operating officer of the DIA. "They had no way of knowing what would happen down the road."

From the beginning, there was a recognition that Detroit was relatively unique in its ownership of an art museum. The cities of New York and Chicago, for example, had subsidized art operations in the 1910s, but they did not actually own the institutions.

"This change marks the beginning of an epoch in the history of Detroit when it shall become a civic function of the municipality to foster art," the DIA said in a 1919 report. "It is an era when art shall become in its broadest sense democratic, with the museum and its valuable collections actually belonging to the people."

In the 1920s, with the automotive industry flourishing, the City of Detroit was flush with cash. The museum went on a spending spree, using taxpayer dollars to acquire world-class artwork, such as Van Gogh's *Self-Portrait with Straw Hat*, Matisse's *The Window*, and numerous pieces by Rembrandt. In 1927, for example, with the Great Depression just a couple years away, the city spent $170,000 to acquire art for the DIA. That same year, crews finished construction on a new $4 million Beaux Arts facility for the museum on Woodward Avenue in what is now known as Midtown Detroit. Three years later, the DIA's director at the time, William Valentiner, procured a masterpiece for the new building when he spotted the missing original of Pieter Bruegel the Elder's *The Wedding Dance* on a trip to London.

Engraved on the façade of the new building were the words

"Dedicated by the People of Detroit to the Knowledge and Enjoyment of Art." Booth commemorated the moment at a ceremony in October 1927 devoting the facility to the people.

"The beauty of art and the spiritual and moral beauties which lie beyond and above the beauty of art alone are as essential in the life of a community as are the material comforts and modern facilities and improvements which it is the pride of every prosperous, enlightened community of today to furnish its citizens," he proclaimed. "And in this spirit today, (on) behalf of the people of Detroit, let us dedicate this building to the lofty purpose for which it was conceived: 'The Knowledge and Enjoyment of Art,' believing that we have seen the completion of a building that will stand for centuries to come."

A FEW WEEKS after investment banker Ken Buckfire started advising the City of Detroit on its restructuring in early 2013, he was sitting in his New York City office when a member of his team walked through the door.

"Ken, I've got good news and bad news," his colleague said. "The good news is the art museum might be worth billions of dollars."

Buckfire didn't make the connection. "What's the bad news?" he replied.

"Well, the city owns it," the colleague explained.

"I said, 'Oh my god,'" Buckfire recalled. "I grew up in Detroit and I didn't even know that."

Buckfire understood the implications. The City of Detroit, already on the verge of insolvency, had an incredible assortment of masterpieces on full display in a sparkling eighty-six-year-old architectural gem on Woodward Avenue.

In the late 1990s, the city had transferred operations of the museum and curation of its sixty-six-thousand-piece collection

to the nonprofit DIA Corporation, which completed a renovation, improved attendance, and convinced voters in Wayne,
Macomb, and Oakland counties to authorize a tax to support
the institution.

Although the nonprofit was responsible for those advancements, the art itself and the museum building were still owned by
the city. Remarkably, a city in profound distress also held a rich
slate of Van Goghs, Rembrandts, Picassos, and Rodins.

The DIA was a shimmering reminder of the city's former
wealth, a source of inspiration for the community, a provider of
education for schoolchildren, and an anchor of economic stability
for Midtown Detroit, one of the city's most vibrant areas.

But in bankruptcy, Detroit emergency manager Kevyn Orr's
team understood that the art—potentially worth billions—would
surely become a target of creditors, including financial giants and
pensioners alike.

"We didn't want to sell it because we understood that the DIA
is like a park, a civic asset. You don't sell your parks," Buckfire said.

But what happens when there's a need of greater proportion?
When contractors, pensioners, employees, and bondholders require
payment? When you can't protect your own citizens?

"The dilemma we faced was if the pension funds are so poorly
funded, a retiree might see his or her pension slashed from $20,000
to $10,000 per year if we couldn't find more funding for the pen-
sion plans. If we don't sell the art, we deserve to get hung," Buckfire
said. "We couldn't subject our retirees to this risk. Then the question is: What do you do about that?"

Jones Day attorney Bruce Bennett set up a conference call with
DIA executives to deliver a sobering lesson on Chapter 9 bankruptcy. The art, he said, was at risk. Creditors would try to extract
value out of the museum. "We knew creditors were going to insist
on it," he said later.

But after the conference call, Bennett believed the executives didn't understand the severity of the situation.

"We had a general impression that the museum thought that they could ignore this," he said.

Orr instructed his team to consider the possibility of monetizing the DIA.

"Philosophically, my view was I have a fiduciary duty, and I have pledged to the governor and everyone else I'm going to do my job," Orr recalled. "I'm atoning for the sins of others. If that means having to inventory the art, look. We have seven Renoirs. Do we need seven? OK? Can we sell a couple and get some coin? Let's just figure out what they're worth and have a discussion. I am going to account for every asset the city has. We may not end up selling them, but there's going to be an inventory. That's got to happen. That's the job."

Orr turned to Bennett and Buckfire—restructuring veterans with a reputation for playing hardball—to deliver a reality check to the DIA.

"They pretty much march straightforward," Orr said. "If you want them to do Sherman, they can do Sherman. But they really don't have a tolerance for any cant."

Their orders? "To send a message that it wasn't capable of being ignored," Bennett said.

Michigan treasurer Andy Dillon, Governor Rick Snyder's point person on troubled cities, pulled Buckfire aside shortly after the city started devising its legal strategies in early 2013, and expressed concern about the political implications for his boss.

"This is a lose-lose for the governor because on the front end if he's putting it in the mix, a certain type of voter is going to be unhappy with him," Dillon said later. "And if there are haircuts that are going to be made and the art is protected, then he put art before pensions. For a politician, it was a loser. So my view was,

'Let the creditors go after that. Don't put the governor in the middle of that.' And my advice wasn't followed."

Bennett and Buckfire told the DIA executives that the museum had limited time to raise hundreds of millions of dollars to make its collection untouchable. With that money—which the city could use to help settle its debts—the entire collection could be transferred to a trust and protected from the auction block. Without that money, Bennett and Buckfire posited, the city might have an obligation to pursue a sale to pay off creditors—and creditors would demand it.

DIA officials were aghast. Selling any art for any purpose, except for purchasing other art, violates the ethical standards of accredited museums. Under those standards, funds from the disposition of art can't even be used to shore up a sagging endowment, renovate an aging wing, pay salaries, or launch marketing campaigns.

"We parted from that meeting knowing that we needed to defend ourselves," DIA chairman Gene Gargaro said. "They were not going to do that."

The visit by Bennett and Buckfire "stiffened our spines," Erickson said. The museum leaders made it clear that they would wage a legal battle against any attempts to liquidate the artwork.

"There was never any doubt in our mind that if we had to, we would litigate it," Erickson said. "We would take it as far as it needed to go because our belief was then, and continues to be, that we hold the collection in trust for the public. It's the tenet that we live by in the museum world."

Buckfire and Bennett didn't care about the museum's tenets. They made it clear that selling art that was paid for with taxpayer dollars might be inevitable. If the DIA got in the way, Orr would have the power in bankruptcy to sever the nonprofit's operating agreement and dismiss the DIA executives, much like bankrupt companies can shed unwanted contracts. Buckfire and Bennett told the DIA to begin raising money.

"We said, 'The DIA Corporation trustees have a real problem,'" Buckfire recalled. "'We don't want to recommend marshaling the art for sale. But if you don't find a way to convey a lot of value to the city in exchange for putting the DIA into a trust, you're making it very hard for us to help you because we have a duty to the city and its creditors and we will not deviate from that.' They said, 'Well, we don't think we have to do anything.'"

Soon after that meeting, word of the city's threats leaked to the *Detroit Free Press*, which published a story on May 24, 2013, saying that Orr was threatening to sell DIA art to satisfy creditors. An explosion of public resentment followed.

"The next day it's in the news," Orr said. "We're sitting there saying, 'Really? You assholes can't keep a secret?' So, it wasn't us. We're going to do this professionally under the cover of darkness, but all hell breaks loose."

Bill Nowling, the colorful but generally measured senior advisor and spokesman for Orr, called a DIA lobbyist and unleashed a torrid rant. "I think I used the F-word [as] every article of the English language," Nowling said later.

"Not only have you not protected yourself, you've put a big target on your back and slathered yourself in honey. Now everybody's going to be gunning for you," Nowling told the lobbyist.

A whirlwind of publicity enveloped Detroit as the world realized that the city's fiscal implosion jeopardized its treasured art museum. Nowling started waking up in the middle of the night with chest pains, believing he was having a heart attack before calming down and going back to sleep. The city was being pummeled with negative stories from throughout the news media.

"Literally it was like sitting in the surf and just getting hammered by waves every day," Nowling said. "You knew they were coming and there was nothing you could do about it. Some were big, some were small."

The preeminent French newspaper *Le Monde* sent a reporter to Detroit for two weeks to investigate the DIA's fate. Nowling met up with him for a dinner interview.

"And I figure he's gonna buy me wine and I don't care because it's gonna be in French and nobody will read it," Nowling recalled.

So he blasted the French reporter. "You guys only care about the art. You don't care about Detroit," he spewed.

"What do you mean?" the befuddled journalist replied.

"The reporters from Germany and London and Paris and Beijing and Japan didn't come here until we started talking about the art. And suddenly they care," Nowling responded.

"Oh, well you can't" sell the art, the French reporter protested.

"So, would you cut old people's pensions? Old, poor, black people's pensions?" Nowling said, recalling his disgust at "Mr. Socialist" from Paris. "Really? They just couldn't get that around their head. It was like that was just a different plane of existence."

The museum's leaders contested that selling a single piece of art would lead to a cascade of events that would kill the regional tax that voters approved in 2012, deprive the museum of donor support because no one would give to a museum that could not control its destiny, and destroy the institution's credibility in the art community. The museum continued its public campaign against Orr's strategists by asking Michigan's Republican attorney general, Bill Schuette, to weigh in.

Schuette argued that the DIA was protected because its collection was held in a "perpetual charitable trust."

"The day he did that was a celebratory day for us," the DIA's Erickson said. "It really underscored the fact that yes, we did have a legal argument. We felt pretty strongly because we had reviewed the historical documents and understood the formation of the museum and the shift to city control. The understanding always was that the collection was held in the public trust both on the part of the founding members of the museum who negotiated the deal with the city and on the part of the city."

But legally, Schuette's opinion was no more binding in federal court than any other brief.

"We gave that very little weight," said Jones Day attorney David Heiman, the city's lead bankruptcy lawyer.

Politically Schuette's brief was an obstacle. But Snyder supported Orr's decision to threaten the DIA despite the political fury that rained down on the city after the threats were publicly disclosed.

"It was a difficult moment, but it had to be done," Snyder said later. "It wasn't an option to take it off the table. From a legal point of view, it had to be on the table. That was not a subjective decision. You need to stop and understand. If you go into bankruptcy, there's a set of ground rules you have to acknowledge you have to follow, which would include the fact that the art had to be on the table."

Endangering the DIA's collection was a reality check for anyone who believed the city could go bankrupt without a realistic threat to its prized possessions. Billionaire philanthropist and art connoisseur A. Alfred Taubman, one of the DIA's biggest donors, was disgusted. "It would be a crime" to sell any art to pay off debt, Taubman, who died nearly two years later, said shortly after the news broke of the DIA's precarious position.

Political pressure encircled the emergency manager's team. Nowling argued privately that threatening the DIA was not only appropriate but justified.

"Our job is not to protect art, but to save Detroit," Nowling told Orr in an email a few days after the DIA's vulnerability was publicized. "We have said ALL options are on the table and being considered. We meant it. This is a financial emergency, and financial emergencies require extraordinary measures, including, maybe, selling art."

Nowling drew an analogy to General Dwight Eisenhower's leadership in Europe on D-Day. "Ike's job was to win the war," Nowling wrote. "He knew that to win the war he had to take Normandy. He also knew that signing the invasion order was tantamount to signing 50,000 death certificates."

To fix Detroit, a few casualties were inevitable. "I don't want to pack up the art, but I wasn't hired to protect it and neither were you," Nowling told his boss.

"If Al Taubman, Keith Crain don't like it, eff them," he wrote, referring to the DIA philanthropist and a Detroit media baron. "They can buy the art and gift it back to the DIA or they can roll the dice and take their chances."

The city, he said, should proffer a forceful defense for the need to consider selling art.

Meanwhile, for retirees who were facing possible cuts to their pensions and health care benefits, the justification for potentially selling art was simple.

Ryan Plecha, an attorney for the city's retiree associations, later described pensioners' philosophy succinctly: "Pills over Picasso."

THE CORE LEGAL ISSUE—whether you could sell the DIA's property at all—was sharply divisive. The DIA argued that the collection was completely shielded from sales because it was held in a public trust, even though no paperwork had been completed to establish such a trust.

The fact that the Detroit Museum of Art trustees had given the collection to the city with no strings attached nearly a century earlier seemed to have exposed the collection to attacks. Detroit's lawyers determined privately that the city at least had the right to sell the approximately 5 percent of the DIA's collection that was purchased with taxpayer dollars: if the city paid for it, the city can sell it. Though the city stopped buying art for the DIA in the 1950s, it had accumulated a substantial collection. The rest of the art was either purchased using donor dollars or given to the museum in some capacity.

Buckfire determined that artwork purchased with taxpayer dollars was a "non-core" asset, and he knew that creditors would not allow the city to devise a restructuring plan that left valuable property untouched. Selling art, he said, would be necessary unless money bubbled up somewhere.

"It's not even a question of if I thought I'd do it. I did. I do," Buckfire said later. "I would have to advise Kevyn appropriately. None of us would want to do that. But the law's the law. We don't have the ability to hide from our responsibilities, as painful as they are. We had to maximize the recoveries to the city's creditors, including the retirees. So yes, we would have recommended selling part of the collection. No doubt about it."

DIA leaders made a nominal effort to gauge the appetite of the wider foundation community to provide funds that might save the museum from a prospective sale. But they ran into a wall. They flew to New York to meet with Darren Walker, president of the Ford Foundation. Walker was sympathetic to the DIA's cause but expressed no interest in providing dollars.

"As I sit here today, I don't see anything I can do to help," Walker told the DIA. "Foundations fund the future. They don't pay for the mistakes of the past."

The brewing fight pitted pensions and services against art. Which do you want to save?

"It really was a false premise," Erickson said. "It's quite emotional to talk about people's pensions, people on fixed incomes losing dollars. My father was an employee of the City of Detroit. My mother gets his survivor benefits. You certainly didn't want to see a big cut in that."

But DIA leaders believed that selling a single painting would destroy the museum and damage the community.

"They feel a little whipsawed," Nowling told Orr in an email about a month before the bankruptcy.

"Things change," Orr responded. "They need to grow up."

IN THE SUMMER of 2013, as the city tumbled into bankruptcy, creditors were already asking for a valuation of the DIA.

"'Asked' is a more polite way of saying 'demanded,'" Buckfire told an official of the New York–based auction house Christie's in an email on July 25.

Buckfire, in fact, had already asked Christie's to conduct a "quick and dirty" assessment of the value of the city-purchased DIA artwork in the spring. Christie's had dispatched experts on impressionist, modern, American, and Islamic art to visit the DIA in early June. They had perused the museum in plainclothes to avoid attention. But the auction house started having second thoughts about conducting a comprehensive assessment after a deluge of negative publicity ensued in the art press. Critics assailed the company for assisting the city.

"All I can think of is, shame on Christie's," wrote *Real Clear Arts* blogger and journalist Judith H. Dobrzynski. "Sure, business is business, but let's remember here that it is NOT the Detroit Institute of Arts that has mismanaged the city and led to the bankruptcy."

Her piece unsettled Christie's executives.

"Our name/brand is being seriously damaged," Christie's president Doug Woodham told fellow executives in an email.

Nowling privately gave Christie's a chance to back out before signing a contract to assess all the city-purchased property at the museum. But the company stuck with its agreement to appraise the city-bought artwork and devise a list of alternatives to selling the collection. A previously warm relationship between the DIA and Christie's became icy as the city forced the museum to cooperate with appraisers.

"These were people we had worked with through the years and had developed relationships with," Erickson said. "They knew how strongly we felt about the sanctity of the collection."

Erickson gave explicit instructions to her staff to provide the bare minimum amount of support to the auction house. "You will facilitate but not assist," she told them.

Collections management staff members, who are accustomed to physically handling the artwork, were assigned to help the Christie's appraisers. But DIA curators—the art experts—were told to keep their mouths shut. "We didn't want to provide Christie's with any inside information that the curators might have on the collection," Erickson said.

Supporters flooded the museum with sympathetic emails and calls, and monetary donations rose. Ordinary trips to the museum took on the feel of hospital visits. It was unclear whether the patient would survive, and people wanted to pay their respects. Visitors looked for signs of distress.

One day, Bruegel's *The Wedding Dance*, an oil-on-wood-panel masterpiece procured with city funds eighty-three years earlier, was hauled off exhibit so that curators could conduct a regular checkup to ensure that temperature and humidity levels weren't causing the paint to crumble. Several visitors approached a security guard to express concern.

"Are you hiding it?" one asked.

———

A PRIZED PAINTING is not worth anything until you convince someone to buy it, so calculating its monetary value is profoundly difficult. But Christie's estimated that 2,773 museum works purchased directly by the city would fetch anywhere from $454 million to $867 million if they were up for sale. The top eleven works, most of them "old master paintings," accounted for 75 percent of the collection's value. Alternatives to selling the museum's treasures, such as renting the art to other museums, were not particularly lucrative or practical, Christie's concluded.

The Wedding Dance topped the list at a market value of anywhere from $100 million to $200 million. Van Gogh's *Self-Portrait with Straw Hat*, an oil-on-artist-board panel painted in 1887, was worth anywhere from $80 million to $150 million. Rembrandt's *The Visitation*, an oil-on-panel work he signed in 1640, was worth $50 million to $90 million.

In the event of a sale, major U.S. museums almost certainly would have refused to bid to avoid upsetting industry standards, risking their accreditation status, and triggering a publicity crisis. But there's no shortage of wealthy private investors in the United States and abroad who would have seized the opportunity.

For Orr, Buckfire, and the city's attorneys, the Christie's assessment set the bar for how much value they needed to extract from the museum to achieve a reasonable restructuring plan. The city's message to the museum was clear: raise the money—or else.

"We told Gargaro that we had no choice," Buckfire said later. "Once the valuation of the art paid for by the city was completed, the DIA people understood, the city would have to find a way to deliver that value to its creditors."

Even if it meant securing an order from bankruptcy judge Steven Rhodes to force a sale.

"If they couldn't raise the money, would I have recommended

sending in U.S. Marshals to take fifty paintings off the wall? Yes," Buckfire said. "And by the way, there still would have been a museum on Woodward Avenue with 59,950 works of art."

Charting a financially sustainable path might mean picking the people of Detroit over a few paintings at the DIA.

"If it came down to selling a Van Gogh so that the city's retirees can live on tuna fish and not cat food, it's not even a close call," Buckfire said. "I'm sorry, but it was all mischaracterized by the DIA. Their position was not well thought through."

CHAPTER 9

You Can't Eat Principles

A few weeks after Detroit filed for bankruptcy, Chief Judge Gerald Rosen of the U.S. District Court for the Eastern District of Michigan headed to Ponte Vedra Beach, Florida, for a golf vacation. Each day, the newly appointed chief mediator in Detroit's bankruptcy crawled out of bed before dawn for a sobering read: Kevyn Orr's initial proposal to Detroit's creditors.

Bonds, pensions, and retiree health care obligations already sucked up about four out of ten of the city's general-fund dollars, and that number was expected to skyrocket to seven out of ten within a few years. Without drastic cuts to the city's liabilities, impoverished neighborhoods would continue to wither under the crushing weight of violent crime, abandoned homes, and unreliable mass transit.

But Orr's proposal, left untouched, would trigger pension cuts of more than 50 percent and massive reductions to retiree health care benefits, not to mention a potential liquidation of the Detroit Institute of Arts.

Once he finished absorbing the gravity of the crisis, Rosen picked

up the phone and began calling attorneys for the city's major creditors to gauge the state of the case. After those conversations, Rosen
concluded that the fates of two crucial parties in the bankruptcy—
the group of more than thirty-two thousand pensioners and the city-
owned DIA—were inextricably linked.

The bankruptcy was already shaping up to pit retirees against
the museum. Pensioners were ready to duel over Orr's plan to slash
their benefits, and the DIA was similarly girding for a battle over
Orr's decision to consider auctioning art. When Rosen called to
discuss the case after his appointment, Mike Nicholson, general
counsel for the United Auto Workers union, suggested that the
State of Michigan buy the DIA and give the money to pensioners.

Rosen liked the concept, but he believed it needed to be bigger.
He grabbed a yellow legal pad and flipped it over. On the cardboard
back, he jotted down notes from his conversations. Then, he started
doodling.

He wrote the word "art" and drew a box around it, symbolically representing a lockbox around the DIA and protecting it from
financial creditors. On the left side of the box, he wrote "state" and
on the right side he wrote "pensions." Then he drew short arrows,
with dollar signs above each, connecting the art box with the state
and pensions.

To resolve the bankruptcy, he theorized, you must transform
a previously binary equation—art versus pensions—into a holistic
formula. Rosen theorized that an injection of outside money would
be necessary to prevent a fire sale, shield pensioners, and reach a
viable bankruptcy blueprint. On the back of the Ampad legal pad,
he jotted down his thoughts: "How much?" "Timeline?" "Protect
art—how?" "What about fed gov't?" "State?" "State museum?"
"Other sources?" "Private donors?" "Foundations?" "DIA?" He
labeled the budding concept, "Art Trust."

David Heiman, the lead Jones Day bankruptcy attorney representing Detroit, was skeptical when Rosen told him he wanted to secure external funds to help resolve the case by protecting the museum and shoring up pensions.

"I said, 'God bless,' but did I believe it was going to happen? Uh, I wanted it to happen, but it wasn't something I spent a lot of time wishing for because it seemed so unusual," Heiman said.

Rosen knew he needed help. One of his first calls was to Eugene Driker, a longtime friend. A statesman in the Detroit legal community during the last half century, Driker was a lifelong resident of Detroit and a partner in the downtown law firm Barris, Sott, Denn & Driker. His calm demeanor, approachability, and reputation for fairness made him a common choice when warring parties needed an arbitrator to resolve their disputes.

Driker was riding his bicycle near his condominium in Glen Arbor, a town tucked in the northwestern corner of Michigan near Traverse City, when his cell phone rang. He pulled to the side of the road. It was Rosen.

"I don't generally [take] cell phone calls while I'm on the bike," Driker said. But he knew about Rosen's mammoth assignment and was deeply concerned about the fate of his hometown.

He quickly agreed to serve on Rosen's mediation team and began reading up on Chapter 9 bankruptcy. With an undergraduate degree in mathematics and deep experience with actuarial issues, Driker headed negotiations with the city's pensioners. He was joined by U.S. District judge Victoria Roberts of the Eastern District of Michigan, a native Detroiter who led negotiations with unions in coordination with Driker.

Rosen also added former Detroit resident and senior U.S. District Court judge Wiley Daniel of the District of Colorado to his team, as well as U.S. Bankruptcy Court judge Elizabeth Perris of the District of Oregon, who had mediated disputes in three municipal bankruptcies in California.

The chief mediator also eventually convinced several others to join his team: former U.S. Bankruptcy and U.S. District Court judge David Coar; U.S. District judge Sean Cox of the Eastern District of Michigan, who had provided oversight for the Detroit Water and Sewerage Department; U.S. District judge David Lawson of the Eastern District of Michigan; and Cooley Law School professor Gina Torielli.

Arguably the first question Rosen needed to answer was whether a federal bailout was possible for Detroit. One big check from Washington could make a lot of debt go away.

But in the immediate months after his appointment as emergency manager, Orr had tried and failed to persuade the White House to deliver cash for Detroit. His former University of Michigan Law School classmate, Valerie Jarrett, a close friend and senior advisor to President Barack Obama, turned Orr down.

U.S. senator Carl Levin, a Democrat representing Michigan and a former member of the Detroit City Council, had told the city privately that a bailout for Detroit was politically impossible on Capitol Hill. But he compiled a list of federal money that the city might be able to tap to boost services, including foreclosure-fallout funds that could be converted into blight-removal dollars.

After he became the lead mediator, Rosen tried Jarrett himself, believing the president might take pity on the Motor City. Detroit is an intensely Democratic town, a bastion of liberalism with a fierce loyalty to union causes and to the president. But the Obama administration had no interest in pursuing a bailout for Detroit. Jarrett said no for a second time.

Rosen turned, instead, to the governor. Rick Snyder was a long-time friend. In 1982, shortly after joining the accounting firm Coopers & Lybrand, Snyder got an apartment in Southfield near Rosen's congressional campaign headquarters. One day, he stopped by.

"You guys could use some help," the future governor told Rosen.

"I was his data analysis person, looking at the history of who voted Republican, Democrat in prior elections," Snyder recalled. "So I had these cool maps showing where he should go walk and where he should try to get votes."

Rosen got trounced. But the campaign sparked a casual friendship between the two. By the fall of 2013, Rosen needed Snyder's help again. Rosen approached with a big request. He told the governor about his nascent concept for deploying state cash to help mitigate pension cuts and save the DIA. Could the governor convince the state Legislature to contribute money to Detroit?

Snyder had bet his political legacy on Detroit's bankruptcy, describing it as tough love that would provide the city a fresh start. But he had already publicly disavowed a bailout—a combustible concept among fellow Republicans in Lansing.

The governor's advisors made it clear to Rosen that the answer was no. Snyder already had his hands full fending off the Tea Party movement in the state's Republican Party and was preparing for a reelection fight in 2014. Convincing the Republican-dominated state Legislature to bail out Detroit would require political capital the governor's team did not believe he could expend.

"I told him [I was] happy to have him come back and have a dialogue as he found information on how we could be helpful," Snyder said later.

ROSEN'S ART TRUST concept conflicted with a coalescing plan devised by creditors to assail the DIA. Against the backdrop of Orr's proposal to deeply slash pensions and health care costs, bond insurer Financial Guaranty Insurance Company identified an opportunity to form an alliance with disenfranchised labor creditors: namely, the Official Committee of Retirees and its investment banker, Lazard's Ron Bloom.

The prospect of a strategic coalition between Wall Street and Main Street to fight Orr's restructuring plan was tantalizing for both sides, if not altogether explosive. Technically, both sides had already formed a legal alliance to oppose the city's first swaps settlement.

But Steve Spencer saw an opening to go further. Spencer, a financial advisor for investment bank Houlihan Lokey, which had been hired to represent FGIC, recognized that the retirees were scrambling for allies.

"Our question was, could we get to a deal with Ron? If we linked up with Ron, we were the most powerful bloc," Spencer said.

In the Motor City, Bloom was a negotiating legend. A former advisor to the United Steelworkers union, he is one of the world's leading labor negotiators in corporate crises. During the Great Recession, Bloom played a crucial role on President Obama's automotive task force, rescuing General Motors and Chrysler and convincing the United Auto Workers union to accept concessions.

FGIC, which had support from its close ally Syncora, proposed to Bloom a unified coalition of the retiree committee and insurers of the city's certificates of participation (COPs). Much like their separate alliance to kill the first swaps deal, the retirees and bond insurers shared a common objective: undermine Orr's debt-cutting roadmap to secure more money for themselves.

Under Spencer's proposal, the COPs insurers and the retirees—collectively representing about 90 percent of Detroit's unsecured liabilities—would publicly release their own restructuring plan for the city. Unlike in corporate bankruptcies, creditors aren't allowed to officially propose restructuring plans to the court in Chapter 9 bankruptcy. But the optics of a coalition of Detroit's biggest creditors would put significant pressure on the city to capitulate.

"If you had unanimous creditor opposition to the city, is the judge really going to approve a plan without any consenting class?" Bloom said later.

Core to the proposal was an agreement to publicly support a liquidation of the most valuable works at the DIA, a monetization of the Detroit Water and Sewerage Department, and a sale of city real estate. Under one version of the plan, the proceeds—estimated at about $4 billion—would be split 50-50 between retirees and financial creditors, according to documents detailing the proposal. The proposal envisioned allowing the city to maintain its plan to invest in basic services with its traditional cash flow, believing that the liquidation of the DIA's most treasured works and the privatization of the water department would supply plenty of cash to free up the regular budget to lift beleaguered city departments.

"Unless you provided for the reinvestment initiative, you never were going to get out of the starting gate," Bloom said. "Whether it was the law or politics, you had to salute that."

As part of the proposed coalition, FGIC and Syncora would be charged with hitting the front lines in the war against the museum, inevitably absorbing a volley of negative publicity and legal attacks. The plan would allow the retirees to enjoy the benefits of a lucrative DIA sell-off, while avoiding the messiness of spearheading an assault on a city jewel. Advisors for the bond insurers and retirees believed that the emergence of an alliance of financial giants and pensioners would shift momentum to their side, giving them significant influence over the city's debt-cutting plan.

Rosen got wind of the talks, which were occurring in November and December 2013.

"We had never come out and said you had to sell the art. But we also never said that you absolutely should not," Bloom said. "We were talking to sell-the-art advocates. They knew we were." He added, "Our theory was that will hopefully get the city and the state to take our effort more seriously."

The two sides were still hashing out details, but the proposed alliance enjoyed "wide support from creditors," Lazard bankers reported in a private presentation December 13, 2013.

Spencer was encouraged by the momentum but still viewed Bloom cautiously.

"We could speak to each other about terms of the deal, but there was only so much I would tell him and only so much I knew he would ever tell me," Spencer said. "But what other option did I have?"

Spencer pressed the retiree committee's advisors to get their client to approve the accord and announce it publicly. The retiree committee scheduled the deal for a vote at a private meeting on the evening of December 19, 2013, and Lazard believed that the panel would embrace the tie-up. But only hours before committee members were set to vote, the governor told the *Detroit News* that he might support a state contribution to help resolve the bankruptcy if the cash were part of a comprehensive settlement. The retiree committee members read the online version of the *Detroit News* story before their meeting and, heartened by the governor's words, voted against the deal with FGIC and Syncora.

Representatives for both sides agreed to continue negotiations. But in true double-agent fashion, Bloom and the retiree committee's lawyers were playing both sides. As they negotiated the deal with the bond insurers, they weighed an alternative plan being hatched by Rosen.

SEVERAL WEEKS AFTER Detroit filed for bankruptcy, Mariam Noland was standing in line at the Gateway Deli across the corner from the federal courthouse in downtown Detroit, when she spotted Rosen.

Noland, a soft-spoken visionary who wields considerable influence in the local philanthropic community as president of the Community Foundation for Southeast Michigan, always felt out of her element when interacting with the judiciary. Her foundation managed a philanthropic fund for the court, so periodically she would have to descend twenty floors of her Fort Street office tower, walk one block to the courthouse, snake through security lines, and make presentations to the judges.

"I was always scared to death of those guys," she said.

She exchanged pleasantries with Rosen, simply acknowledging the judge's new assignment as chief mediator in Detroit's bankruptcy.

"Geez, it's really nice you're handling this," she told the judge. "And if there's anything I can do, let me know."

She didn't mean anything by it. "It was just a throwaway," Noland said later. That is, she would love to help but didn't envision any role for a small nonprofit in a municipal bankruptcy involving $18 billion in liabilities.

She grabbed her takeout order, and they parted ways. Soon after the chance encounter, Rosen called. "Can you come see me sometime?" he asked.

"Sure," she replied.

"How about today?" the judge implored.

That afternoon, Noland traipsed up to the judge's chambers on the seventh floor of the courthouse. Beautiful wooden bookcases, strewn with souvenirs from the judge's legal career and personal pursuits, dominated the sides of the room. On one shelf sat Winston Churchill memorabilia.

As she entered the room, she saw Rosen and then, next to him, his friend and fellow mediator, Eugene Driker. "It's like, OK, this is going to be serious," Noland recalled.

Rosen and Driker spelled out their proposal. They wanted

to raise hundreds of millions of dollars from foundations to help resolve the bankruptcy by reducing pension cuts and saving the DIA from a sell-off.

"They knew that a lot of money would help," she said. "They also made it clear that they needed this money very fast."

Noland pondered the moment. "Foundations don't move fast," she was thinking. "They don't fund things that have already happened. They never fund public agencies, like paying pensions. If that's been done anywhere, I don't know."

She thought the judge's idea was categorically implausible. "Are you crazy?" she thought.

"I did not say that," she remembered. "I thought that. So I said, 'Sure.'"

Back at her office, Noland followed through on her promise. She plunged through her Rolodex, firing off calls to the leaders of about a dozen nonprofit foundations, including notable philanthropic groups with Detroit connections, such as the Ford Foundation, the Kresge Foundation, the Knight Foundation, and the Mott Foundation. With Detroit's bankruptcy occupying national headlines, she figured it wouldn't be difficult to at least intrigue her fellow nonprofit leaders with the prospect of helping the city in some capacity.

"I said, 'Would you be willing to come listen to the judge?' To a person they said either, 'Yes I can come,' or they said, 'I can't, but we'll have our board chair there.' Everyone said, 'Yes,'" she recalled.

They set a date to meet with the judge: Tuesday, November 5, 2013.

NOT LONG AFTER becoming president of the Ford Foundation in early September 2013, Darren Walker had outlined a plan to expand the foundation's commitment to Detroit. Henry Ford's son, Edsel

Ford, established the Ford Foundation in 1936. But the foundation moved its headquarters to New York more than three decades later, diminishing its ties to the Motor City. Walker believed that it was imperative to honor the Ford family and the foundation's corporate heritage by reestablishing a connection to Detroit. Still, when Walker got Noland's call a few weeks after starting his new job, he was interested but skeptical.

"When someone calls a foundation and there's a problem, they usually want you to help," he said later. "That's what we do at foundations. We help solve problems. But this problem was so monumental that I couldn't imagine what a foundation could do to help."

Nonetheless, Walker agreed to make the trip from New York to Detroit for the November 5 meeting.

Alberto Ibargüen, CEO of the Knight Foundation, had visited Detroit a few weeks before Noland called to invite him to the same meeting. The Knight Foundation was founded by the Knight Newspapers family, whose media properties once included the *Detroit Free Press*. Because of that heritage, Knight had devoted millions of dollars in grants during the last several decades to Detroit initiatives with a focus on journalism, entrepreneurship, and the arts.

Ibargüen had brought Knight's board of directors to Detroit for a board meeting simply to gain a better understanding of the city's challenges and opportunities. Detroit emergency manager Kevyn Orr even gave a private talk to the board.

"He was extraordinarily articulate, tough, clear, and put everything on the table," Ibargüen said. "That was actually the first meeting at which I remember somebody in authority talking about the art as an asset that needed to be addressed in some fashion."

Ibargüen walked away from the meeting with "zero inkling" that the Knight Foundation would have any role in trying to resolve the bankruptcy, but he did have a better understanding of the downsides of Chapter 9. At the time, Ibargüen, who calls himself a "recovering lawyer," was serving on the board of American Airlines, which was weeks away from emerging from a successful Chapter 11 bankruptcy. In Chapter 9, he learned, creditors have an incentive to drag out the fight to avoid taking cuts as long as possible.

"The city's not going anyplace," Ibargüen said. "So there's a kind of built-in advantage to anyone who can dig in and say, 'I'm not moving. You owe me a hundred cents on the dollar.'"

No one understood the realities on the ground more than Orr, who was making little progress in mediation several months into the bankruptcy. When Rosen pitched the concept of securing foundation funding to help reduce pension cuts and save the DIA, Orr was skeptical.

"I'm looking at him thinking, 'Do you understand how philanthropies work? There's charity, and there's philanthropy. And philanthropies don't just give money away,'" Orr said.

Go for it, Orr told Rosen, but don't get your hopes up.

The city's attorneys maintained their aggressive stance in mediation, pushing for steep pension cuts and questioning whether Rosen's Art Trust would come to fruition. "I think people thought . . . 'Can this really happen?'" said Heather Lennox, a Jones Day attorney who helped lead negotiations with pensioners. "Because it never had before."

AS THE MEETING with foundation leaders approached, Rosen set up a dinner at his home with Rip Rapson, his doubles tennis partner in the 1970s while they were both congressional aides in Washington, D.C.

Rapson was CEO of the Michigan-based Kresge Foundation, whose $3.5 billion endowment and commitment to philanthropy in Detroit made it a prime candidate to contribute to the Art Trust. Over the last several years, Rapson had directed a philanthropic funding blitz in Detroit, plunging money into the Detroit Future City project to explore new land use opportunities and backing the construction of a new streetcar line on Woodward Avenue.

Rosen tested his idea on Rapson, saying he wanted to raise $500 million from foundations but needed to identify any potential land mines in his approach. Rapson laughed.

"Judge, that's a huge amount of capital to ask on such short notice with so relatively few actors," Rapson said.

"Well what do you mean?" Rosen responded.

"At the end of the day you only have two or three foundations that are capable of making the kind of contributions you need to get to this number," Rapson responded. "This is a very difficult sell to smaller organizations for whom this will be seen as outside their scope of authority and expertise."

Rapson told the judge that he would need the Ford Foundation and the Kresge Foundation to make major contributions to keep his proposal alive.

"The judge was really fixated on the art," Rapson recalled later. "He said, 'I really just have to take the art off the table because otherwise it's going to be litigated.' I said, 'Well, with all due respect, that optic will not be helpful to you. It's got to be seen as somehow playing into your argument that it expedites the bankruptcy.'"

That was Rosen's mission.

"So it's really important that you don't put the foundations in the position of seeming to come to the rescue of the art institute," Rapson told Rosen. "And, similarly, it's probably going to be a fine line you're going to walk because we also can't be seen as coming to the rescue of the pensioners."

Rosen absorbed his friend's advice. "Are you willing to keep an open mind?" Rosen asked.

Rapson, agreeing to send two colleagues to Rosen's upcoming

meeting as he headed to South Africa on a previously scheduled trip, said, "Of course."

But "I assume what you'll get from your meeting is a lot of polite silence," Rapson told Rosen.

WITH THE WIND whipping on Election Day in Detroit, the leaders of a dozen foundations meandered into the judge's stately conference room on the seventh floor of the Theodore Levin U.S. Courthouse on West Lafayette Boulevard, not knowing exactly what to expect.

Rosen had asked his fellow mediators to attend the meeting to lend gravity to the conversation. Driker felt passionately that for the idea to work, the mediation team would have to compile enough money to make a meaningful dent on pension cuts and ensure the DIA never encountered a similar situation again.

"I was convinced that you could never get anybody to put any money into this process unless they were sure that the money would solve the problem," Driker said.

Driker liked the idea, but he doubted the foundations would jump at the chance to get involved.

"I was expecting their reaction would be, 'We'll get back to you. Don't call us, we'll call you,'" Driker said.

On the agenda Rosen prepared for the meeting, he channeled Churchill: "A pessimist sees the danger in every opportunity. An optimist sees the opportunity in every danger."

The mediators were lined up in a row of chairs at a rectangular conference table. Rosen sat in the middle, flanked by his team. He proceeded to lay out the city's problems, like an investigator splashing an interrogation table with grim photos of a crime scene. And he gave the foundation leaders a crash course in municipal bankruptcy.

It "was pretty depressing. The amount of liabilities that the city owed. The political quagmire. The possibility that there could be years and years of litigation and public discord—with the nation seeing Detroit as just this place of dysfunction," Walker said. "It was pretty sobering."

Without an influx of external funding, Rosen believed that the bankruptcy would devolve into a brawl between the city, its creditors, the DIA, and political leaders—with the city's neglected residents left to fend for themselves as crime worsened and blight proliferated.

"But you can solve this," Rosen told the foundation leaders.

"Boy," Ibargüen thought to himself, "this is a stretch."

Walker didn't mince words. "What you're asking us to do is to help correct the bad decisions of leadership in the past," Walker told the mediators.

Foundations invest in the future. "Foundations don't often get engaged in fixing something that was created by a mayor or a pension board," Walker recalled later. "Period."

But the conversation gradually turned more productive as the mediators explained the unique nature of their proposal. By the end of the meeting, Ibargüen began to see the logic in the judge's equation for solving the bankruptcy.

"You keep the cultural treasure. It's a symbolic victory for the city. You take care of most of the pension obligations. You put the money into the economy because the people still live there. And as the city is going forward, it has a lot less money to pay out as a regular expense of running the city. All of it made sense to me," Ibargüen said.

As the meeting ended, the mood was buoyant.

"At the outset, we thought that the focus of many of the foundations would be to salvage the art, to salvage the DIA—and a second in priority would be to preserve the pensions to the extent possible," Driker said. "The overarching consideration by those in attendance was neither of those. It was more to save the city. The reaction of some of the leading foundations was that the art and the pensions were important pieces of all of this, but the most important outcome was to save Detroit. That was kind of breathtaking."

Afterward, several attendees headed to Noland's house in a suburb east of Detroit for a dinner gathering. Noland's home, designed by Finnish architect Eliel Saarinen and restored to its original condition, is a common gathering spot for community leaders to discuss vexing challenges.

Rosen, Driker, Walker, Ibargüen, and Mott Foundation CEO Bill White joined Noland and her husband, James Kelly, for a catered meal, which had gone dry as the courthouse meeting tarried. In the home's signature round dining room, the leaders talked about the heroics of Rosen's idol, Churchill, and discussed their common interests, including baseball and golf.

"If people are going to give money, they have to know each other. It's like any other business," Noland said later.

Ibargüen savored the conversations about baseball with Rosen, whose father had been a minor league player in the Chicago Cubs' farm system.

"In my world, baseball is life. I grew up in the Caribbean, listening to simulcasts in Spanish of the New York Yankees games on the radio because we didn't have a television," Ibargüen said. "It was as if we had known each other for a long time."

Walker's presence at the meeting was particularly crucial, because everyone involved in the budding deal knew that without the Ford Foundation, they would have no chance of raising the kind of cash the mediators wanted. The Ford Foundation's endowment totaled more than $10 billion, compared with $3.5 billion for the Kresge Foundation and more than $2 billion each for the Knight Foundation and the Mott Foundation.

As the dinner came to a close, Walker and Ibargüen, good friends from long before the meeting, hopped into a cab and headed for their hotel rooms in downtown Detroit. When the evening started, they were skeptical. But after several hours of conversation, they had both become believers.

Ibargüen exuded enthusiasm. "This isn't going to happen if you don't step up," Ibargüen told Walker as the clock neared midnight, "and you need to step up soon because we could lose momentum and this thing could go off the rails at any time."

Walker knew it. "I really did feel inspired by his words," Walker remembered later.

The two foundation executives weighed their chances of convincing their respective boards to green-light pledges.

"For this to work, Ford has to really come in big," Walker told Ibargüen.

Ibargüen was impressed. "Darren had been president of the Ford Foundation for about thirty-seven minutes at that point. Really, he had just started a month or two before. But he was determined that there has to be an end to the alienation between Detroit and the Ford Foundation," Ibargüen said later. "For me, it was a real opportunity for Knight because we're already a comparatively major philanthropic funder in Detroit."

He turned to Walker in the cab. "How big is big?" he inquired.

"It's got to be fifty or a hundred million," Walker responded.

Ibargüen sensed an opportunity to nudge his friend: "I ignored the fifty, because I'm committed at this point in my own mind," he recalled.

Ibargüen challenged Walker. "If you do a hundred, I have to do twenty—and by the way you're getting away with murder because on an asset basis, you're seven times bigger than we are, and I shouldn't be putting up that much money."

They laughed. "I think we have a deal," Walker said, smiling.

"Alberto," he added, "this is going to be a hundred-million-dollar taxi ride."

In the days that followed, the other foundation leaders who attended the meeting reported back to their colleagues. Rapson, returning from his trip to South Africa, had become a big believer. But several of the smaller foundations privately expressed skepticism at first.

"I had gotten calls from more than half of the folks who said, 'There's no way we're doing this, so what do we do?'" Rapson recalled.

Walker and Rapson agreed that they needed to jointly champion the cause to give confidence to the smaller foundations that the deal would work. They began campaigning behind the scenes with their foundation counterparts, formed committees to explore the legal implications of the proposal, and maintained contact with Rosen as they made progress.

Rapson saw the bankruptcy as a crossroads for Detroit—and for the Kresge Foundation's investments in the city.

"We had spent the previous four or five years investing in the kind of civic scaffolding that we believed would be necessary for Detroit's recovery over time," Rapson said. "Our sense is that that scaffolding was powerful and would stand the test of time, but not if a bankruptcy obliterated all of the work and the effort and the investment that had gone into it. The bankruptcy clearly had the potential to undo years and years of careful investment and build-out of the kinds of building blocks that a community needs in order to be successful."

Walker, Rapson, Ibargüen, and Noland simultaneously embarked on a campaign to convince their trustees and other foundations to approve funding to help resolve the city's bankruptcy. They urged the Mott Foundation, the Kellogg Foundation, the Erb

Foundation, the Hudson-Webber Foundation, and others to consider donations.

A few weeks later, Rosen met with Walker to discuss the prospective deal at the Ford Foundation headquarters in New York. As the judge entered Walker's office, he noticed Nelson Mandela images hanging on the wall. "You know, Nelson Mandela said, 'The impossible's always impossible until you do it,'" Rosen told Walker.

Walker's eyes lit up. "You're so right," he told the chief mediator.

But the deal wasn't done yet. On the wall of Walker's office also hung a *New Yorker* cartoon depicting an older man chasing after a dapper young chap who is throwing money out the window. "Just a minute, young man," the older character proclaims. "That's not the way we do things at the Ford Foundation!"

Walker looked at Rosen and pointed to the cartoon. Rosen didn't miss a beat. "If you want to reconnect Ford with Detroit, you should do it in a meaningful way," he said to Walker.

Meanwhile, at Knight, Ibargüen delivered a request for $20 million at a board meeting in early December 2013. At the conclusion of his infectious presentation, trustee Beverly Knight Olson asked to be recognized. Throughout the presentation she had remained silent.

"She usually is not a fan of big grants, and this would be, if we did it, one of the biggest we had ever done," Ibargüen recalled later. "I had no idea what she was going to say."

"I think this is wonderful," she proclaimed. "I think this is exactly what we ought to do. I think this is exactly what my father and my uncle set up the foundation for. But I don't think $20 million is enough. I think we should do thirty."

Ibargüen was floored. With tears in her eyes, Olson recalled her uncle.

"I think we should do more because Jack Knight loved Detroit, and the *Free Press* was his paper," she said.

"At that point," Ibargüen recalled, "it was done."

The Knight Foundation board voted to authorize a $30 million pledge, and Ibargüen quickly excused himself from the meeting. He called Walker. "Listen, you piker, I just went up ten million. I've got thirty. You better deliver more than a hundred," he said.

"I'm inspired, I'm inspired!" Walker said. "I'm going to ask for 125."

That night, the Ford Foundation board held a phone meeting and authorized a pledge of $125 million to Detroit. After securing authorization from his board and similar actions at the other foundations, Walker called Rosen to deliver the news.

"Darren, when the history of this bankruptcy is written, you will be a hero of this bankruptcy," Rosen told him.

Kresge, doubling down on its huge investment in Detroit, pledged an astounding $100 million, an enormous sum for its size. More pledges streamed in. Kellogg gave $40 million; William Davidson Foundation, $25 million; Community Foundation for Southeast Michigan, $10 million; Mott, $10 million; Erb, $10 million; Hudson-Webber, $10 million; and McGregor Fund, $6 million. Inspired by their efforts, one individual philanthropist, A. Paul Schaap, pledged $5 million through his family foundation, and other individuals donated tens of thousands of dollars as well.

In a matter of weeks, several leading national and local foundations had hurdled their respective bureaucratic barriers and pooled their resources to lift up Detroit. Rosen's idea was irresistibly novel.

"It was creative and it was ingenious—the solution that he crafted," Walker said. "It was disruptive and it pushed us to our limits in thinking about how we could problem-solve. For me, it had all of the elements of something truly transformative—and that's what I think philanthropy should be doing."

For Walker, aiding pensioners was a critical component of the deal. "As a foundation that supports the idea of work and labor practices that are fair and equitable to workers, we felt that a huge injustice was done to the retirees. And that injustice is, in part, what emboldened us to act," he said.

Saving the DIA was similarly a key priority. "We believe that cultural institutions are an essential part of any great city or community," Walker said. "Those cultural institutions are anchors, and those anchors are essential to the civic pride and the level of education and knowledge. For us it was not an either/or."

Yet for the deal to work, the state would have to make a meaningful contribution too. Without the state, there simply wasn't enough money to justify the city relinquishing ownership of the DIA to an independent trust.

"It gave the judge the leverage he needed—the leverage to go back to the state, the leverage with the pensioners. It was brilliant," Noland said.

As news of the confidential foundation negotiations leaked to the media in the fall, *Detroit Free Press* reporters John Gallagher and Mark Stryker dubbed the emerging deal the "grand bargain." The mediators adopted the term, other news media began using it, and the phrase stuck.

Rosen summoned Driker. "It's time to go back to the governor," he said.

ROSEN AND DRIKER, armed with good news, drove to Lansing to ask Snyder for money a second time. The judge disclosed that the Ford Foundation had pledged $125 million and the Kresge Foundation had agreed to contribute $100 million. Altogether, he projected at the time that the city would eventually compile $350 million in foundation pledges. The governor was astounded.

"Really?!" he said to Rosen and Driker. "What do you think the state should do?"

Rosen didn't hesitate. "I think you should at least match the foundations," he said.

The governor agreed, making a strategic political pivot almost immediately.

"I could see that being potentially a great solution," Snyder recalled later. "I think the foundations showing leadership was a great way to say this was an added thing that otherwise wouldn't be available in the bankruptcy."

In a manner of speaking, the proposed accord was reminiscent of venture capital, an industry in which Snyder had spent more than a decade before becoming governor. In venture capital, investors often seek the financial certainty of syndicated deals by lining up additional investors, essentially channeling matching funds, and solidifying the core investment.

"In a lot of ways, that's the value," Snyder observed later. "You were getting incremental new dollars that otherwise wouldn't be there to help solve the problem."

But the governor's support—and the backing of the foundations—was contingent upon the DIA kicking in money too. Orr, who approved of Rosen's efforts but hadn't yet fully endorsed the deal, wanted $100 million from the DIA. He believed a nine-figure commitment would be more palatable to Judge Rhodes, who retained the power to approve or reject the deal. That figure was approximately equal to the size of the museum's entire endowment, illustrating the depth of the fundraising challenge the DIA would be facing if it committed to that amount.

"It's completely unfeasible to do that and continue to raise what we do to cover expenses and what we've committed to raise in endowment dollars," DIA chief operating officer Annmarie Erickson said publicly at the time.

Without the DIA in the grand bargain, the deal was likely to dissolve. Privately, the foundation leaders grew impatient with the DIA's recalcitrance in the face of their own generosity.

"We're putting up a huge percentage of our unrestricted grant-making for twenty years," Noland said later. "You'd like someone to step up."

Snyder invited DIA chairman Gene Gargaro to join him for a ceremony on January 24, 2014, in Washington, D.C., where the governor was set to receive an award from Americans for the Arts at the U.S. Conference of Mayors for, of all things, supporting the arts. As the ceremony approached, Snyder popped open a web browser and started downloading the DIA's financial statements from the museum's website. The CPA governor began examining the museum's finances and determined independently that the DIA could free up millions of dollars in funding.

The night before the ceremony in Washington, Snyder called Rosen, sounding almost giddy. He told Rosen that he had identified ways for the DIA to squeeze more cash out of its endowment. "I went through the DIA's financials," he told the judge. "I'm going to ask them for $100 million."

Rosen, who so far had privately persuaded the DIA to commit $50 million, believed the governor's request would fall flat. "Governor," he told his old campaign friend sarcastically, "get the award first."

After the ceremony, Snyder and Gargaro slipped into a private room to discuss the grand bargain. "All this business about the museum dragging its feet or not participating was simply our thoughtful and careful efforts to make sure we could fulfill our degree of participation," Gargaro told the governor. "And I'm here to commit to you $50 million."

The governor expressed appreciation for Gargaro's gesture. But he sent a clear message. That's not enough. It had to be a hundred spread out over twenty years.

"This solves the problem," Snyder said. The grand bargain, if approved, would allow the museum to become an independent institution, shielding its artwork from bankruptcy sales and permanently protecting the collection from the threat of the city's financial woes.

The governor told Gargaro that he believed the museum could afford it.

"I can't tell you what he saw there, but in reality I live with those financial statements," Gargaro said later. "He didn't see anything there that I didn't know about. But I didn't debate his financial acumen. I just listened. We were making a deal, and the deal was bigger than any details in the financials."

Plus, Gargaro recognized that the governor was facing immense political pressure in Lansing.

"He was hearing, I'm sure, from Cadillac and Traverse City and Muskegon and other places: 'What's in this grand bargain for us, and why isn't the DIA at the table?'" he recalled later.

Still, the DIA chairman pushed back. "Well, if it's 100, what's to keep it from being 150 or 200?" he asked Snyder.

"Gene," the governor replied, "if you could commit to 100, I'll commit to you that it will not be a dollar more than 100."

Gargaro, who had spent the better portion of 2013 unsuccessfully seeking a solution to the DIA's crisis, accepted Snyder's offer. He reached across the table and shook the governor's hand.

"We're in for $100 million," he told Snyder.

A few days later, the DIA's board signed off on the pledge in an emergency meeting and publicly backed the grand bargain for the first time. Still, concern lingered over the commitment. When Gargaro called Erickson, the museum's chief operating officer, to recount his conversation with the governor, she felt deflated at first.

"I felt like, damn, we've been working so hard to balance the budget and do things responsibly. Years before the city even considered changing pensions, we froze our defined benefit pension plan and went to a defined contribution plan," she said. "We worked with our unions on work rules, we went through periods of salary freezes, we had years where there were no raises. I thought, we've been suffering and suffering to run this place responsibly, and this is what it got us. A $100 million bill."

She also couldn't shake the feeling that raising $100 million for the grand bargain would damage the museum's capacity to raise outside funds for its endowment, an endeavor that was supposed to make the DIA financially sustainable without regional taxpayer support by 2023.

"If you look at it from a practical standpoint, a hundred million dollars to get control of the collection? That's a pittance," Erickson said. "But for an institution that's historically been financially challenged, a hundred million dollars is an enormous amount of money."

Gargaro's enthusiasm for the grand bargain washed away Erickson's reluctance. "Gene was completely confident that we could do this. He never, never wavered. And it's hard not to believe when the chairman of your board is saying, 'We're going to hunker down and do this together,'" she said.

The DIA hit the fundraising trail quickly. The natural place to start was the Big Three automakers: General Motors, Ford, and Fiat Chrysler. All three companies had been on the sidelines during Detroit's bankruptcy, but they quickly bought into the grand bargain as an opportunity to help lift their hometown.

GM and the GM Foundation pledged a combination of $10 million, while the Ford Motor Company Fund—not to be confused with the Ford Foundation—also pledged $10 million. Chrysler kicked in $6 million.

Several major Detroit businesses also chipped in. Penske Corporation pledged $10 million, Detroit billionaire Dan Gilbert's companies pledged $5 million, and the Detroit-based DTE Energy Foundation pledged $5 million. Several other foundations and companies with major operations in the Detroit area also made seven-figure gifts.

By the summer of 2014, it became clear that the DIA would swiftly achieve its target of raising $100 million over twenty years for the grand bargain.

AS A CONCEPT, the grand bargain gained momentum. But it was far from fully formed. The city's retiree groups withheld their support in confidential mediation sessions, pushing the city to free up more cash for pensioners.

After Rosen publicly revealed the foundation commitments, Orr officially integrated the concept of the grand bargain into his bankruptcy restructuring plan. On February 21, 2014, Orr's team filed the first version of its debt-cutting plan of adjustment with the U.S. Bankruptcy Court, publicly revealing the city's official offers to pensioners and financial creditors. The plan of adjustment showed the harrowing effects of the city's fiscal calamity on the lives of real people and the balance sheets of financial giants. It spared no one.

To put Detroit on a financially sustainable path for the first time in half a century, Orr proposed monthly pension check cuts of 34 percent for civilian pensioners and 10 percent for police and fire pensioners if they voted to reject the grand-bargain cash. If pensioners voted to accept the grand bargain and relinquish their right to sue the state over the bankruptcy, however, those cuts would fall to 26 percent and 6 percent, respectively.

"We weren't sure whether it was so grand," said Robert Gordon, lead attorney for the city's pension funds.

As retirees refused to give in, Orr delivered a new proposal in March 2014 with even steeper proposed cuts to pensioners.

He raised the threatened cut to police and fire pensioners if they rejected the grand bargain from 10 percent to 14 percent. He also proposed a complex plan to claw back excessive annuity bonuses that the city's pension funds had distributed during the last decade—a destructive policy that had helped plunge the city into insolvency.

Shirley Lightsey, president of the Detroit Retired City Employees Association and a member of the Official Committee of Retirees, was mortified. Fellow retirees were terrified. "Some people were so upset they were making themselves sick," she said later. "It was enough to make anybody lose sleep at night because you had worked all your life and thought you were safe."

What concerned her most were retirees whose quality of care in assisted living centers and nursing homes was directly correlated with their monthly income. "The care they get is based on what's coming in," she said. "You could actually see the difference because of their income level. When you really think about it, it's frightening. It kept me awake nights."

Protesters had gathered on February 24, 2014, at the Historic King Solomon Baptist Church to excoriate the plan of adjustment, promising to "shut the city down." David Sole, a Detroit Water and Sewerage Department retiree, wore a T-shirt that read, "Hands Off My Pension!"

"We're calling on 20,000 retirees to come out in your wheelchairs, in your walkers, and their children and grandchildren," Sole said.

Distressed pensioners flooded the city's retiree associations, pension boards, and retiree committee with letters, emails, and phone calls. Some retirees urged their lawyers to refuse to give in, to fight until the end, even if that means appealing all the way to the Supreme Court.

The collective cry of retirees called for a liquidation of the DIA to avoid drastic pension cuts. "If it's a choice of somebody eating or selling the art," Lightsey said, recalling the prevailing sentiment, "sell the art."

Retirees argued it was better to sell "the building, the land, the people that are in there," added Don Taylor, president of the Retired Detroit Police and Fire Fighter Association.

But the solidification of the grand-bargain funding had fundamentally altered the conversation. It was free money that would evaporate if pensioners completely refused to consider the deal. Rejecting the foundation donations altogether could make the retirees appear unreasonable.

As the grand-bargain funding was materializing, Judge Rhodes had called members of the retiree committee into his courtroom to warn them against refusing to consider cuts to pension and health care benefits. "Profound change," he said, might be necessary.

"Now is not the time for defiant swagger or for dismissive pound-the-table, take-it-or-leave-it proposals that are nothing but a one-way ticket to Chapter 18," the judge said. "This is bankruptcy jargon for a second Chapter 9."

The city simply cannot agree to pay pensioners any more than it can afford, Rhodes warned.

"If the plan . . . promises more to creditors than the city can reasonably be expected to pay, it will fail, and history will judge each and every one of us accordingly," he said.

The grand bargain offered pensioners an avenue to extract value out of the DIA without fighting an uncertain, costly, and lengthy legal battle over the right to sell artwork. Accordingly, its emergence arrested the brewing deal between the retiree committee, Syncora, and FGIC, an alliance that likely would have led to a public fight to liquidate the most valuable works at the museum. Instead, the retiree committee, the city's two pension funds, and the city's major retiree associations trained their sights on pressuring Orr to improve his offer to pensioners.

Ron Bloom cut off discussions with Houlihan Lokey investment banker and FGIC advisor Steve Spencer, who believed an alliance between the financial creditors and retirees could exert immense pressure on the city to sell art.

"The art was a great promise," Bloom, the Lazard investment banker negotiating on behalf of the retiree committee, said later. "But no one could ever figure out how you were going to actually implement it. How were you going to actually convince the judge to force the city to sell the art? And even if you convince the judge, how are you going to convince the state not to legislate away the city's obligation to do it?"

Political sense led Bloom to conclude that trying to dismantle the DIA by establishing a partnership between the retirees and the financial creditors was a losing proposition.

"If you're going to go up against the governor of the state and the entire Michigan political establishment, you better come ready to do some pretty serious battle," Bloom said. "We concluded that at the end of the day, an alliance with the city and the state—even if we didn't get everything we wanted—was far more likely to succeed at the courthouse."

Spencer was left in the cold.

"Ron was the most dangerous person for us to negotiate with because if he locked up the support of the governor, then all the financial creditors were screwed, and we were the low man on the totem pole," he said. "When we started negotiating with Ron, we knew it was a Faustian bargain."

THE GRAND BARGAIN looked appealing to the retiree committee, but not at the level of pension cuts that Orr first proposed. Lightsey and Taylor privately pressured their fellow members of the retiree committee to negotiate a reasonable deal with the city, embracing the grand bargain rather than waging a protracted fight. Retiree committee negotiators demanded concessions on pension cuts but agreed to give ground on health care benefits, which have few legal protections in bankruptcy.

In a groundbreaking accord, representatives for the major retiree groups—including the Official Committee of Retirees, the General Retirement System pension board, the Police and Fire Retirement System pension board, and the two retiree associations—reached agreements with the city in the spring of 2014 to recommend that pensioners support the grand bargain in exchange for dramatically lower cuts than Orr had originally proposed.

Police officers and firefighters got the best deal. Because their pension fund had been managed more responsibly, it was in better shape. So they did not have to endure any cuts to their monthly pensions. Instead, their cuts were limited to a reduction in their annual cost-of-living-adjustment (COLA) increases, from 2.25 percent to 1 percent.

Representatives for general city pensioners agreed to steeper cuts because their pension fund was worse off. They agreed to recommend that pensioners accept a 4.5 percent base cut to their monthly pension checks and the total elimination of COLA increases. They also agreed to install a new layer of oversight to prevent board members from making imprudent investments. In addition, negotiators agreed to recommend that general pensioners give back a portion of the excessive annuity bonuses that were paid out from 2003 to 2013. This claw back—which pensioners could pay in a lump sum or subtract from their regular monthly pension checks—would amount to bigger overall cuts for individuals who benefited most from the annuity bonuses in the period leading up to Detroit's bankruptcy. To soften the blow, the city agreed to cap the highest possible cut to anyone's monthly pension check at 20 percent.

Health care cuts were drastic: the city agreed to pay $450 million to two new and independent health care trusts, called Voluntary Employee Beneficiary Associations, which would administer significantly reduced health care benefits for retirees. The cuts amounted to about a 90 percent reduction in the value of retiree health care insurance. That was steeper than Orr's original proposal of 80 percent cuts, but negotiators came to believe that a combination of Medicare, public health-care exchanges, and spouses' private plans would soften the blow on individual retirees. Consequently, after the initial $450 million to start the trusts, the city would never again pay for retiree health care benefits, offering sharp relief to the annual budget and freeing up money to invest in public services.

Despite the breakthrough at the bargaining table, lowered pension cuts were completely contingent upon a vote of approval from each individual class of retirees: the civilian pensioners and the police and fire pensioners. As part of his agreement with the pension groups, Orr revised his plan of adjustment to give retirees an extraordinary incentive to vote yes. Without their vote of approval, the base cuts would balloon from 4.5 percent to 27 percent for general retirees. For police and fire retirees, the cuts would include an elimination of their COLA increases if they voted no.

Still, the benefit reductions were dramatically lower than what the city had first proposed in mediation: cuts of more than 50 percent to general retirees. The influx of grand-bargain funds, dedicated solely to pensioners for the sake of preserving the DIA, significantly reduced the impact of the city's insolvency on retirees.

"I don't think the pensioners who are taking hits appreciate this, but never has a class of creditors got a targeted allocation of funds," Orr said later. "The reason it was fair and equitable was we weren't doing it."

Meaning, the city wasn't setting aside a special pot of its own money specifically for a favored group of creditors. The money was coming from foundations, the state, and the DIA's corporate donors. "If you don't accept it, it's going to go away," Orr said. "But it's never happened before. It's beyond fair."

The city's team had struck the pension settlement with negotiators for the retiree groups. But the real decision-makers were the pensioners themselves. Bankruptcy law requires each class of creditors—general pensioners and uniformed pensioners—to vote on the proposed cuts through a secret ballot.

If pensioners in both classes voted "yes," the city would accept the grand-bargain money and pensioners would relinquish their right to sue the State of Michigan over cuts. If they voted "no," however, the city likely would ask Rhodes to impose the larger cuts. The fact that negotiators agreed to support the grand bargain was significant. But it would be meaningless without an official vote of approval from pensioners.

Gerald Galazka, a retiree who worked in the city's recreation department for thirty-five years, considered the pension cuts a grievous strike at helpless retirees.

"It is my belief that diminishing pension benefits is not only illegal but morally reprehensible. Individuals that worked 30 years or more for the city had very little to do with the mismanagement, corruption, and investment decisions made by city officials and trustees that managed taxpayer dollars and pension funds," Galazka said.

The indignation of some retirees confounded Lightsey, who had come to believe that a wholesale rejection of cuts—based purely on the principle that pensions should never be touched—reflected a complete detachment from Detroit's fiscal wreckage and legal realities. To be sure, she remained upset at the bankruptcy's effects on her constituents. At the beginning of the case, she too believed that pensioners should appeal all the way to the Supreme Court to defend their rights, if necessary. But the grand bargain changed things. She rejected the belief that retirees should fight the bankruptcy indefinitely, arguing that jeopardizing the unexpected gift of outside funding lacked basic pragmatism. The certainty of manageable cuts—made possible by the grand bargain—was better than the risk of devastating cuts with a small hope of a successful challenge to Rhodes's ruling allowing pension reductions.

One day Lightsey was riding in a car with Ryan Plecha, a close advisor and Lippitt O'Keefe Gornbein attorney representing her retiree association, when her frustration boiled over.

"What's wrong with these people?" she asked rhetorically. "Don't they understand they can't eat principles?"

She continued to stew. "What principles?" she said. "You can't eat principles."

If pensioners rejected the grand bargain based on the principle that they should not have to accept any cuts, they risked devastating their finances.

Lightsey repeated her line over and over, and it started to catch on. Plecha added a kicker.

"And uncertainty doesn't pay the bills," he chimed in.

They soon realized that they had stumbled onto a catchphrase with a sensible punch: "You can't eat principles, and uncertainty doesn't pay the bills."

It was relatable and unassailable. Plecha designed a button with plans to distribute it to retirees.

"You Can't Eat Principles" is emblazoned at the top of the pin. "Uncertainty Doesn't Pay the Bills" it reads at the bottom.

In the middle of the button is a depiction of the *Spirit of Detroit*, a bronze statue that sits outside city hall. Written across the *Spirit of Detroit*'s chest on the pin was a rallying cry aimed at pensioners: "VOTE YES."

CHAPTER 10

Haircuts

David Heiman didn't even need a haircut. His short-cropped light-gray hair was fine.

But when Judge Gerald Rosen interrupted an intense mediation session to announce that it was time for his regular haircut, the Jones Day bankruptcy attorney figured he would tag along for a trim. It had been weeks since Kevyn Orr's team proposed the first version of a plan of adjustment in February 2014. Although funds for the grand bargain were beginning to materialize, the City of Detroit was making no progress in its bid to reach a settlement with its unlimited-tax general obligation (UTGO) bondholders, a group of financial creditors that was incensed at the city's attempt to cut its debt.

The city had proposed payouts of twenty cents on the dollar for all of its unsecured bondholders, which roiled Wall Street. The municipal finance community had always believed that bonds receive a higher priority in the grand scheme of municipal debt than pension obligations. But the city had made a better offer to pensioners, effectively favoring retirees over bondholders. That reflected a precedent that Wall Street was desperate to avoid.

"That mediation had been going on for a long time," Heiman said. "It was getting nowhere fast."

The city's UTGO bondholders, led in the confidential negotiation sessions by investment firm Blackstone restructuring chief Tim Coleman, held about $388 million in debt that Detroit had issued over the previous fifteen years for specific purposes—such as to finance infrastructure projects throughout the city.

But Jones Day argued that Chapter 9 bankruptcy eliminated the city's pledge to use its "full faith and credit" to pay bondholders in full. Detroit wanted to divert the stream of tax revenue that voters had authorized for UTGO projects into its general fund, where it could be used to pay for police, fire, and other basic services.

The UTGO bond insurers—Assured, Ambac, and National Public Finance Guarantee—feared that Detroit's attempt to treat their debt as general unsecured obligations could entice other cities to consider a similar move to improve their balance sheets.

After they reached an impasse, Coleman and Heiman tagged along with the judge to Francesco's Barber Shop on the ninth floor of the Ford Building on Griswold Street in downtown Detroit. They warned Frankie the barber that they would be discussing confidential material that must remain secret under the court's mediation privilege.

"You know," Heiman told Coleman, "we're probably just gonna have to litigate this and get the court to decide."

As Frankie the barber trimmed away, Rosen's phone rang. It was Governor Rick Snyder.

"Guess where I am?" Rosen told Snyder. "I'm at the barber shop. We're talking about UTGOs."

"Let me know if there's something we can do to help," Snyder replied.

Frankie the barber jumped in.

"Tell the governor I saw him on TV," Frankie told Rosen. "It looks like a butcher's been at his hair."

The mood lightened as the negotiators resuscitated their attempt to reach a settlement. Heiman and Coleman started to find common ground.

One of Rosen's mediators, Chapter 9 veteran and U.S. bankruptcy judge Elizabeth Perris of Oregon, had already concluded that the city could not legally divert UTGO tax revenue to its general fund without the consent of bondholders. That added ammunition to the bondholders' bargaining position.

And bankruptcy judge Steven Rhodes had urged the sides to reach a settlement to avoid a court judgment.

"The decision here is most likely all or nothing," Rhodes had told them in open court on February 19, 2014. "One side is going to win and the other side is going to lose—and that's going to be very happy on one side and very tough on the other side."

Neither side in the UTGO dispute wanted to take its chances. With Frankie clipping away, the negotiators reached a deal in principle that would ultimately trim the UTGO claims, keeping the full taxing authority in place and diverting a portion to low-income pensioners.

After the trip to the barbershop, Rosen called the governor back to give him the good news. After an additional round of talks over the details of their deal, the bondholders agreed to accept a 26 percent haircut, with the savings devoted to helping vulnerable retirees avoid falling below the poverty line because of the city's proposed pension cuts. The deal created an annual pot of nearly $2 million to help those pensioners.

"That was a very pivotal moment in that barbershop. That was really the first settlement," Heiman said. "At the time, it was funny. And it's funny now. But it was the real thing."

They called it the "Haircut at the Haircut." Several weeks later, the city reached a deal with its limited-tax general obligation (LTGO) bondholders too. With a weaker legal case for repayment, they agreed to accept thirty-four cents on the dollar for their debt. Collectively, the bond settlements removed two substantial hurdles preventing the City of Detroit from reaching a consensual restructuring plan.

Those deals, combined with the grand bargain, positioned the city's chief adversaries—bond insurers Syncora and Financial Guaranty Insurance Company—as the only major holdout creditors in the bankruptcy.

The swaps that had been subject to several rounds of settlement talks were set to be paid off at their expense. After Rhodes rejected the city's first two swaps settlements with UBS and Bank of America Merrill Lynch, Orr had threatened to sue the banks over the legality of Kwame Kilpatrick's original deal, authorizing Jones Day to prepare a lawsuit. The city's lawyers came within minutes of filing the suit on January 31, but held off only after the banks signaled a willingness to give in. Instead of engaging in a legal battle before Rhodes—who had already revealed that he believed the swaps were illegal—the banks caved and officially agreed in March to an $85 million payout.

FGIC and Syncora regurgitated their previous objections to oppose the third swaps settlement. But their chances of killing it were minimal.

The night before Rhodes was set to rule on the final deal, Syncora attorney Stephen Hackney was having dinner with his mom, a Michigan resident, at a seafood restaurant in downtown Detroit's Renaissance Center. With her son constantly in the news, she had plans to catch him in action in court the next day.

"She came to see her son get sacrificed at the altar of Judge Rhodes," Hackney later corrected.

Fellow Syncora attorney Ryan Bennett spotted Orr and the Jones Day team having dinner across the restaurant overlooking the Detroit River.

Unbeknownst to Hackney, Bennett walked over to the city's table. "Guys, if you want to have some fun, Hackney's mom is here and sitting over there at that table," Bennett said.

Orr and Heiman seized the opportunity. They waltzed over to Hackney's table and complimented their fierce rival.

"Your son's a nice guy. He's doing a great job," Orr told Hackney's mom.

He hadn't thought twice about it. "Always meet a boy's mom," Orr said later. "Steve was deposing me every other day, but be big, man. We're professionals. Hey, it's business. Try not to be a prick."

Hackney savored the moment. "It was an example of Orr's statesmanship that I thought carried him through the case," he said.

Hackney was, indeed, sacrificed the next day. Rhodes approved the $85 million settlement, thus saving the city at least $145 million off the original swaps deal that he had torpedoed.

In the courtroom, however, the battle between Detroit and Syncora persisted. Syncora and FGIC continued to plant roadblocks in a bid to derail the city's momentum and gain bargaining leverage. Fed up with the bond insurers' obstinacy and encouraged by Rhodes's revelation that he believed the certificates-of-participation (COPs) deal was illegal, the city placed Syncora and FGIC in its crosshairs and filed a new lawsuit seeking to wipe out the original $1.4 billion COPs deal altogether. If successful, it would be the first time in about three decades that a U.S. municipality successfully invalidated a debt deal retroactively.

The virtually unprecedented move required the city to effectively sue itself with a lawsuit targeting the shell corporations that Kilpatrick's administration had created, staffed, and funded. The suit claimed that the entire transaction was "a sham."

The lawsuit inflamed tensions with Syncora and FGIC.

Their position was simple: "You took my money. You're not gonna pay me. I want your firstborn and salt of the earth," Orr explained.

ALTHOUGH RETIREE NEGOTIATORS had agreed not to pursue a liquidation of the Detroit Institute of Arts as part of the grand bargain, Syncora and FGIC had other ideas. They demanded a valuation of the entire museum, not just the artwork purchased with city funds that auction house Christie's had appraised. The Christie's assessment covered only 5 percent of the DIA's collection. But an assessment of the entire collection would also include pieces that individuals had donated to the museum, including those given with restrictions attached. FGIC's attorneys and advisors resolved to build a case that the city should tap the collection to pay off creditors, regardless of the museum's ethical standards. At the same time, Syncora blasted the city with a litany of procedural attempts to slow down the bankruptcy.

To undermine the grand bargain, FGIC advisor Steve Spencer figured he had to prove that the entire art collection was worth far more than the $816 million over twenty years in pledges that Rosen would eventually obtain to preserve the museum as an independent institution and reduce pension cuts. Rhodes would get the final say on the grand bargain, as long as retirees voted to accept the deal. But Syncora and FGIC called the grand bargain a fraudulent conveyance of a valuable asset to a favored group of creditors. Pensioners would receive the benefits of the DIA's monetization, while the bond insurers were left with scraps.

The city wouldn't consider alternative deals for the DIA, but Spencer had no problem doing so on his own. He devised a plan to solicit bids from prospective investors against the city's will.

"We weren't going to roll over on this," he said.

Spencer sent representatives to examine the museum's artwork in person, combed historical documents for relevant information, and solicited input from art experts on the collection. With that information and the estimates already produced by Christie's, Spencer compiled a 259-page pitch book detailing the museum's major assets and began distributing the materials to prospective buyers in the art world. He had turned the DIA's collection into a kind of luxury catalog for wealthy suitors. Four investors delivered tentative bids.

One group, a coalition of Catalyst Acquisition Group and Bell Capital Partners, offered $1.75 billion for the entire museum. Beijing-based Poly International Auction, a Chinese version of Christie's, said it would pay up to $1 billion for the DIA's Chinese art collection. New York–based Art Capital Group offered to extend a $3 billion loan to the City of Detroit with the DIA as collateral—a loan that would almost certainly require the city to sell art to service the debt. Finally, China-based Yuan Capital singled out 116 works for which it was willing to pay up to $1.5 billion, backed by a consortium of investors.

The prospective offers helped FGIC construct a case that the museum was worth far more than the city had procured through the grand bargain.

"Spencer's plan was super creative," Hackney said.

But city officials swiftly dismissed the alternative bids, choosing to stick with the grand bargain instead of finding a more lucrative route. "It was like, 'ping,'" Hackney said, flicking his finger as if to instantly dismiss the plan. "They just didn't care, which was sad because Spencer actually spent a lot of time thinking about this."

Orr gave little credence to the bids.

"I knew they were going to go out and find some oligarchs to come in here and say, 'We'll give you a gazillion dollars for the art,'" Orr said later. "And the reality is, that's what they'll say then. Then they'll go do their due diligence and say, 'Oh, we didn't really mean *that* gazillion dollars—we meant *this* negative gazillion dollars over here.' So it's all speculation."

Even though the bids weren't binding, the plan was designed to place public pressure on the emergency manager to consider alternatives to the grand bargain. But Orr didn't budge.

"It's like . . . *Apocalypse Now*. Motor goes off. He sniffs, 'It smells like victory,'" he said. "We didn't give a shit about the pressure."

In addition, the city argued that the legal dustup surrounding the prospective sale of DIA property would cast uncertainty over any attempts to sell the treasures, leading to a protracted court battle that would delay the revitalization of Detroit.

"There are a lot of issues, like how would you ever sell it? Who's going to buy it?" Heiman said. The most ideal solution, he said, was to identify "a middle ground for the art: find value but not remove the art from its availability to the Detroit area because of its importance to the future of the city."

After spending the first half of the bankruptcy at odds over Orr's plan to consider selling DIA property, the museum's lawyers joined forces with the city's attorneys to oppose Syncora and FGIC. The DIA was central to the vitality of its Midtown Detroit neighborhood and part of the lifeblood of the city, museum supporters suggested.

"This institution lifts the city above being just another impoverished city. The DIA is a hundred-plus-year investment in the human potential of Detroit, in the human capital of Detroit," DIA chief operating officer Annmarie Erickson said later. "We are one of the major educational institutions in the city. We provide services to social service groups in the city. We are much more than a building with paintings and sculpture in it. We are a member of the community. And we bring something very special to this community that would be devastating to lose."

FGIC and Syncora asked Rhodes to force the city to cooperate with the potential DIA bidders, but he refused. Having failed in their attempt to strong-arm city officials into talking with the outside bidders, FGIC and Syncora resolved to dig up dirt on the museum itself. Hackney popped a gigantic subpoena on the DIA, forcing the museum to unearth a swath of documents, many dating back a century. He demanded documents within the DIA's possession that shed light on the donation of the Detroit Museum of Art to the city in 1919, ownership records pertaining to all sixty-six thousand pieces in the city's collection, financial statements and tax documents, membership records, appraisals, insurance documents, communications with the city regarding the art and the grand bargain, and a host of other records.

"We were literally going through over a hundred years of documents—hundreds of thousands of pages. It taxed everyone," Erickson said. "It was just mind-boggling."

Syncora's persistent legal attacks and objections drew an escalating series of insults from the city's lawyers. Detroit accused Syncora of executing a "schizophrenic" strategy, conducting a legal "ambush," deploying an "exceedingly adversarial" approach, and using a "scorched-earth litigation strategy." Robert Hertzberg, an attorney for Pepper Hamilton, which was assisting Jones Day in representing the city, looked utterly disgusted one day when he accused Syncora of taking a "carpet-bombing approach" in an attempt to obliterate the grand bargain. Hackney complained to Rhodes about the suggestion that Syncora was "committing war crimes," calling it "unhealthy" to use such terminology to describe a legal battle.

Rhodes grew impatient at the squabbling.

"Let's keep the war analogies to a minimum, if not eliminate them from our discussion altogether," Rhodes lectured the attorneys from the bench in April.

As the bond insurers continued their assault on the grand bargain, the city plotted a preemptive strike. Instead of pretending the
grand bargain properly valued the museum, the city authorized its
own assessment of the entire DIA.

Orr hired Michael Plummer, a consultant with Artvest Partners and a former Christie's executive, to estimate the value of the
whole museum. After an extensive market analysis, he concluded
that the museum was worth anywhere from $2.8 billion to $4.6
billion.

"A number of other objects in the DIA collection have not had
comparables that have come on the market in seventy to a hundred
years," Plummer wrote.

His figures added weight to the creditors' assertion that the
grand bargain did not deliver enough money to justify relinquishing ownership of the museum. But Plummer added a crucial caveat.
Those figures were the ideal book value for the art. In a fire-sale
scenario, he estimated that the DIA's property would fetch only
$1.1 billion to $1.8 billion.

What's more, he presented a detailed argument for why auctioning the DIA's collection would be troublesome and uncertain.
For one thing, most museums would likely boycott the sale as a
protest against the process. In addition, there was no guarantee
the city would prevail in the inevitable legal fight over the right to
sell the collection, a battle that would surely draw lawsuits from
art donors, the attorney general, and, of course, the DIA itself. By
comparison, when Brandeis University had tried to shutter its Rose
Art Museum in 2009 and liquidate its collection to shore up the
university's finances, a legal imbroglio followed, and the university
eventually abandoned its plan. Even if the city had the indisputable
right to sell art, a rapid liquidation would result in smaller returns
than if the collection was sold over time, Plummer noted.

The ripple effects of even a partial sale would be sweeping, he said. "Selling the most valuable works in the DIA collection would deprive the museum of its core attraction, drastically reduce attendance and related revenues, drive away potential donors of future gifts and endowments, and in all likelihood, ultimately force the closure of the DIA due to a loss of economic sustainability, resulting in a full liquidation," Plummer concluded.

Syncora and FGIC continued their assault. For starters, they argued, the city wouldn't necessarily have to sell off the DIA's property all at once.

"Anything can be sold over time," James H. M. Sprayregen, lead Kirkland & Ellis attorney for Syncora, said later. "They made us into a caricature. Like, 'They're saying you've got to sell it tomorrow, and that would be a disaster.' Well of course that would be a disaster. But where there's a will, there's a way. And there was no will. There were a lot of different ways you could have done something creative, and the answer was, 'No way.'"

In a counterstrike, FGIC retained an art expert, Victor Wiener, a former executive director of the Appraisers Association of America and former Christie's fine arts director, to conduct a competing evaluation of the entire DIA.

In less than two weeks, Wiener pegged the value of the entire museum collection at more than $8 billion, with the 387 most valuable pieces accounting for about half of the value.

Wiener even suggested that the museum's treasured *Detroit Industry* murals by Mexican artist Diego Rivera—which are part of the physical structure of the DIA—could be sold. "The removal of frescoes in a setting such as a major museum today would be performed with state-of-the-art technology that would leave the works in essentially perfect condition in a new location," he said.

For the administrators of the DIA, talk of literally ripping walls out of the building was excruciating.

"It was pretty awful," Erickson said. "I can't minimize the stress we were under. The idea that the collection could be raided was horrifying for all of us. We knew there were a whole lot of resources on their side. But at the risk of sounding Pollyannaish, I always felt that we were right. That somehow, in the end, right was going to prevail over millions of dollars and lawyers. I felt we had the moral high ground on this one, and I was willing to stand there."

Moral high ground, of course, means little in bankruptcy court.

And what's more morally acceptable: Keeping a priceless art collection or selling some paintings to increase public safety? Maintaining a treasured museum or liquidating it to make creditors go away? In that acute sense, Detroit's bankruptcy introduced a philosophical, ethical, and legal dilemma that no other municipality had ever faced. But even if selling art to pay creditors and invest in city services was morally acceptable, was it financially prudent?

Rhodes had hinted in his eligibility ruling that putting art on the auction block might not be sensible.

"When the expenses of an enterprise exceed its revenue, a one-time infusion of cash, whether from an asset sale or from a borrowing, only delays the inevitable financial failure unless, in the meantime, the enterprise sufficiently reduces its expenses or enhances its income," Rhodes said. "The City of Detroit itself has proven the reality of this many, many times."

The city's lawyers nonetheless clung to a careful middle ground in their arguments before Rhodes regarding the DIA and the grand bargain. They never publicly articulated an opinion on whether art could be sold. Instead, they simply argued that the city did not have to sell the art, that determining whether art could be sold would take ages, and that dispensing art in a quick sale would compromise the value of the collection. Recognizing that selling art would require a legal fight, the city argued that the grand bargain was an acceptable alternative—especially because it was free money.

But Hackney questioned the conventional wisdom that the

foundations would give money only to the pensioners. In June 2014 he slapped a subpoena on the foundations involved in the grand bargain, demanding access to all documents revealing their communications regarding the deal and up to twenty-five years' worth of records on the foundations' activities.

"All of my friends called here and said, 'We've never been subpoenaed!' It was shock. 'Hey, we're trying to do good,'" Mariam Noland, president of the Community Foundation for Southeast Michigan, said later.

The foundations cobbled together a plan to fight the subpoena, hiring Doug Bernstein, a veteran bankruptcy lawyer with metro Detroit firm Plunkett Cooney, to file a motion asking Rhodes to quash Syncora's request.

"I can imagine how your clients feel," Hackney told Bernstein by phone with a dash of sympathy. But Bernstein accused Syncora of intimidating the foundations and asked Rhodes to kill the subpoena.

"The foundations believe that the subpoenas have been issued for no other reason than to convince the foundations that no good deed goes unpunished and that they should reconsider their agreement to commit funds to aid the city," Bernstein told Rhodes in a court hearing.

Hackney insisted that information on the foundations' motives was relevant and that Syncora was not trying to harass or intimidate anyone.

"It's not fair, and it's not a description of how I operate in this case," he said. "Whether the foundations were the ones that imposed on the city the requirement that all monies go to the retiree classes or whether the city was the one that proposed that to the foundations" is relevant.

Rhodes disagreed. He rejected Syncora's subpoena, handing

the insurer another loss in the courtroom and allowing the foundations' deliberations to remain secret.

Knight Foundation CEO Alberto Ibargüen felt vindicated.

"My attitude was always, 'I've been sued by people with a better case than you, and we still won,'" the foundation leader, a former newspaper publisher, said. "I felt we were on absolutely rock-solid grounds from the very beginning. This was volunteer money. We were under zero obligation whatsoever."

Even as the battle with the bond insurers marched on, Erickson, the museum's chief operating officer, offered an olive branch to one of the bond-insurance attorneys who interrogated her in a deposition about the DIA's role in the bankruptcy.

"He shook my hand and said, 'I really like art,'" Erickson recalled. "I said, 'Come visit the museum.'"

CHAPTER 11

Fixing the City

Placing Detroit on a sustainable path required more than bankruptcy. Fixing the balance sheet was only one part of Kevyn Orr's job as emergency manager. His directive from Governor Rick Snyder also entailed a push to overhaul basic services and restore sensibility to the city's bureaucracy. Under Mayor Dave Bing and the Detroit City Council, the city government had plunged deeper into disarray. After Orr's appointment, he turned his attention to restoring order.

One day, Bill Nowling, Orr's senior advisor and spokesman, walked down to the mayor's office, fully expecting to discuss city operations with Bing's staff.

"No one was there. Those offices were empty," Nowling said. "Where's the bureaucracy that's running this city? Who's running this shit? Nobody was."

Political gridlock and dysfunction had come to define Detroit. But Orr's arrival left the City Council and the mayor mostly powerless. Orr was free to overhaul services without their approval. Before his arrival, political leaders had mulled an offer from Snyder to transform Belle Isle into a state park. The island, on the Detroit River between the United States and Canada, was once an example of Detroit's beauty, but it had fallen into disrepair save for a few nice trails, lookouts, and gathering spots. The governor promised to invest heavily in upgrades for the nearly one-thousand-acre park.

Architecturally notable buildings on the island needed basic repairs, with busted heating and air-conditioning systems, aging water pipes, burnt-out lights, and broken windows. The island, remarkably, was actually sinking into the Detroit River, a geological phenomenon the city could not afford to combat. Trash cans littered the island's canals. Beaches were strewn with garbage. Restrooms were closed or repugnant.

"I walked into one of the toilets. I wouldn't let my dog go in one of those toilets. People had defecated on the floor," Orr recalled. "You drive across the island and look at the boat club, and the fucking pool is falling into the river. I mean, the foundation is disastrous."

It cost Detroit about $6 million per year to operate the island, a figure that did not include the price of upgrades. But Detroit City Council members, in one of their final acts before Orr's appointment, had rejected the governor's offer to invest in the island and turn it into a state park on long-term lease from the city.

When Orr arrived, he reversed the City Council's actions. The city could no longer pretend it had resources that it didn't possess. He signed the lease. A year later, state officials had completed an extraordinary amount of improvements, putting Belle Isle on the path to being a jewel once again. The savings and upgrades were meaningful, but Orr said later that he had been most concerned about the prospect that the city's creditors would pursue the island.

"It's a thousand acres. At $100,000, charitably, per acre, that's $100 million. That's real money. Waterfront property that faces Canada. That motivated me more than the $6 million per year it cost us to manage it," Orr said. "At that point, I said, 'Let me get this the hell out of here before it becomes a part of the conversation of the city's assets.'"

Before Snyder appointed Orr, Detroit's sanitation services were floundering too. Residents reported sharply inconsistent garbage pickup times. Detroit was one of the only major cities in the United States without a substantive recycling program. For a city already battling immense issues with illegal dumping, unreliable trash pickup only added to the problem.

"The state of solid-waste pickup in the city was unbelievable to us," said Conway MacKenzie consultant Chuck Moore, a restructuring expert hired to identify ways to overhaul the city government. "When you look at what the residents were dealing with, they would have their garbage getting picked up at midnight or even later."

At Moore's recommendation, Orr privatized the system, handing operations over to two firms, Rizzo Environmental Services and Advanced Disposal, which agreed to take over waste collection at essentially the same cost with approximately the same number of workers. The companies almost immediately restored trash collection in Detroit to normal municipal standards, created a recycling program, and increased the frequency of bulk pickup.

"People were thrilled," said Stacy Fox, whom Orr appointed as deputy emergency manager. "People would stand up and applaud."

Even early opponents of change quickly turned into believers. One of those early opponents was Mike Duggan, a former Wayne County prosecutor and politico who was credited with turning around the Detroit Medical Center hospital system as CEO. A stocky, bald, middle-aged guy with a gravelly voice and a penchant for rumpled suits, Duggan had soared to a victory in the city's mayoral election in November 2013 after waging an improbable write-in campaign in the primary. The triumph made him the first white mayor of the city in four decades. He replaced Bing, who chose not to run for reelection amid widespread discontent with his leadership and a distant relationship with Orr.

Duggan's reputation as a political bulldog manifested from the beginning. An avid opponent of privatizing services, he demanded control of city services from Orr, having portrayed himself as a fix-it man for city government and campaigned on a promise to oust the unelected emergency manager.

After demolishing his opponent in the general election, Duggan drew up plans to lace in some anti-Orr blasts during his victory speech on Election Night. But Fox, a Duggan supporter and friend since their days as law students at the University of Michigan, pleaded with the mayor-elect to set aside the rhetoric.

"Do we really need to go there?" Fox asked the mayor-elect as he prepared to deliver his speech. "I get it. You want him out, and everybody knows that, and that was clear throughout your campaign. But now we know we have to work together. So let's find the way you do that."

The mayor-elect edited the anti-Orr remarks out of his speech. It was a pragmatic acknowledgment that he would have to collaborate with the emergency manager to achieve anything after taking office. Orr, who held all the political power in the city, was only halfway through an eighteen-month appointment before the city's leaders could theoretically try to vote him out under the state's emergency manager law.

Still, Duggan's arrival created tension with Orr. For weeks after Duggan's election, the two were engaged in a standoff over their respective roles in charting the city's path. Their first face-to-face meeting after the election was like a "bad blind date," Orr said later.

"I'm sure like any elected official, he felt, 'Why do I have to deal with this?'" Orr said. "I felt like, 'Dude, right now I've been in City Hall longer than you have, OK? I know more about it than you do. So I've walked away from my fairly comfortable lifestyle to come here and help you, and I'm not gonna take crap from anybody because I've got a job to do and I've got to get out of here.'"

But Orr needed Duggan. Although the emergency manager had restored financial sanity to Detroit and made smart strategic decisions about certain city services, the bankruptcy was monopolizing his attention. An emerging turnaround of the police department, the selection of private trash operators, and the transfer of Belle Isle were his primary accomplishments on services by the time Duggan took office in January 2014. But fending off Syncora, FGIC, and the rest of the city's creditors was an all-consuming affair.

"I knew Mike was a good operator, and I knew we weren't good at it," Fox said. "So the sooner we could find common ground on areas of operation, it would benefit everybody."

After establishing a modicum of trust and understanding, Orr agreed to put Duggan in control of several key aspects of the city. Duggan assumed responsibility for implementing the city's plan to demolish abandoned homes, leading the comprehensive overhaul of the city's dilapidated street-lighting system, and overseeing the fire department. The new mayor also got control of the city's day-to-day spending and operational decision-making. In one of his first moves, Duggan recruited a municipal information-technology expert, Louisville, Kentucky's Beth Niblock, to join the city as chief information officer. Niblock quickly began overhauling the city's ancient computers, networks, and software.

"Our objectives were the same as Mike's—to return the city to full democracy," Fox said. "But that being said, Kevyn had a set of responsibilities under the law that he couldn't just hand over."

Orr maintained control of the bankruptcy, the city's overall finances, and the police department, the latter of which angered Duggan.

"Kevyn wouldn't let him have it," said Rich Baird, advisor to Snyder. "He appealed to the governor, and the governor said, 'No, I have to support my emergency manger. He will determine the timing of these transition items.'"

As part of a power-sharing agreement reached between Orr and Duggan before he took office, Duggan had agreed to abandon his campaign promise to fight the city's then-yet-to-be-released plan of adjustment. That move would later allow Duggan to gain the political benefits of a vastly improved municipal balance sheet while evading the inconvenient side effects of a battle to slash the city's liabilities. Orr absorbed the political pressure, giving Duggan runway to devise an operational strategy to remake the city's bureaucracy.

Within months, the lighting overhaul was on a fast track, and the city's effort to demolish abandoned homes was picking up steam. Duggan projected in early 2014 that by the end of 2015 all the streetlights would be back on in the City of Detroit—a remarkable feat. With Orr and Duggan on good terms, the city government appeared, for the first time in recent memory, to be headed in the right direction.

DESPITE THE OPERATIONAL progress under Orr and Duggan, the Detroit Water and Sewerage Department (DWSD) was in a state of disrepair. After a combination of leadership failures and financial shortcomings over the course of several decades, the city-owned system was malfunctioning at a rapid rate.

A majority of the three thousand miles of water pipes within the city limits were between seventy and ninety years old, with some dating back to before the Great Depression. Over a three-year stretch, the system experienced more than five thousand water main breaks within the city's borders. Although water quality was fine, fixing the infrastructure would take hundreds of millions of dollars, perhaps billions. In addition to DWSD's infrastructure problems, the department had been dogged by corruption.

DWSD operated under federal oversight for about thirty-five years after authorities discovered in the 1970s that the department had violated the Clean Water Act and flouted federal pollution standards. In the 2000s, Mayor Kwame Kilpatrick leveraged his position to steer water contracts to his buddy, Bobby Ferguson, who also extorted contractors to win business. One of the people involved in the conspiracy was the director of DWSD during Kilpatrick's reign, Victor Mercado, who eventually admitted his guilt and was sentenced to eight months in a halfway house.

Past corruption notwithstanding, after Kilpatrick's ouster, the Bing administration made strides in helping DWSD become compliant with federal regulations. In an acknowledgment of that progress, U.S. district judge Sean Cox terminated federal oversight of the water department the week Orr took office.

Despite the department's many troubles, Detroit's water system was still one of the city's only major assets in the bankruptcy, with about four million customers in metro Detroit, servicing communities in Wayne, Macomb, and Oakland counties.

Almost contemporaneously with Orr's appointment, a committee established by Cox—consisting of several city executives and City Council members—had recommended translating DWSD's customer base into a source of revenue by leasing the water system to a new, independent authority. The proposal envisioned the authority paying the city $50 million per year for the right to operate the system and collect customer payments. The committee believed the city could use the lease payments to finance basic services through its general fund. The deal would have been similar to arrangements in cities such as Washington, D.C., and Jacksonville, Florida.

The city's investment bank, Miller Buckfire, which had already explored potential DWSD monetization options on behalf of the

state, adopted a version of the regional authority concept on behalf
of the city shortly after Cox's committee made its recommendation.
The investment bank proposed transferring the assets of the water
department to an independent authority that would effectively
assume day-to-day operations and lease the system from the city.

Ken Buckfire believed that Wall Street investors would extend
better bond interest rates to a water authority that did not have
the word "Detroit" in its name, thus reducing operating costs and
improving the financial position of the system. The proposed deal
would provide new revenue for the city's beleaguered general fund.

But politicians in the suburbs that paid for water from the city
recoiled at Buckfire's aggressive stance in the negotiation process.
County officials accused Buckfire of trying to extract value from
the department at the expense of suburban ratepayers. Oakland
County politicians were particularly upset at the prospect of their
taxpayers helping to foot the bill for Detroit's revitalization. And
they questioned whether Detroit's leaders were capable of spending
lease revenue responsibly.

"Why would they do anything but attempt to return to the old
ways of providing benefits to the friends and family of the past?"
said Bob Daddow, a deputy executive of Oakland County, in an
email to Buckfire.

For metro Detroit, squabbling between the city and suburban
counties was reflective of the kind of bickering they've engaged
in for decades. Like dysfunctional family members unwilling to
acknowledge that their destinies are intertwined, Detroit and
its surrounding counties have utterly failed at regional planning,
except for a small burst of progress in recent years. For example,
metro Detroit lacks a cohesive regional transportation system,
making mass-transit travel between some communities difficult or
impossible.

Privately, creditors wanted Detroit to hammer the counties in the water negotiations. Ron Bloom, the Lazard investment banker advising the Official Committee of Retirees, had concluded that the city held most of the bargaining chips in the water negotiation process. He believed the city didn't even need the counties' support to establish an independent authority because it controlled the asset, a legacy of the city's former wealth.

Furthermore, Bloom concluded that Detroit water rates were exceptionally low when compared with those in other major urban areas. Rates were 64 percent higher in New York and 74 percent higher in Washington, D.C., for example. Quite simply, creditors believed, Detroit could extract more value from its water system by turning it over to a private authority.

There was no shortage of outsized personalities in the water deal negotiations. Buckfire's reputation as a tough negotiator clashed with Oakland County executive L. Brooks Patterson, who threw a public fit over Detroit's proposal, which had Orr's endorsement.

Patterson, a Republican, is well respected in political circles for his financial acumen but remains infamous for a sharp wit that occasionally manifests in imprudent rhetoric. In the throes of negotiations over the proposed water deal, Patterson became engulfed in a controversy over his remarks in a *New Yorker* profile.

"Anytime I talk about Detroit, it will not be positive," he told the magazine. "Therefore, I'm called a Detroit basher. The truth hurts, you know? Tough shit."

Patterson's comments, including an insensitive racial remark, ignited a controversy among the city's supporters, who viewed the article as the latest example of Patterson's dismissiveness toward Detroit. So it was no small irony when Patterson took offense at what he viewed as Buckfire's dismissiveness.

Buckfire "came in and dealt with us like we were a bunch of country bumpkins," Patterson told the *Detroit Free Press* at the time.

The water deal negotiations fell apart.

"He said I was treating him like a country bumpkin, and I wasn't," Buckfire, who lived in Oakland County as a kid, said later. "My mother was very upset about that. She said, 'I'm not going to vote for him again.' I said, 'Mom, you don't live there anymore. You can't vote for him.' She said, 'I'll come back and not vote for him.'"

But even Buckfire, generally unshakable at the bargaining table, was dismayed at Oakland County's stance.

"The counties, which have always hated Detroit, just didn't want the city to have the money, despite the fact it would have had no impact on rates," he said.

Patterson rejected the suggestion that he opposed Detroit's revitalization.

"I'm a Detroiter by birth. I went to school there. I was raised there. I have no animosity toward the city. From my perspective, selflessly, I hope they come all the way back," he said later.

A revitalized Detroit would make it easier to promote the region, he insisted. "For years now, I've had to explain Detroit away. I hope they recover. I really do," he said.

Patterson's opposition to the water deal centered on Buckfire's proposal to transfer the system's assets to an external authority that would pay the City of Detroit about $50 million annually over forty years. Buckfire theorized that the authority would be able to afford the lease payment because under the city's bankruptcy plan, cuts to pensions and retiree health care insurance would save DWSD an equal amount in costs over four decades. Buckfire's proposal called for the lease payments to be deposited back into the city's general fund so that the city could hire police officers and firefighters and tear down abandoned homes. But if DWSD was left in place after the bankruptcy with no separate authority taking over, its costs would have plummeted because of the cuts to pensions and health care, and the city would have been legally required to lower water rates for its suburban customers.

"It would have been a pure gift for Oakland County on the backs of our retirees. Mathematically he knew I was right," Buckfire said later. "What he really wanted was a rate reduction."

Patterson swiftly dismissed Buckfire's assessment. "I have no idea what he's talking about," Patterson recalled. He said his position was simple: you can't extract value out of the water department for the city's benefit.

"If it has any kind of cash flow, it has to go back into the system and not in the general fund. That's one of the tenets. The money stays in the system because we've got the huge cost of rebuilding and upgrading," Patterson said. "We can't let the water department become a cash cow to fund the [city]."

Buckfire was not about to allow Oakland County to enjoy collateral benefits from Detroit's bankruptcy. "Of course not," he said. "Oakland County and Macomb County for forty years got rich off the decline of Detroit. They really did because the entire tax base moved up there. Their nightmare was that Detroit would rise again and attract people and businesses away from Oakland and Macomb counties."

After several months of negotiations failed to produce a deal, Oakland County deputy executive Gerald Poisson wrote a letter to Orr dated April 7, 2014, calling the city "desperate" and slamming what he called a "descent into name calling."

Detroit and the counties had reached an impasse. The same day as the letter, Oakland, Macomb, and Wayne counties filed official legal objections in court to Detroit's plan of adjustment, asking Judge Steven Rhodes to block the city's bankruptcy restructuring because of the effort to regionalize the water system.

AS TALKS FALTERED, Orr brought out a new weapon. He solicited bids for private operators to run or purchase the water system, which would have enormous consequences for the counties.

"This was in the beginning of 2014 when all those nastygrams were going back and forth between us and Bob Daddow and Brooks," Orr said. "I finally got to the breaking point and said, 'Fuck it. It's outta here. We're doing it because we have to do it.'"

The city identified Chicago-based water operator Veolia as a leading candidate to take over the system in a privatization. Under the originally proposed regional authority, the counties would have gotten seats on a board of directors that would still control water rates, theoretically protecting ratepayers from exorbitant increases. But under a private operator, water rates would be hard to control. A private operator would squeeze superfluous costs out of the system, potentially laying off workers and maximizing profits at the expense of taxpayers. That was a politically disastrous scenario for elected officials in the counties, whom voters could punish at the ballot box.

Daddow, a deputy executive for Patterson, had already warned the governor's chief of staff, Dennis Muchmore, of a political explosion if the city's water deal efforts forced the counties to pick up the costs of Detroit's dilapidated infrastructure.

"If there is any exposure of the suburbs assuming financial responsibility for Detroit's morass, mismanagement, and corruption over the years, I seriously doubt that there would be any votes" to support the deal from county board members, Daddow told Muchmore in an email in December 2013. "God help this region if Orr chooses to try to privatize this matter with the increased costs that brings—it would light up" the region.

Rhodes put an end to the public bickering over the water deal by ordering the parties into confidential mediation, saying in court that he had a "sense" that "a regional water authority is not only in the best interest of the city but also in the best interest of all the customers of the city's water department." Those customers suffered the consequences of the city's lack of basic maintenance of its pipes and water treatment facilities.

"If we do not take advantage of this unique opportunity, the opportunity will, in all likelihood, be lost forever," Rhodes opined.

U.S. District Judge Cox, whom chief mediator Gerald Rosen had appointed to lead the regional water deal mediation talks, forced the squabbling city and counties to the bargaining table. Snyder dispatched his senior advisor, Rich Baird, to facilitate the conversation, and Orr invited Duggan into the negotiations.

Colleagues insist that Baird's devotion is to Snyder, not to an ideology, despite a few dustups with Democrats during the governor's first term. On the flip side, Duggan is a hardcore Democrat whose ideological principles few would question. The two opposites attracted.

"Rich was the governor's advisor, and therefore speaking to Rich is like talking to the governor, which gave Rich a lot of power," Buckfire observed.

Patterson steadfastly refused to allow the prospective regional authority to divert cash into Detroit's general fund. But Duggan found common ground with the Republican Oakland County executive. Like Patterson, he believed that leveraging the water system to create a new source of revenue for Detroit's public services was unrealistic because of the immense amount of ancient pipes that would require massive reinvestment.

"We were dramatically underinvested in the Detroit infrastructure," Duggan said. "That's got to get fixed."

Cox organized a meeting between Patterson and Orr to clear the air. "Sean Cox was instrumental because he was brought in after we sort of had the blowup," Orr said. Orr and Patterson met for dinner at a steakhouse in the ritzy Oakland County suburb of Birmingham, where they gulped wine together.

"It's just me and Brooks. We start laughing, drinking. I'm picking his brain. It was a very nice event. We actually like each other,"

Orr recalled. "The next day Bob Daddow calls to say, 'What can we do to get this deal done?'"

Patterson transformed into a supporter of Orr. "We got along really well," Patterson said later. "I think Orr's up to the task."

Orr refused to blame Buckfire for the temporary breakdown in negotiations. "If there's any failing, it's not Ken's. It's my failure to recognize the value of relationships and taking that up quicker," Orr said. "Once we did that, boom, boom, we're off and running."

But in the midst of the mediation, an unexpected public outcry over the city's effort to force delinquent accountholders to pay their water bills threatened to undercut the momentum.

NEARLY HALF OF Detroit water accounts were delinquent as of March 2014, amounting to $118 million in unpaid water bills. Facing pressure to shore up its finances, DWSD cracked down on delinquent ratepayers by shutting off water to residents at a pace of three thousand per week.

The rampant delinquencies reflected a diversity of circumstances, ranging from poor residents who simply couldn't afford to pay, to enraged citizens who refused to pay on the basis that the city was not meeting their basic needs, to scofflaw residents who could easily afford to pay, to rich businesses that didn't pay for no reason at all.

The shutoffs proceeded uneventfully until the United Nations issued a statement in June calling water a "human right," blasting the city, and suggesting that the shutoffs might violate international laws. A flurry of protests ensued as outraged activists implored Detroit to restore water access for the poor. Ten people were arrested at one rally.

"This is literally a jungle out here," said Meeko Williams of the

Detroit Water Brigade at one rally, where volunteers distributed jugs of water, coolers, and filtration straws to residents who had their water shut off. "People are surviving however they can."

The controversy was emblematic of the conflict among a bankrupt city that could no longer afford to give away water for free, a low-income populace with many folks barely scraping by, and a bureaucracy that failed to educate residents about available financial assistance. Orr was exasperated at the maverick water department's indiscriminate handling of the shutoffs.

Duggan said he was better equipped to manage the water issues.

"Okay, you go deal with the department," Orr told the mayor.

Orr handed over control of DWSD to Duggan, deepening the mayor's management of day-to-day operations in the city while the emergency manager maintained control of the bankruptcy. Duggan quelled the controversy by temporarily suspending shutoffs so that the city could distribute information on assistance funds. He also embarked on a plan to overhaul basic management processes in the water department. For example, the department often failed to respond to water main breaks in the evening because repair specialists worked day shifts. Entire neighborhoods would be flooded until the next morning, when someone was finally dispatched to the scene.

"I was trying to get the damn water main breaks to get shut off and stop screwing people around," Duggan said later. "That's all I was trying to do."

The moratorium on shutoffs dampened public hysteria over the issue.

Still, complicating the path to a regional authority was Orr's plan to force the city's secured water bondholders to exchange their debt early, effectively impairing their bonds, the legal term for forcing them to accept new terms they had not agreed to. That incensed Wall Street, and all the major insurers of the city's water and sewer debt filed official objections to the plan of adjustment. The ratings agencies threatened to punish DWSD with a lowered bond rating if Orr proceeded with his plan to force bondholders to accept reduced interest rates. A lowered bond rating would undermine the budding regional water deal.

"I'd never even heard of this rating classification before. It wasn't 'D' for default. It was worse than 'D,'" said Amanda Van Dusen, a Miller Canfield attorney helping Detroit negotiate a resolution to the bond dispute. "That was going to hurt the ability of the system to borrow money going forward. We all know from the water main breaks this was a system that has a lot of needs."

To smooth out the dispute with Wall Street, the city made an offer to disgruntled investors to buy back bonds by issuing new secured DWSD debt at more favorable terms for the city, a refinancing concept suggested by Citigroup Global Markets head of public finance David Brownstein. That deal saved the water department more than $100 million on a present value basis—which could be invested in infrastructure repairs—and provided assurances that a restructured water department wouldn't hurt bondholders. The refinancing was optional, but 93 percent of the objecting debt holders exchanged their bonds voluntarily.

With the debt issue resolved, the water and sewer bondholders dropped their objections to Orr's plan of adjustment, and the path to a water authority was clear. Facing pressure to get a deal done rather than risk having one imposed by Rhodes, the counties caved. In a historic breakthrough, the city and the counties signed a tentative forty-year deal in September 2014 to establish the independent Great Lakes Water Authority, which would lease the city's water assets in exchange for $50 million in annual payments to help finance infrastructure improvements. That would foot the bill for a massive overhaul of the city's water system, though the deal prevented the city from using the money for public safety or other services as Buckfire originally wanted.

In a nod to the shutoff crisis, the deal also carved out an annual stream of $4.5 million to help low-income Detroiters pay their bills and limited water-rate increases to protect ratepayers from sudden spikes. The new authority would have six members, with two appointed by the mayor of Detroit, one by the governor, and one each by the counties. But five of six votes would be required to raise rates or issue debt, requiring near-regional unity to make substantive decisions.

Leaders in all three counties quickly dropped their objections to Detroit's restructuring plan, removing one of the last remaining obstacles preventing the city from exiting bankruptcy.

CHAPTER 12

"Get the Damn Buttons"

In conservative western Michigan, distrust of Detroit has accumulated like an arterial plaque. Resentment against corruption, unions, and racial politics in Detroit is commonplace. Some residents in the state's southwest corner even identify more with the Windy City of Chicago than with the Motor City, which they view as a postindustrial anachronism, not as a crucial cog in Michigan's economic engine.

When Governor Rick Snyder, who enjoyed wide support from voters on the west side of the state, embraced the grand bargain and asked the state Legislature to match the foundations' pledge to help rescue Detroit, it was a stunning political maneuver. At the outset of the bankruptcy, few political insiders believed Republicans in Lansing would ever entertain the idea of dishing out cash for Detroit. Anything remotely resembling a bailout was out of the question.

"I personally started with a no-way, no-how," Jase Bolger, the Republican Speaker of the House, said later. "There was no-way, no-how we were going to participate in business as usual. We're not interested in a bailout."

Snyder had already pledged his support to Judge Gerald Rosen, the bankruptcy's chief mediator, and to Gene Gargaro, chairman of the Detroit Institute of Arts, for the state's portion of the grand-bargain contribution. But there was no political assurance that he could wrangle the votes from members of his own party, let alone Democrats furious at the prospect of pension cuts for retirees and union members.

Without state money, the grand bargain would collapse; the city would not have enough money to justify preserving the DIA and keeping pension cuts low. Kevyn Orr would be forced either to put the DIA on the auction block or to pursue steeper cuts to pensions—or possibly to do both.

Orr set out for a Lansing lobbying blitz, but after a first round of meetings with legislators, the outlook for the grand bargain appeared grim.

"There were legislators who were really pissed off, and I'm the lightning rod," Orr said.

Legislators vented to Orr: "'What about my district? I'm out here in Lapeer and I don't get a dime!' 'They made their bed. Let them lie in it.' There was a lot of that," he recalled. "That didn't go so well."

The governor, Rosen, Orr, and state legislators who already supported the grand bargain crafted a dual message to persuade cynics. For Democrats, the sell was simple. Detroit is loaded with reliably Democratic voters and union backers who would never forgive legislators if they abandoned the city.

For Republicans, the sell was more complex. Some Republicans grasped the significance of Detroit as a driver of economic development for the state. Without a vibrant metropolitan city, Michigan would lag in its pursuit of young professionals who favor urban nightlife over suburbia. What's more, Detroit's dreadful global reputation would continue to make it difficult to attract investors and tourists to the entire region, depriving the state of jobs and tax dollars.

But the central thrust of Snyder's pitch to fellow Republicans was that contributing to the grand bargain was itself a bargain. The deal required pensioners to vote to give up their rights to sue the state over pension cuts. Although the law seemed to make it clear that pensions can be cut in bankruptcy, there remained the possibility that retirees and unions could persuade an appellate judge to overturn Judge Steven Rhodes's ruling and require the state to make up the entire pension shortfall, estimated at $3.5 billion when the case started. If that came to pass, the payments would blast a hole in the state budget.

In addition, the grand bargain was constructed to ensure that no pensioners fell below the poverty line. Without it, a sizable number of retirees could require Medicaid and other social services, compounding the financial consequences for the state budget. But for a one-time contribution of $195 million—the present value of $350 million over twenty years—the state could minimize those risks.

For Snyder, the prototypical CPA thinker, those numbers made sense.

"By having this grand-bargain pool of resources, we could actually help people significantly that otherwise might fall into the social safety net. You have all the personal tragedy that would come with that. In addition, that would be an expensive item for the public sector, whether it be the state government or the federal government," Snyder said later. "Isn't it better to keep people self-sufficient rather than having them fall into the social safety net?"

The top Republican in the state Senate, majority leader Randy Richardville, had unsuccessfully pushed a bill in 2013 that would have protected the DIA from a sale in a bankruptcy. The grand bargain, coming a year later, would accomplish the same objective. He embraced it, though he refused to call it a bailout.

"In a very conservative caucus, there were members that were concerned about that messaging," Richardville said. Instead, "you could call it an insurance policy against the state budget getting hit."

To broaden the appeal of the grand bargain, supporters explained the statewide effects of Detroit's bankruptcy.

"Every single ZIP code in the state of Michigan had at least one [Detroit] retiree," said Don Taylor, president of the Retired Detroit Police and Fire Fighter Association and member of the Official Committee of Retirees, who lobbied legislators to back the deal. "It just showed it wasn't just a Detroit issue. It was going to affect the economies of a lot of smaller areas because the people wouldn't have spendable income or may lose their homes."

On her eightieth birthday, May 15, 2014, Shirley Lightsey, president of the Detroit Retired City Employees Association and a member of the retiree committee, drove to Lansing to testify in support of the grand bargain. Her testimony came about seven months after she testified in court against Detroit's eligibility for bankruptcy and blasted Orr for calling pensions "sacrosanct." In short, Lightsey and Taylor had convinced their fellow members of the retiree committee to recommend that fellow pensioners accept the grand bargain instead of holding out for something better that might not come. Now they needed to convince lawmakers to approve the state's portion of the grand-bargain funding before lobbying for individual pensioners to accept the plan. In her testimony, Lightsey urged the state Legislature to recognize that by voting to accept the grand bargain, retirees would be giving up their right to sue over pension cuts.

"This is no small concession for proud citizens to forgo this right and set their constitutional protections aside. To give up such appellate rights is difficult and heartbreaking, but the pension treatment that could result from a cram down and the uncertainty of appellate action is exponentially worse and unacceptable," Lightsey said.

An unlikely bipartisan coalition between Republican representative John Walsh of Livonia and Democratic representative Thomas Stallworth III of Detroit emerged to soothe the concerns of their fellow legislators in Lansing.

Grand-bargain supporters also orchestrated bipartisan legislation to establish a financial oversight board that would take effect at the conclusion of Orr's tenure, whenever that might come, and ensure that Detroit did not slip back into old fiscal habits. After Detroit's elected officials regained political control of the city, the financial review board would retain the authority to veto budgets, reject debt, and approve major contracts, including union deals—possibly for more than a decade.

Mayor Mike Duggan and City Council president Brenda Jones, both Democrats, like all other elected officials in Detroit, threw their support behind the grand bargain, helping to win over many fellow Democrats in the state Legislature. But they pushed for a quick sunset on the oversight board's authority.

"I'm one that believes in democracy," Jones said. "Once the elected officials show that we can do the job that we were elected to do, let us do our job without someone looking over our shoulders."

Duggan and Jones eventually committed to supporting the creation of the nine-member oversight commission after legislators agreed to give them each a seat on the board and to remove the commission's powers upon three straight years of balanced budgets and debt payments.

The creation of an oversight board fulfilled one of the emergency management team's earliest priorities.

"Nobody on Wall Street has any illusions about what can happen to the city when it's not being held accountable," said Ken

Buckfire, who had pushed hard for an oversight board from the outset in his discussions with the governor's administration before Orr's appointment. "The city had proven for decades that it's not accountable. It wasn't responsible. So if the city expects to borrow from the capital markets again, the markets will expect that someone will be ultimately responsible for ensuring that the city does not repeat the sins of the past."

Despite growing support for the grand bargain and oversight legislation, Bolger fired a last-second shot at the city's unions. He announced in late April that he would not back the final deal until there was some form of financial contribution from active-employee unions for the grand bargain. It was not enough that retirees would have to accept cuts in the deal. He viewed his request as an appropriate call for shared sacrifice, but his detractors viewed it as a bid to extract blood from political enemies.

Foundation leaders backing the grand bargain panicked, fearing that Bolger's new play could derail their efforts. Privately, Snyder and Richardville tried to talk Bolger out of it, but the Speaker would not budge. He wanted the active unions—whose members included vested pensioners—to feel some pain if the state was helping them out.

"I understand that he wanted them to have skin in the game, but I believed, because they already were in significant trouble, that their skin was already in the game," Richardville said.

Rosen, who had been trekking to Lansing for private meetings with legislators about the grand bargain, pressed the city's labor creditors for support too. The United Auto Workers union, which had tried to stop the early bankruptcy filing with its furious rush to the courthouse in July 2013, agreed to help. The UAW and the Michigan Building and Construction Trades Council agreed to raise a few million dollars to offset retiree health care cuts, a concession that satisfied Bolger.

"We had to be convinced that there was something different— that this was a true turnaround," Bolger said later. "I saw it as essential that everybody come together and participate in the recovery, or else it would be too easy to slip back into the bad habits that brought Detroit there."

The basic need to put Detroit on the path to renewal resonated for some legislators. Republican representative Al Pscholka's district counts more fans of the Chicago Bears than the Detroit Lions. But he still backed the grand bargain.

"I hail from southwest Michigan, but today I stand with Detroit and its path back to prosperity," Pscholka said on the floor of the House chambers as members voted on the aid package on May 22, 2014.

In a historic round of votes, the state House and then the state Senate overwhelmingly supported the package of bills required to deliver the grand-bargain funding and oversight. In an office in Lansing, the typically unexcitable Snyder threw his arms around Orr and Bill Nowling, Orr's senior advisor, in celebration. For the governor, who signed the package into law, it was a remarkable political victory, a surmounting of enormous odds in a state that had been bitterly divided over the course of its anchor city.

"I think he saw this as a call," said Nowling, who had served as Snyder's campaign press secretary in 2010. "He campaigned in Detroit. Victory speech in Detroit. It didn't get us any votes in Detroit. But there's a current of the population that cares about Detroit. They want to see it fixed."

WITH THE GRAND-BARGAIN funding in hand and the necessary legislation signed, the city still needed pensioners to acquiesce—far from a sure thing in a bankruptcy marked by street protests and emotional pleas from retirees to spare them from financial pain.

Although the grand bargain minimized the impact of Detroit's fiscal crisis on vulnerable retirees, many pensioners still believed that they should not have to accept cuts.

For the city to officially accept the grand-bargain funding and limit cuts to retirees, members of both groups—general pensioners and police and fire pensioners—were required to vote to accept the deal. In a separate vote, retirees were also given the chance to vote on Orr's plan to dramatically slash their health care insurance.

Over the course of sixty days in the late spring and early summer of 2014, thousands of retirees cast ballots. Some vocal opponents tried to convince retirees to vote "no" and roll the dice with an appellate fight.

Rosen and mediator Eugene Driker, architects of the grand bargain, grew nervous that a vocal minority would sway what they believed was a silent majority to kill the deal. As the weeks passed and retirees cast their votes, Rosen summoned Nowling to his chambers in the federal courthouse for a chiding.

"He's talked to five people who are voting no, and he thinks it's a representative sample," Nowling recalled, sarcastically.

Rosen wanted a coordinated media blitz to convince retirees to back the grand bargain.

"'Bill,'" Rosen told the emergency manager's spokesman, "'you're not doing enough. You don't know what you're doing. You're not treating it like a political campaign.'"

Nowling quietly seethed.

"My normal inclination is to blow my lid," he said. "But these are federal judges and Eugene Driker, who I have great respect for. I'm just going to sit here and eat a turd."

Nowling had prepared a marketing plan to campaign for a "yes" vote—but he didn't want to deploy it unless it was necessary.

"I knew that would be a whole fucking mess as soon as I start spending taxpayer dollars," he said.

So he held off. Nonetheless, Rosen pressured Orr to do something to seal the deal.

Shirley Lightsey, member of the retiree committee and president of the Detroit Retired City Employees Association, suggested the city fund the purchase of the buttons that her attorney, Ryan Plecha, had designed, emblazoned with their catchphrase, "You can't eat principles, and uncertainty doesn't pay the bills."

She wanted to distribute them to pensioners at community meetings to maintain momentum for the grand-bargain vote.

"So I said, 'OK, we'll order the buttons,'" Orr recalled.

But his assistant told him that the bankrupt city didn't have petty cash to pay for them. Orr was exasperated.

"I'll pay for the fucking buttons," he told his assistant, laughing later as he recalled the absurdity of the moment.

He dug for his personal credit card and authorized the purchase.

"I paid for those buttons—just to get it done and show the mediators that we're making a move," Orr said. "That settled them down just long enough to get the vote in. They had been spooled up, man."

He paused for a moment, reflecting on the matter incredulously. "Six hundred bucks of buttons," he sighed, shaking his head. "Get the damn buttons."

As ballots dribbled in day after day, Nowling crunched the numbers. Retirees were voting "yes" in droves.

"I did twelve different scenarios on the vote. There was no way we were going to lose it. And I knew it. I knew exactly who had voted and how they voted," Nowling said.

Still, to correct misperceptions about the deal, the city's retiree associations, pension funds, and the Official Committee of Retirees held meetings to recommend a "yes" vote to members.

And, in the middle of the vote, the city's largest union,

AFSCME, which represented general city workers, reached a long-in-the-making collective bargaining agreement in confidential mediation sessions overseen by U.S. District Court judge Victoria Roberts. After Orr made a key concession not to privatize services such as the transportation department, AFSCME agreed to recommend a "yes" vote to its members. Meanwhile, with a few days to spare before all votes were due, one of Orr's most ardent adversaries, the city's largest police union, also reached a contract of its own after securing long-overdue pay increases. The police union's officials then recommended a "yes" vote on the grand bargain to members with vested pensions.

With all the votes counted, pensioners had voted overwhelmingly to endorse the deal. Police and firefighter voters accepted it by a margin of 82 percent to 18 percent, while general city voters accepted by a margin of 73 percent to 27 percent.

In a remarkable display of personal sacrifice, retirees approved 90 percent cuts to their health care benefits by an even wider margin in a separate vote. They accepted those drastic reductions by a margin of 88 percent to 12 percent. For Orr, Snyder, and Rosen, the vote was an immensely gratifying endorsement of a hard-fought bankruptcy plan.

But the city's remaining enemies, Syncora and FGIC, had no intention of accepting the results of the vote.

CHAPTER 13

The Empty Cabin

The newspaper advertisement screamed, "Motor City Going Out of Business Sale!"

"Hurry Before It's All Gone!"

"The Entire City Is for Sale—Everything Must Go!"

"Largest Inventory of Abandoned Property on the Planet! Acres upon acres of beautiful former Homes, Schools, Businesses, Churches, Dreams. Many historic places, from bungalows to entire housing projects."

"Hurry! They aren't making them like this anymore."

The spoof, the brainchild of a provocative social artist calling himself Jerry Vile, was published in *Metro Times*, an alternative Detroit weekly, about a month after the city filed for bankruptcy. It advertised sales on stop signs, streetlights, manhole covers, pensions, union cards, and police chief uniforms. The Detroit Institute of Arts, the spoof ad said, would hit the auction block in a sale at a local Holiday Inn.

"Fill Your Walls—Nothing over $39.95," the ad declared.

In another stunt in May 2014, Vile orchestrated a creative protest on the grounds of the DIA itself, spearing about a hundred sticks with plastic flamingos—painted to look like vultures—into the museum's shimmering green lawn. If the grand bargain's opponents were vultures, their critics would say that bond insurers Syncora and Financial Guaranty Insurance Company played the role of carrion-eating fowl.

As the grand bargain careened rapidly toward a capstone trial that could result in huge losses for Syncora and FGIC, it became clear that Judge Steven Rhodes might have to decide whether to approve the city's request to wipe out the insurers' claims over their objections. Absent a mediated settlement, the companies were left with only each other as allies.

"You know where you're going to end up," Judge Gerald Rosen, the chief mediator and architect of the grand bargain, told the creditors as they failed to make progress in summer mediation sessions with the city. "A bankruptcy is like a train. First, it's at the station. People who buy the first tickets get the best seats on the train. People who buy the second tickets get the second-best seats on the train. People who buy the last tickets get run over by the train."

Syncora and FGIC were the last ones at the ticket booth. With the grand bargain incorporated into the proposed bankruptcy plan by midsummer, the city was offering six times higher payback for pensioners than for the bond insurers based on a percentage of their unsecured debt.

"You never understood whether or not they fully got how great their deal was," Kirkland & Ellis attorney Stephen Hackney, the leader of Syncora's ground game, said later. "Congratulations that the firemen are in favor of a deal that says their pensions aren't going to get cut at all. That's not necessarily something that blows my skirt up. We were all looking at, like, nothing."

In bankruptcy, unsecured creditors with similar legal standing are supposed to be treated similarly. There's room for some discrimination in treatment, but it must be justified. Pensioners, who were considered unsecured creditors for the purposes of the bankruptcy, argued that they deserved better treatment because they were more vulnerable than financial creditors and because they were relinquishing their rights to sue the state in exchange for grand-bargain money that would not otherwise exist. They argued that their pensions had greater legal protections than the certificates-of-participation (COPs) debt, which the judge had said was likely based on an illegal structure.

Still, Syncora was incensed that the grand bargain was designed explicitly to benefit pensioners. The debt Syncora and FGIC had guaranteed was actually used to fund pensions. Yet, because of the debt's dubious legal structure, the pension lenders were being treated differently in court than the pensioners. As a matter of public perception, helpless pensioners curry more sympathy than villainous financial creditors. Hackney knew this.

"I guess an interesting question is: Does it matter if you don't do right by FGIC and Syncora? I think most people would say, 'Who cares about a couple of swap insurers? It only matters in some ineffable macroeconomic way that we'll never really track down.' But I think process matters a lot," Hackney said later. "I think if you don't do things the right way, there's a cost to that that becomes difficult to assess. And because it's difficult to assess, maybe that's why no one cares about it."

AS A YOUNG BOY, Gerald Rosen had visited a summer camp in Charlevoix, Michigan, where counselors would force misbehaving kids to spend a few minutes alone in an empty cabin in the woods as punishment. During the bankruptcy, a picture of an empty cabin hung on the wall in Rosen's judicial chambers, a gift from mediator and friend Eugene Driker. As a negotiation tactic in Detroit's bankruptcy, Rosen replicated his camp experience with creditors who refused to cooperate. He shut them out of negotiations until they were ready to be nice. Syncora spent a lot of time in Rosen's empty cabin. There, the insurer's attorneys grew increasingly upset at what they perceived to be the chief mediator's brazenness.

For one thing, Rosen had issued a series of press statements about individual settlements spawning from secret mediation proceedings. He wrote them himself and authorized their distribution through the court's public relations arm, sometimes before creditors were fully comfortable with the announcements.

"There was this idea that if you announce it, it was a fait accompli, or something like that. People can't back out," said Dentons attorney Carole Neville, lawyer for the Official Committee of Retirees. Before the "details were worked out, the settlements got announced. It was so frustrating."

Rosen also had surprised people involved in the case by conducting confidential sessions with members of the state Legislature and the Detroit City Council, away from the spotlight of the media, to build momentum for the grand bargain. And he appeared at press conferences promoting the deal, making public statements that left creditors stunned at the sight of the lead mediator openly discussing the case.

At a press conference held on June 9, 2014, to celebrate grand-bargain donations, Rosen implicitly acknowledged the tightrope he was walking.

"Judges," he began, "aren't used to attending press conferences."

Nonetheless, he launched into a speech endorsing the proposed deal and praising the bipartisan coalition of politicians who supported it.

"I'm not a politician, but through all of this I couldn't help but notice that I was asking the state's leaders to do this in an election year. Not an easy task," Rosen proclaimed. "I couldn't help but

THE EMPTY CABIN 207

think that maybe we're setting a template here in Michigan for how things should be done."

The proposed bankruptcy settlement, he said, would not be "possible without all of us keeping a clear vision firmly in mind about who this is really about. It's about Detroit's retirees, who have given decades and decades of their lives devoted to Detroit."

The judge's remarks only reinforced Syncora's belief that the grand bargain—which Rosen had originally dubbed the "Art Trust"—was designed explicitly to benefit retirees and no one else.

"The debtor—the city—to me didn't seem actually in control of the case from the beginning. I think the big decisions weren't really made by them, like the art and the pensions," said James H. M. Sprayregen, the Kirkland & Ellis attorney who oversaw Syncora's case.

The grand bargain was principally Rosen's brainchild, and it had become bigger than the bankruptcy. By securing altruistic pledges from foundations and announcing them before the city had released its first plan of adjustment, Rosen built so much momentum for his own solution that no reasonable leader of the city or the retiree groups could reject it. For them, rejecting the grand bargain in favor of some alternative route—say, liquidating the DIA to satisfy creditors and reinvest in the city—would have been ludicrous. You don't refuse more than $800 million in free money.

"That was a different dynamic than almost any other case," Sprayregen said. "Mediation is kind of a misnomer here. Traditional mediations are to settle disputes amongst parties. That's not really what this was. It was more of a political activity, which is not necessarily critical. It's just the facts of life."

As Syncora observed Rosen's maneuverings, it realized that mediator and grand-bargain co-creator Eugene Driker's wife, Elaine, was a former member of the DIA board of directors. Collectively, the insurer believed, Rosen's public support of the grand bargain and Elaine Driker's connection to the DIA tainted a supposedly impartial mediation process.

The Kirkland lawyers pondered an explosive tactic. After spending the duration of the bankruptcy negotiations attacking the city, Syncora pivoted. The company's legal team plotted an attack on the process of the bankruptcy itself and the propriety of mediation sessions that culminated in a deal favoring unsecured pension creditors over unsecured bond insurers.

In August, Sprayregen and Hackney filed an official objection to the city's bankruptcy plan on the grounds that "agenda-driven, conflicted" Rosen and Eugene Driker had displayed "naked favoritism" by colluding to preserve the DIA for the "sole benefit" of pensioners.

"The grand bargain was orchestrated to maximize recoveries for politically favored, insider creditors while protecting the museum assets from all other creditors and the city itself," the attorneys wrote. "Neither Judge Rosen nor Mr. Driker ever disclosed any biases or conflicts of interest that might affect their ability to serve as impartial mediators in this case, but, while Syncora takes no pleasure in saying it, both were biased and conflicted from the beginning."

Syncora noted Elaine Driker's previous ties to the DIA and said mediators in other cases "have been disqualified for far less glaring conflicts of interest than Mr. Driker's here."

Rosen had said publicly that the grand bargain "is really all about" helping Detroit retirees, the insurer noted.

Kirkland argued that Rosen's deal trampled Syncora's rights to a fair recovery through the bankruptcy process and would strip the city of a valuable asset—the DIA—that could help pay creditors and fund services.

The audacity of Syncora's accusations rippled through the tight-knit community of attorneys, advisors, bankers, and politicians involved in the case. To publicly accuse mediators—including the District Court's chief judge—of violating ethical guidelines and conspiring to pursue their own agenda for political purposes was virtually unprecedented. The groundswell of public support in metro Detroit for the grand bargain made the accusations all the more astonishing.

"We got lots of calls after we did that from people saying, 'That was ballsy to do, but that's exactly what everybody's been thinking and saying,'" Sprayregen said. "There was nothing in there that was surprising. The surprising thing is we were willing to sign it and put our name to it."

When the filing hit, the Drikers were driving south on Interstate 75, returning from their northern Michigan condominium to check on their Detroit home after a rainstorm had pummeled the region.

Eugene Driker saw the caller ID on his phone and picked up.

"Wait until you hear this," Rosen said.

He read Syncora's attack to Driker, word for word.

"There's a good reason you shouldn't talk on the cell phone while you're driving," Driker said later. "I almost drove off the road when I heard that. It was shock, disbelief, anger, puzzlement. I was dismayed. And obviously my dear wife wasn't thrilled about her name getting dragged into this either."

By this stage in the case—quite possibly too late to derail the announced plan of adjustment—Syncora was laying the groundwork for an appeal.

"We believed that was where the real battle was," Sprayregen said. "We had a lot of people look at that before we filed it. We knew it was incendiary—incredibly incendiary."

But the objection contained a fatal flaw. At the beginning of the bankruptcy, materials documenting each individual mediator's potential conflicts of interest had been distributed to all attorneys involved in the case. Those materials included an emailed disclosure on September 9, 2013, of Elaine Driker's prior connections to the DIA. Somehow, Kirkland's scrupulous attorneys had missed it.

"The minute I got home, I dug out the disclosure letter I had sent to Judge Rosen the year before," Eugene Driker said. The mediator had properly disclosed his wife's connection to the museum. The city's Jones Day attorneys pounced on Kirkland's blunder.

"Desperation is seldom pretty, and here it is particularly ugly as it has led Syncora into a strategy of distortions, half-truths, and outright falsehoods," Jones Day attorneys wrote in a court filing. "By making this false and defamatory accusation, it is Syncora that has crossed the line."

The city openly suggested that Rhodes should consider punishing Syncora's attorneys by imposing sanctions or even ordering a formal apology.

"They really stepped in it," Jones Day attorney David Heiman, the city's lead lawyer, said later.

Grand-bargain supporters agreed.

"I love Steve Hackney. I think he's a wonderful lawyer. I think they really went overboard, and I frankly was pissed off," said Dentons attorney Carole Neville, lawyer for the Official Committee of Retirees. "It was total bullshit what they did. I was really angry at Steve for that. I think they were just willing to rock the boat as far as they could go. But I think it was a little bit of a misstep."

Judge Rhodes convened a hearing on August 25, 2014, to start the process of considering sanctions against Kirkland.

Hackney's defense was simple: I'm doing my job.

He did not back down.

"It is important for all of us to remember that we have arranged for ourselves here an adversarial system that doesn't just encourage people to fight zealously on behalf of their clients. It requires you to. As an advocate on behalf of Syncora, I am here to fight for their rights," Hackney told Rhodes. "We genuinely believe that the plan that has emerged out of the mediation process, the cornerstone of which is the grand bargain, is a tainted plan. We believe it did slit the bonds of propriety."

Fighting for Syncora meant fighting for a "hated minority" in the case, Hackney admitted.

"It is often a lawyer's duty to challenge the rectitude of certain public actions. That is one of the hard things about being a lawyer," he said in court. "You have to say things from time to time that are unpopular."

"Well," Rhodes interrupted, "but that's not an unlimited obligation."

No, it's not. But Hackney pressed further. It's critical, he argued, to ascertain whether the decision to favor pensioners over Syncora and FGIC sprung from the mediators, the pensioners, the foundations, the city, or elsewhere.

"And why is that relevant?" Rhodes pressed.

"It's relevant because the mediators are supposed to be impartial, and what you can't do is bring your own view of what matters—of what really matters—to the mediation," Hackney said. "You facilitate."

He had articulated Syncora's most compelling argument against the grand bargain. In a court of law, is it fair to favor one set of creditors over another, owing to one's conscience? But Rhodes exposed a hole in Syncora's assertion that mediators had conspired to shortchange financial creditors. What about the Christmas Eve Massacre, he pointed out? The city had tried to give a truckload of cash to UBS and Bank of America Merrill Lynch at Rosen's personal recommendation.

"Now, explain to me how that demonstrates a bias against financial creditors by the mediators," Rhodes said.

Rosen's slipup on the swaps settlement had, remarkably, come to serve as a vindication that the mediators weren't biased against financial creditors. If they were, Rosen never would have recommended a lucrative deal that favored the banks. In a rebuke of Syncora's accusations, Rhodes ruled that the insurer "falsely asserted" that Driker had failed to reveal his wife's connections to the DIA.

Allegations that Rosen and Driker "colluded" to design a biased restructuring plan were "scandalous and defamatory," as well as "legally and factually unwarranted, unprofessional, and unjust," Rhodes ruled. He ordered Syncora to prove why its attorneys should not be slapped with sanctions.

Until that moment, Rhodes had not publicly protested Syncora's zealousness.

"In virtually all respects, I had no problem with it. I appreciated it," Rhodes said later. "They were really good lawyers."

But the accusations against the mediators profoundly troubled him.

"To this day I do not understand it, or what the strategy was behind it, or what they thought they would gain by it," Rhodes said later. "It was so out of character for how they had been conducting themselves throughout the case. I was deeply disappointed by it. I was. I felt that was totally unjustified."

Put simply, mediators are not capable of collusion, Rhodes had ruled, because only the city and its creditors can strike a deal. The mediators can only make suggestions and attempt to bring the parties together.

"They were in no position to 'collude' with anyone, to 'orchestrate' or 'engineer' anything, to 'execute a transaction,' or to 'pick winners and losers.' These allegations misunderstand the nature of mediation," Rhodes ruled. "As much respect and gratitude as the mediators deserve for their dedication and skill in their accomplishments in this case, they could not impose their will, their plans, their agenda, or their bias upon the parties through the mediation process, assuming they had any of those."

Besides, Rhodes concluded, even if a plan emerged out of mediation that unfairly discriminated against financial creditors, it's the court's responsibility to block the deal.

"That was the protection that the creditors received when this court disapproved the city's settlement with the swaps," Rhodes wrote. "The mediators' record of accomplishment in this case establishes but one plan, one agenda, one bias—to settle as much of the case as they can and to do so tirelessly and selflessly."

The judge was particularly aggravated at Syncora's attack on the Drikers. But he declined to order an apology.

"Although not because a public apology is not warranted here," Rhodes ruled. "It is, and to Mrs. Driker, too. Rather, the court concludes that a coerced and therefore insincere apology is not a true apology at all; it is not an acknowledgment of a mistake or an expression of regret."

For the first time in the bankruptcy, the dustup between Detroit and Syncora had devolved into a grisly feud. The prospect of mutual reconciliation appeared impossible.

"Rhodes put a lot of blood on the floor," Hackney said later.

CHAPTER 14

One Bullet, Two Creditors

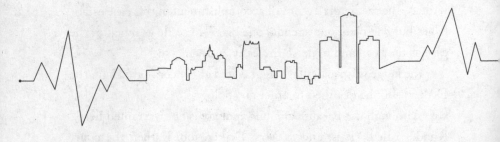

The emergence of the grand bargain, settlements between Detroit and unsecured bondholders, and the resolution of the water authority dispute left Syncora and Financial Guaranty Insurance Company as the only major parties trying to stop Detroit's bankruptcy plan. Throughout the case, they had been joined in a common goal: forcing Detroit to pay off $1.4 billion in pension obligation certificates-of-participation (COPs) debt and the underlying interest-rate swaps at a higher rate than Kevyn Orr's proposal of pennies on the dollar. Where the allies' strategies diverged, however, was primarily in style and aggression.

The Weil, Gotshal & Manges attorneys and Houlihan Lokey financial advisors representing FGIC, including lawyers Alfredo Perez and Ed Soto and banker Steve Spencer, were fighting a boxing match, adhering to the rigid structure and well-established rules of the federal bankruptcy process. That strategy had given Weil, Gotshal & Manges and Houlihan Lokey the upper hand in many past bankruptcies.

In contrast, the Kirkland & Ellis attorneys representing Syncora—James H. M. Sprayregen, Stephen Hackney, and Ryan

Bennett—attacked the process of Detroit's bankruptcy itself, questioned the ethics of the mediators, attempted to block the overhaul of the city's dilapidated lighting department, slammed the brisk pace of the case, and blasted the city for privileging pensioners.

FGIC had tailored its focus more narrowly, primarily emphasizing its effort to prove that the Detroit Institute of Arts was worth far more than the city was willing to admit, thus making the grand bargain appear to be drastically undervalued. But the Kirkland attorneys did much of the heavy lifting as the lead objector.

"I think FGIC took a very gentlemanly position. They let Syncora be the asshole and they just said, 'Me, too.' But they said it very nicely," said retiree committee attorney Carole Neville of Dentons.

To exit bankruptcy, Detroit faced a final hurdle: convincing Judge Steven Rhodes to approve its plan of adjustment at a historic trial called a plan confirmation hearing. The proceedings required the city to present reams of evidence on Detroit's financial condition, bankruptcy settlements, and future investment priorities, as well as witnesses to testify in favor of the plan. Confirmation required Detroit to prove that the plan was legal, served the best interests of its creditors, did not discriminate unfairly among creditors, and was feasible to implement.

But the lens through which courts should assess the fairness of a municipal bankruptcy plan is a matter of debate in the legal profession. How do you determine whether a restructuring plan discriminates fairly or unfairly against creditors? Two popular measures in corporate bankruptcy, the Markell Test and the Aztec Test, adopt different criteria on how to define fairness.

Which one would Rhodes use to gauge the fairness of the city's plan?

Days before the trial was set to begin in early September 2014, Hackney stepped to the podium at an otherwise routine hearing and asked the judge directly.

Which test "is the one that you think is appropriate?" Hackney prodded. "The Aztec Test or the so-called Markell Test?"

Rhodes crossed his arms. "There is a third alternative," he said.

Hackney paused for a moment, his brow furrowed. "The Rhodes test?" he inquired.

The judge nodded slowly.

BY SLASHING MORE THAN $7 billion in liabilities—including substantial reductions to pensions, retiree health care benefits, general obligation bonds, and debt insured by FGIC and Syncora—Detroit's plan of adjustment would scrub its balance sheet of 75 percent of the legacy costs that had prevented it from investing in core city services. To protect the most vulnerable, the unlimited-tax general obligation bond settlement negotiated in the downtown Detroit barbershop, known as the "Haircut at the Haircut," would carve out a dedicated pool of resources to soften the blow on low-income pensioners.

With the debt reductions, cost cuts, and projected new revenue, the city would have $1.72 billion over ten years to spend on services that it would not have had without the bankruptcy, according to the city's projections. About one-fourth would be devoted to blight removal, with the rest dedicated to hiring police officers and firefighters, investing in public safety equipment, upgrading dilapidated computer systems, purchasing buses, improving infrastructure, and giving base-pay raises to employees who had endured steep cuts.

Over approximately a year of mediation with city unions, Orr's team also had negotiated new five-year contracts with the city's entire workforce, spanning about four-dozen bargaining units. Those deals required active workers to contribute to their pension plans, work longer to earn pensions, and give up the right to include overtime pay in the calculation of monthly benefits. The new active pensions were less generous than those from the previous system, but they guaranteed a minimum level of benefits for workers. Orr's team had wanted to move workers to a 401(k)-style plan altogether.

"We wanted a defined contribution plan, which is where people are going in the future, and the unions were having none of that," Jones Day attorney Heather Lennox said later.

For Rhodes, the crucial question was whether Orr's efforts offered a feasible route to restore basic services to residents and prevent Detroit from relapsing. He would decide the matter during the plan confirmation trial beginning in early September 2014. For Jones Day attorney and Chapter 9 veteran Bruce Bennett, the answer was clear.

"I think we got Detroit as much relief as anyone could have ever hoped for," he said later. "Under the circumstances, I think it's the best we could do, and it's the best anyone could have done."

Attorneys for Syncora and FGIC, however, believed the plan of adjustment was discriminatory in its treatment of financial creditors. Although the emergence of the grand bargain theoretically allowed the city to use other financial resources to reach settlements with financial creditors, the grand bargain was explicitly designed to benefit pensioners.

But it was the only way the foundations involved would commit.

"The money could only be used to fund pensions," Alberto Ibargüen, CEO of the Knight Foundation, said later. "If the money was going to be used to increase the payout to creditors, we weren't going to contribute. That was actually a really critical point. I can just assure you that if there was any inkling that the money was simply going to go into a general pot, I don't think there's any foundation that would have contributed."

Whether it's legal to direct outside funds to one favored class of creditors, though, was a matter of dispute as the trial opened.

With the grand-bargain money factored in, the city's plan called for compensating pensioners for 59 percent to 60 percent of their unfunded claims. But when excluding the grand-bargain contributions, the plan called for compensating pensioners for 39 percent to 48 percent of their unfunded claims.

Syncora and FGIC were being offered no more than 10 percent payment. And if the city won its lawsuit to delegitimize the debt deal those insurers had backed, they would get nothing. Questions surrounding the legality and fairness of the grand bargain became crucial to the fate of the city's entire bankruptcy plan. Without it, the plan would dissolve and the city would be forced to renegotiate with creditors, a process that could take years. To gauge whether it was fair, one had to assess the alternatives. Could the DIA have been legally liquidated? And if so, could it have been liquidated for more money than the grand bargain supplied?

Bennett said the very fact that there was a dispute over the legality of liquidating the DIA was reason enough to justify the grand bargain. Privately, the city had concluded that it had the right to sell art paid for with taxpayer dollars if it wanted to. But publicly, it argued that a conclusive answer to that question could take eons to determine, with lawyers for the DIA, the attorney general, and the museum's donors waging a vigorous battle against sales. A battle of that sort could thrust the entire bankruptcy into a land of uncertainty.

"We don't have to resolve that question," Bennett said later, recalling the plan confirmation trial. "What we have to decide is that it's a big fight and that it could go either way, and one of the ways it could go is you can't have sales. That's as far as I thought the city needed to go."

All the city was required to demonstrate, Bennett maintained, was that the settlement fell within a legally definable "range of reasonableness." Since one potential outcome of a battle over the legality of selling DIA property was a ban on doing so, the range of reasonableness started at zero, he argued. As such, an $816 million deal to save the museum was perfectly acceptable.

Predictably, Syncora and FGIC launched a vigorous, final counterattack on the grand bargain in the plan confirmation trial, arguing in court that it equaled a fraudulent transfer and that $816 million was insufficient to allow the museum to permanently escape city ownership. In fact, they argued that the real value of the grand bargain was far lower than $816 million—an oft-cited figure that valued the state's $195 million upfront contribution at $350 million over twenty years when projecting interest, while nonprofit and corporate donors were contributing $466 million over the same stretch.

The bond insurers' argument was based on a method of calculation called present value, which requires settlements to be evaluated in the context of how much a deal is worth up front, compared with how much it's worth over time. Inflation and the prospect of investment returns mean, for example, that $1 million is worth much more today than $1 million in payments spread over twenty years. It's the same reason that lottery winners are given a choice between a larger figure of annual payments over several decades, or a smaller up-front payment. Because the foundation and DIA donor pledges would be paid out over two decades, the grand bargain was worth only about $455 million in today's dollars, the creditors argued.

What's more, FGIC said, the DIA's argument that its collection can't be sold is a myth. The assertion that the museum was held in a public trust or charitable trust—ideas the DIA and the attorney general had perpetuated—was unsupported because no legal work had been done to execute such a transaction, the insurer argued.

Even if donors of some of the museum's sixty-six thousand pieces had managed to convince the city to accept artwork with strings attached—such as a restriction that the art never leave the museum—bankruptcy is designed to sever such contracts, FGIC attorney Alfredo Perez argued.

Earlier in the case, the city's Bennett had insisted that sorting through the DIA's immense records would be akin to hunting through a massive warehouse like the one at the end of the Indiana Jones film *Raiders of the Lost Ark*, when the U.S. government hauls the Ark of the Covenant into safe storage.

But the DIA documents, it turns out, were "extremely well maintained" and sortable, Perez proffered during the plan confirmation trial. Going through the process of securing the judge's approval to sell art, contrary to conventional wisdom, would not be difficult, Perez said.

Rhodes poked a hole in FGIC's argument, however.

"Let me ask you this hypothetical question," he prodded Perez. "If the city owned the schools that its children were educated in, or if the city owned the libraries and the books in the libraries in the city, would you want those sold and monetized, too?"

No, Perez said. Of course not. That would be unthinkable.

"Where do we draw the line?" the judge asked.

"Well, but where do you draw the line on the other side?" Perez retorted.

Rhodes didn't take the bait: "No, I'm asking you. Where do you draw the line? What about the libraries? Would you sell them too?"

"I would not sell the libraries," Perez said.

Here was the double standard the judge sought to expose. "But books are, what, more important, more significant, more valuable than art?" he asked.

Perez briefly hesitated. "I don't know what intrinsic value the library has," he said.

Somewhere, Ben Franklin rolled over in his grave. "Assume it had really valuable books in it," Rhodes said.

"Well, then perhaps, then perhaps," Perez acknowledged.

What if a "school building happened to be sitting on an oil well?" Rhodes supposed.

You wouldn't supplant innocent students and teachers, would you?

Actually, yes. Yes, you would, Perez said. "You'd have to argue that, right? And the city would probably have done that, your honor," FGIC's attorney asserted.

In this case, the oil well had taken the form of an art museum, with a spigot of art proceeds diverted to bolster pensions instead of financial creditors. That violates the basic commandments of bankruptcy, Syncora attorney Marc Kieselstein had maintained in a blistering opening statement during the trial.

"We are not in a house of worship or an ecclesiastical court," he preached. "There are no verities, there are no truths we hold to be self evident, there is no received wisdom, there is no gospel according to Mr. Buckfire or Mr. Orr. And nothing is true simply because the debtor fervently desires that it be true."

Detroit cannot favor vulnerable retirees over financial creditors in consideration of the "human dimension" of pension cuts, Kieselstein argued. Orr himself had, earlier in the case, said publicly that pensioners must be treated equally with other creditors. Somewhere along the way, he had changed his mind, Kieselstein said.

"This isn't *Back to the Future*. Mr. Orr is not Marty McFly. We can't pile into the DeLorean, go back in time" and allow Orr to alter his opinion, Kieselstein said. "Neither the law nor the space-time continuum allow for that."

As a matter of political policy, it's acceptable to prioritize people over lenders. But not in court, Kieselstein said.

"You could stop the trial right here," Kieselstein proclaimed. The "human dimension," he argued, cannot be considered when designing a plan of adjustment.

After spending nearly three hours blasting the city during his opening statement, Kieselstein channeled another theological doctrine—predestination.

That's "the idea that from the outset some are saved and some are damned, and who falls into which category is ordained by a higher power. But if you fall into the latter category, your fate is sealed, and no human force can change that," he said. "And you can probably guess what category we think we landed in. It's not the one with the pearly gates."

But the court has the power to change Syncora's fate, Kieselstein said.

"The rule of law means nothing is preordained and nothing is predestined," he said.

After concluding his attempt at a systematic dismantling of the grand bargain, Kieselstein motioned toward his seat.

But Rhodes was not done with him. "I have a question for you, sir," the judge offered.

What's the price Detroit must pay to end this brawl?

"I need a percentage," Rhodes demanded, wanting to ascertain what portion of its debt Syncora wanted paid back in order to drop its objections and accept a settlement.

Equal treatment, Kieselstein said. "Something that's within shouting distance of what the actives and retirees are getting, your honor," he said.

"What's the percentage?" Rhodes demanded again.

Kieselstein desperately sought a route back to his seat at the objecting attorneys' table.

"I'd have to consult with my client," he pleaded, shrinking away from the inquiry. "I don't have authority to answer that question, your honor."

To reveal Syncora's demands would be to compromise the insurer's bargaining position with the city. Kieselstein wanted nothing to do with that.

But Rhodes clearly wanted a deal. Allowing the trial to carry on with Syncora and FGIC maintaining their objections would ensure that doubt lingered over the city's future during the inevitable appeals process.

"I want a percentage and I want it now," Rhodes said. "You've made some very powerful arguments."

As their clash intensified in significance, Kieselstein sought refuge in the confidentiality of mediation. "I'm going to be violating your mediation order," he said.

"I want you to just give me a number," Rhodes said.

"Seventy-five cents, your honor," Kieselstein caved.

But where, the judge asked, would that money come from? Detroit is broke. The city was offering Syncora and FGIC only ten cents on the dollar, at most. To pay them seventy-five cents on the dollar would require several hundred million dollars that the city did not have.

There could be a combination of ways, Syncora's attorney offered. But, of course, the most obvious method for finding additional value in the city's estate would be to abandon the grand bargain and extract cash from the DIA's holdings.

FGIC's Perez offered support for his ally, saying it was unconscionable for the city to favor pensioners over Syncora and FGIC.

"They've got a billion-five of our cash, and we're the bad guys. How could that be?" Perez said. "Cities sell art. They could sell a hundred pieces and we would all go home happy."

"A hundred pieces will get you to the seventy-five percent Mr. Kieselstein wants to get for his client?" Rhodes asked.

"Probably would. And we might be even more reasonable than him," Perez said.

The jittery crowd in the courtroom released a wave of nervous laughter.

"We're the more reasonable twin," Perez said.

BANKRUPTCY TRIALS BEAR a strong resemblance to criminal trials. Suspects on trial for murder can change their plea to guilty in the middle of the proceeding if things aren't going their way and they don't want to take their chances with the jury. Sometimes that means making a deal with the prosecutor to testify against a co-conspirator.

Likewise, in bankruptcy, debtors and creditors battling over a restructuring plan can resolve their differences in the middle of a trial, reaching settlements and rendering the proceeding something of a formality. And allies can turn on each other in a heartbeat.

Throughout Detroit's bankruptcy, Syncora and FGIC had conspired to derail the city's restructuring plan. Both faced the seemingly inevitable in the form of an approved plan of adjustment, wiping out their debt. Syncora's team of Kirkland attorneys had done most of the heavy lifting on the case, in large part because their client was in a more precarious financial position. Early in the bankruptcy, industry observers had speculated that a negative outcome in Detroit's restructuring could bankrupt Syncora. For Syncora, the outcome of the trial was almost certain to be unsightly, even though the company's finances had improved for unrelated reasons during the bankruptcy.

Despite a steady stream of objections to procedural moves and substantive issues throughout the bankruptcy, the company had repeatedly failed to win the judge's approval in court, save a few sporadic victories. Chances were slim that Rhodes would tank the grand bargain, effectively rendering the foundation gifts void and sending the city scrambling to reach new deals with pensioners, bondholders, and other creditors. That gave the city an extraordinary built-in advantage at trial.

If Syncora and FGIC refused to give up and reach settlements, the city was prepared to ask Rhodes to cram down the plan of adjustment, forcibly imposing the restructuring plan on creditors.

"I assumed and believed that they would not settle and that I would have to consider the city's request to cram down the plan over their objections," Rhodes said later.

Kirkland's vigorous opposition to the city —which included scores of court filings, subpoenas, and objections—and its willingness to parlay that aggressive approach into an appellate campaign made a deal seem unlikely.

"To me, it was quite wasteful, because my own feeling was that at some point we would just have to cram them down," Jones Day attorney David Heiman said later. "It would be a lot better to have them in the deal. But I didn't really expect that. The reason was we could not pay them anything."

The deals with retirees, bondholders, and swap holders Bank of America Merrill Lynch and UBS had sapped most of the city's capacity to offer cash to Syncora and FGIC. In the end, Syncora decided there was value in turning its back on its partner. Plus, it had its eye on assets in addition to cash. Only a few weeks after Detroit filed for bankruptcy in 2013, Syncora had, for reasons completely unrelated to the city's insolvency, assumed control of the company that operates an international tunnel underneath the Detroit River that connects travelers to Windsor, Ontario. This remarkable coincidence had given the insurer a vested interest in maintaining a good relationship with the city, which owned the U.S. portion of the tunnel.

"Only in Detroit could this happen," Ken Buckfire, the city's investment banker, said later. "It's so ironic."

As their public court battle reached a bitter crescendo during the plan confirmation trial, Syncora attorney Ryan Bennett quietly approached mediator Gerald Rosen with an entrée. The insurer had identified several plots of city-owned land near the tunnel that it was interested in obtaining, he said. He also explained a theory of Kirkland's: if the city reached a deal with Syncora, FGIC would be forced to settle because it could not possibly continue the fight on its own.

"The premise was that look, this is Judge Rosen's case. So if I can get Judge Rosen to champion my deal, these other guys at Jones Day and Miller Buckfire will pick it up and run with it," Bennett said. "So that was my strategy, and it worked."

Rosen, whom Syncora had just recently accused of collusion, was receptive to that approach—his desire to resolve the bankruptcy winning out over any personal resentment.

Syncora's nascent business ties to Detroit would work to the city's advantage. With the bankruptcy trial ongoing, negotiators for Syncora and the city huddled secretly in the federal courthouse and crafted a settlement that resolved their differences and transformed the insurer from fierce enemy into committed proponent of Detroit's future.

They reached tentative terms a week into the trial and announced their official accord several days later. The deal included a combination of a stream of debt payments, an extension on Syncora's operating lease of the Detroit-to-Windsor tunnel, credits to acquire and develop property near the tunnel, and a lease on a parking garage in the city's lucrative entertainment and sports district. As part of the deal, Syncora was required to invest in infrastructure improvements at the dilapidated parking garage and had a significant incentive to develop the tunnel-area property. Technically, the deal equaled thirteen cents on the dollar in cash for Syncora's claims—better than the maximum ten cents Orr had publicly offered for months—though it's difficult to measure the settlement's full value because it's dependent on future developments. The value could be much higher if Syncora makes smart business decisions and reaps profits.

"The way our deal is structured, we do well if Detroit does well, which I thought was creative," said Kirkland lawyer James H. M. Sprayregen, Syncora's lead attorney.

For Kirkland, there was one thing left to do. In a September 15 court filing, the insurer apologized privately and publicly to Rosen as well as to Eugene and Elaine Driker for accusing them of subversive activity. It acknowledged that Elaine Driker's connection to the DIA had, indeed, been adequately disclosed.

"We are deeply sorry for the mistake we made and for any unfounded aspersions it may have cast on Chief Judge Rosen and the Drikers," the Kirkland attorneys wrote.

They added an extra layer of praise for Rosen: "We observed first-hand his remarkable skill as a mediator; his tenacity and perseverance under incredibly trying circumstances; and his great personal sacrifices, which included many long hours and making himself available at any time and on short notice. This was a herculean effort, and without Rosen's steady hand and calm under pressure, the settlement would not have been achieved."

Sprayregen called Driker personally to say he was sorry.

"He was very apologetic. I had never met the man," Driker said. "It's never too late to apologize."

But Syncora's lawyers made no other apologies for their general aggression in the case.

"Kirkland made a lot of money, but I thought it was kind of unnecessary," Sprayregen said. "I don't want to be defensive, but I actually don't think we were taken seriously until we went on the offensive. We made one mistake, which was unfortunate, and we had to deal with that."

The personal accusations were regrettable.

"But the fundamental allegations of the way the process was working? I don't believe anybody wanted an appellate court to see those," Sprayregen said.

Rhodes, however, believed that the mediation process in Detroit's bankruptcy set a national standard for how municipal bankruptcies can be resolved. Forcing parties to negotiate while the litigation conveyer belt is humming along pressures everyone to make a deal instead of taking their chances in the courtroom. But the one element of Detroit's bankruptcy that probably won't be replicated elsewhere is the grand bargain.

"The concept of a mediator going outside of the role of just settling a dispute and soliciting money to help settle that dispute is unprecedented in the history of bankruptcy and in the history of mediation as far as I know," Rhodes said later.

Despite his distaste for Syncora's attack on the mediators and the grand bargain, Rhodes was satisfied by Kirkland's apology and settlement, and he dropped his threat of sanctions afterward.

Removing emotions from the equation, Kevyn Orr, who still calls Sprayregen a friend, viewed Kirkland's strategy throughout the case as part of a master plan that went far beyond Detroit.

"I know Jamie isn't this Kumbaya guy," Orr said later. "There are several guys who will do anything for their client, and Jamie's one of them. Sure enough, true to form, cue central casting, he almost got his ass sent to jail for his client. Why? No. 1, part of it is they will go to the wall for their client. That's their brand. No. 2, it's marketing. He's able now to say to any other clients out there, 'Look at what I did. I was willing to go down in flames for you in Detroit. I was willing to go to jail. You need to hire me.'"

THE STUNNING ACCORD between Detroit and Syncora dealt a death-blow to FGIC, which had now lost its only remaining ally.

"We had one bullet, but two creditors," said Ken Buckfire, Detroit's investment banker. "So we shot FGIC first."

The divorce between the insurers was too much for FGIC to handle. Appearing visibly shaken the next morning in court, FGIC attorney Alfredo Perez asked the judge for a delay in the trial. "I love Alfredo, but he looked green to me," Hackney said.

Hackney had prepared more than eighty pages of questions he would use to blast Orr on the witness stand during cross-examination later in the trial. But with his sudden unexpected departure, FGIC's attorneys, who had counted on Kirkland to continue to take the lead in the case, were caught off guard.

"We were cognizant of the litigation preparation being its own asset and we knew that FGIC had not invested in the trial as much as we had," Sprayregen said. "We knew if we settled prior to them, they were almost for sure going to have to settle."

He was right. A few weeks later, FGIC's own negotiations with the city intensified. After vigorously contesting the grand bargain and accusing the city of underweighting the value of the Detroit Institute of Arts, the insurer's fight to force the city to monetize the art had suffered a devastating setback.

FGIC advisor Steve Spencer, who had tirelessly procured tentative bids for the DIA from foreign investors earlier in the bankruptcy, remained frustrated at the grand bargain. Rosen, Spencer said later, made a "major tactical error" by signaling so early in the case that he wanted to save the DIA for pensioners, instead of dangling the fate of the museum for months as a bargaining chip to force retirees and unions into a better deal.

"He gave it all away to the pensions. He didn't have to. But that's what hurt all of the financial creditors," Spencer said.

But Spencer realized that there was nothing left for his client. Waging a bitter appeal increasingly appeared fruitless.

"The pensions would have screamed bloody murder. That would

have been just a goddamned bloodbath, you know?" Spencer said later. "And for what? Another penny or two for us? Ugh. No. There was also the possibility that if the court continued looking for ways to try and screw the financial creditors, that we ended up with a donut. So it was a perilous fight."

FGIC continued arguing against the grand bargain for a few weeks in the plan confirmation trial. But after a marathon negotiating session the night of October 14, 2014, in Rosen's conference room, and with the help of close Snyder advisor Rich Baird, FGIC gave up its fight, reaching a historic settlement with Orr and effectively transforming the largest municipal bankruptcy in U.S. history into a consensual restructuring deal.

With little cash to spare, Detroit instead gave up a combination of future debt payments and rights to develop the land underneath the Detroit Red Wings' riverfront Joe Louis Arena, which is slated to be demolished after the hockey team departs for a new downtown stadium in 2017. As part of the settlement, FGIC agreed to procure a deal to transform the property into a massive hotel complex that could also include residential, office, and retail space. The state would pay for demolition costs, estimated at several million dollars, to sweeten the pot. Like Syncora, FGIC technically got thirteen cents on the dollar in cash for its claims, though the deal is worth more when factoring in the value of its development accord.

The upside of the Joe Louis Arena deal was enough to satisfy FGIC. Spencer had become familiar with the property after waking early every morning in his room at the Westin Book Cadillac hotel and taking a jog through the streets of downtown Detroit, down to the riverfront, and around the arena.

"At 6:15 in the morning you can do a lot of really good diligence," Spencer said. "We got some very good parcels."

After striking the deal at about 3:00 a.m. on October 15, 2014, the negotiators gathered for a photo to commemorate the occasion. They were beaming.

Rosen approached Spencer. "You guys fought in a very respectful, principled way," the judge told Spencer. "That's the way you do it. You've done a good job for your client here, and I hope they realize that. You've done a yeoman's work, and I appreciate it."

Under the cover of darkness in downtown Detroit, Spencer walked out of the courthouse with a clarity of purpose.

"As much as I disagree with a lot of things Judge Rosen did, his comments were still meaningful to me," Spencer said. "At least we could bury the hatchet on this one. You at least do respect me as a professional."

The last thing Spencer did before leaving Detroit was visit the DIA one more time, staring longingly at the museum's treasured paintings, sculptures, and artifacts.

"I love art. I actually do," he said. "There's part of me that thinks it's really wonderful that the museum collection is staying intact for public viewing. But even as I walked through, I looked at it and said, 'There's so much that could have been done here.'"

WITH ALL OF the city's major creditors supporting the plan, the only lingering question preventing Detroit from exiting bankruptcy was this: Does the plan do enough to put the city on the track to financial sustainability with a legitimate shot at restoring adequate services?

Like a prosecutor who must prove guilt beyond a reasonable doubt, the burden of proof lay with the city. From the moment he declared Detroit to be "service delivery insolvent"—that is, functionally and financially unable to provide adequate services to its residents—Rhodes ensured that the lives of ordinary Detroiters would remain of paramount concern in the bankruptcy. Amid a firestorm of legal disputes, everyone agreed the city's 688,000 residents deserved better police, more efficient fire protection, improved mass transportation, and a streamlined bureaucracy.

The plan of adjustment carved out a path to divert cash flow from creditors to city services, theoretically fueling a revitalized and more responsive government during the next decade. And Orr had made considerable progress on several fronts in restructuring city government. But there were setbacks. For example, he discarded a hope of privatizing the city's bus system after an outside contractor refused to take the deal.

In a report prepared at Rhodes's request, Phoenix Management consultant Martha Kopacz concluded that Detroit's bankruptcy plan would put it on a financially feasible path—but only by a slim margin. She cautioned that the day-to-day execution of the plan of adjustment would prove vital to its success. Funding for the city's reinvestment initiatives, which Orr had estimated would total $1.72 billion over ten years, was not altogether guaranteed to happen.

About 51 percent of that investment budget would come from debt reductions achieved in the bankruptcy. But the rest assumed that the city's officials would collect additional revenue and slash expenses, as outlined in the plan of adjustment, long after Orr's departure. For example, Orr's budget projected that the city would collect $483 million over ten years in additional revenue by increasing bus fares, raising parking fees, and collecting more taxes on income and property, among other actions. And it projected $358 million over ten years in lower expenses in the city's daily operations, through measures such as eliminating city-run Belle Isle operations, outsourcing income-tax collection to the State of Michigan, and conducting less maintenance after investments in new police and fire equipment.

These expectations mean that the plan of adjustment would rely heavily on Duggan's ability to overhaul the city's dysfunctional bureaucracy. He would have to find ways to boost revenue and deliver cost savings to fund service improvements. With good execution, the city would have enough money to add about seven hundred employees to its workforce, including new police officers and firefighters. It would fund a blight-removal campaign. It would provide cash to invest in basic software and computers to drastically improve communication among city employees. It would fund the purchase of more than one hundred new buses over eight years, transforming mass transit in a city where it's not uncommon to wait an hour in the cold for the bus to come.

These are things that Detroit deserves. The fact that Orr prioritized a major investment plan in city services for residents over repaying disgruntled creditors was a first in municipal bankruptcy.

"There are people out there that still say what happened is offensive or outrageous," Jones Day attorney Bruce Bennett said later. "I clearly don't."

He just needed the judge to agree.

CHAPTER 15

The Rhodes Test

On Friday, November 7, 2014, grand-bargain supporters streamed into the chambers of U.S. District Court chief judge Gerald Rosen of the Eastern District of Michigan. They gathered around a TV to watch a closed-circuit feed of Judge Steven Rhodes delivering his ruling on Detroit's plan of adjustment.

Supporters packed the courtroom too. Detroit emergency manager Kevyn Orr sat at the city attorneys' table, listening intently. In the audience, Speaker of the House Jase Bolger, whose skepticism about the grand bargain had morphed into support, found a seat on the wooden pews. Mayor Mike Duggan and City Council president Brenda Jones—both of whom backed Orr's restructuring plan after initially opposing his appointment—also sat in the courtroom.

At 1:00 p.m. on the dot, a beep sounded, and the reliably prompt judge strode slowly through the door and made his way to the bench. Without preamble, he approved the city's plan of adjustment, setting the stage for Detroit's bankruptcy to end less than a year and a half after it started.

"In Chapter 9 of the bankruptcy code, the federal government offers help to the states in solving a problem that, under our constitutional structure, the states cannot solve by themselves. That problem is the adjustment of the debts of an insolvent municipality," Rhodes said. "Today, this federal bankruptcy court grants that help to the State of Michigan and the City of Detroit."

Cheers erupted in Rosen's chambers. A court photographer snapped pictures of the occasion. Governor Rick Snyder smiled wildly, with Rosen, advisor Rich Baird, and former campaign spokesman Bill Nowling among those by his side.

In overflow seating in the jury box in the quiet courtroom, mediator Eugene Driker and his wife, Elaine, sat intently listening to the ruling. Lifelong residents of Detroit, they relished the moment.

"I'd been practicing law since 1961, so there weren't too many mountains for me yet to climb professionally. And this was the opportunity of a lifetime to work on something so interesting and consequential with such very talented people on all sides of it," Eugene Driker said. "I never met so many smart people and so many people dedicated to rescuing Detroit. So it was an honor. It was the thrill of a lifetime."

After his appointment of Orr as emergency manager, Snyder's critics had dubbed him a dictator. They plastered demonic images of the governor onto posters, portraying him as a racially insensitive, despotic tyrant with no regard for the welfare of the citizens of Detroit.

But what emerged from the city's bankruptcy was not an ideological trampling of democracy or union rights. What emerged from the bankruptcy was a plan that, for the first time in decades, offered hope to the people of the City of Detroit.

Three days before the judge's ruling—with the grand bargain solidified and Detroit on the doorstep of exiting bankruptcy—Michigan voters had reelected Snyder to a second term. At least two polls suggested that voters supported Snyder in part because of his leadership in Detroit. And a separate poll commissioned by the *Detroit News* and WDIV-TV showed that in Detroit proper, 85 percent of voters believed that the city would be better off after the bankruptcy.

Snyder never viewed his takeover of Detroit as an affront to democracy.

"I just took it as doing my job," he said. "I'm not going to shirk my responsibilities because people have a different perspective. And I do represent every citizen of the State of Michigan. When people said there was no elected official, I was elected by all the people of the State of Michigan to do my job to represent all the citizens of this state well. And that, in particular, includes the seven hundred thousand residents of the City of Detroit."

Opponents accused Snyder and Orr of shattering promises that were made to retirees who relied on pensions and health care benefits and promises that were made to bondholders who relied on the city's financial wherewithal. But the city had broken those promises years ago—perhaps decades ago—by failing to reach labor deals it could afford and by borrowing to pay the bills instead of correcting course to avoid a fiscal iceberg. Snyder and Orr simply acknowledged the city's reality and tried to do something about it.

"People don't appreciate what a good executive Rick Snyder is. And I mean that," said Orr, who said he remains a Democrat at heart but can work for anyone with a bias for pragmatism and principles. "He came in his first administration and decided he was going to take on Detroit. People had spent three years telling him he was doing this plantation-style takeover of the jewels of the city. He never wavered from his commitment to do the right thing. He never told me what I should do—other than, 'Do the right thing.'"

Orr knew that his boss's political legacy was on the line.

"He bet the farm, and it was unclear who was going to win that bet for the better part of the year," Orr said.

AFTER APPROVING DETROIT'S plan of adjustment, Rhodes urged city leaders, unions, and politicians to recalibrate their approach to pension policies, which had played a critical role in Detroit's bankruptcy. Labor leaders must stop bargaining for short-term political benefits and start placing their emphasis on the long-term health of pension plans. Political leaders, the judge suggested, must monitor municipal pensions to ensure that they don't slip into insolvency and jeopardize people's livelihoods. City officials must prioritize pension payments in their budgeting, something Detroit had neglected for years.

The city paid a heavy price to rectify its fiscal mess. Although several firms agreed to reduce their bills in solidarity with pensioners and bondholders who accepted cuts, city-paid lawyers, financial advisors, accountants, and consultants still collected more than $170 million for their work in the case. Rhodes deemed the bankruptcy bill fair considering the complexity, speed, and size of the case. But the cost, representing about one-sixth of the city's annual budget, serves as a warning for other municipalities that are flirting with fiscal disaster.

"What happened in Detroit must never happen again," Rhodes said.

Despite the difficulties pensioners were facing because of Detroit's insolvency, selling Detroit Institute of Arts property would have been a terrible outcome, Rhodes said. The grand bargain would allow the city to transfer ownership of the museum's collection and property to the nonprofit DIA Corporation, the legal entity that was already operating the institution and will now permanently care for its collection. Anything else would have compromised the cultural, educational, creative, and community values the museum embodies, Rhodes argued.

"Every great city in the world actively pursues these values," he said in his ruling. "They are the values that Detroit must pursue to uplift, inspire, and enrich its residents and its visitors."

He went a step further, stunning people involved in the case by opining that any attempts to sell art "almost certainly" would have failed on legal grounds.

"To sell the DIA art would only deepen Detroit's fiscal, economic, and social problems. To sell the DIA art would be to forfeit Detroit's future," Rhodes added.

Annmarie Erickson, chief operating officer of the DIA, was euphoric.

"Our litigator came up to me and said, 'What would have happened if we had litigated it?' I said, 'We'll never know,'" Erickson recalled.

Was the city's plan fair to creditors? Yes, Rhodes said. It's a "matter of conscience."

"Several factors naturally inform this judgment," he said, including his own "experience, education, and sense of morality."

That, then, is the Rhodes Test. Conscience dictates fairness.

The judge thanked the mediators, including Rosen, whose appointment he called "the smartest thing I did in this case."

"Never before have bankruptcy mediators proactively sought to marshal the community's financial resources to solve a community problem. Most importantly, they knew that their work was not simply about resolving a bankruptcy case. It was about fixing a broken city. Where would this case be without them?" Rhodes said.

Bankruptcy resurrected Detroit.

"In every case, we have a debtor who needs help, who made mistakes, who took unwarranted risks, who accepted bad advice, who exercised bad judgment, who was too long in denial, or who had just plain bad luck," Rhodes said in his ruling, echoing a refrain he's long embraced. "But no matter, our society holds dear the value of a fresh start and of second chances. That value is manifested with brilliant clarity in our bankruptcy laws."

He turned his attention to the elected officials who will be charged with implementing the plan of adjustment. During their first year working together, Mayor Duggan and Council President Jones had forged a healthy working relationship, providing hope that Detroit could move past political dysfunction and desperation.

The city, Rhodes said, is ready to govern itself again. "Please make me right," he said.

"Before I conclude, I want to address the people of the City of Detroit, whose passion for this city is remarkable in its breadth, in its expression, and in its unwavering endurance. I just said that your leaders are about to get the city back. Actually, of course, it is you who are about to get your city back. It is your city. A large number of you told me that you were angry that your city was taken away from you and put into bankruptcy. . . .

"I urge you now not to forget your anger. Your enduring and collective memory of what happened here, and your memory of your anger about it, will be exactly what will prevent this from ever happening again," Rhodes said. "And so I ask you, for the good of the city's fresh start, to move past your anger. Move past it and join in the work that is necessary to fix this city."

The grand bargain to resolve Detroit's bankruptcy echoes a "much grander bargain" in America, he said.

"It is the bargain by which we interact with each other and with our government, all for the common good. That grander bargain, enshrined in our constitution, is democracy," he said. "It is now time to restore democracy to the people of the City of Detroit. I urge you to participate in it. And I hope that you will soon realize its full potential."

———

FOR DETROIT, EMERGENCY management had lasted about twenty-one months. Kevyn Orr had given operational power back to the city's elected officials in September 2014, retaining control of only the bankruptcy for the final months of his tenure. He officially resigned effective December 10, the day Detroit legally exited Chapter 9 bankruptcy. His departure restored the full powers of the City Council and the mayor—with the exception of the state oversight board, which will ensure the city pays its bills on time and doesn't borrow exorbitantly.

Orr's legacy is this: he gave Detroit a second chance at life. He restored the city's finances. He put the city on a track to revitalization. With Snyder's political backing, he made hard decisions that leaders from Detroit's past had refused to make. "I hope his legacy is that he took on an enormous—and some might say impossible—challenge and met that challenge with grace, dignity, professionalism, and proficiency," Rhodes said later. "Of all of us who were challenged by Detroit's insolvency, he had the most challenging and difficult job of all."

A few months after the bankruptcy's conclusion and his departure from Detroit, Orr returned to the city for a variety of events heralding the outcome. The man whose tenure in Detroit started as a source of considerable political discord and social angst took a seat in a nondescript coffee shop at the MotorCity Casino Hotel in Detroit, going almost unnoticed at first.

The city, Orr surmised, needs more than the financial overhaul it received through bankruptcy. It now needs a cultural expectation that Detroit can be great again. Detroiters do not only deserve more from their leaders. They must demand more.

"It's habit, it's expectations, it's learned behavior—it's almost a feeling of, 'We don't deserve to have that going on here,'" Orr said. "You do deserve to have a nice neighborhood. You do deserve to have nice streets. You do deserve police protection. You do deserve to have a future."

As Orr discussed the city's future, an unidentified middle-aged man walked by at a brisk pace. He noticed the former emergency manager sitting in the coffee lounge and stopped in his tracks.

The man walked up and extended his hand.

Orr paused, his eyes betraying a momentary sense of bewilderment. They shook hands.

"Hey," the man said. "Good job. Good job."

Orr smiled. "Thank you very much, sir," he said. "I appreciate that."

And the man walked off.

FOLLOWING THE BANKRUPTCY'S conclusion in December, the Detroit Institute of Arts, now forever shielded from the city's creditors, served as the host for a day of reconciliation. Rosen invited two of the DIA's most ardent opponents during the case to tour the museum. After bond insurer Syncora's bitter feud with Detroit ended in a groundbreaking settlement, Syncora executive Claude LeBlanc and Kirkland & Ellis attorney James H. M. Sprayregen traversed what would have been forbidden territory a few months earlier.

On a late Monday afternoon—the one day of the week the museum is closed to the public—Syncora's bankruptcy strategists strolled through the hushed exhibits for two hours alongside Rosen, DIA chairman Gene Gargaro, and DIA director Graham Beal.

They gazed admiringly at masterpieces by Van Gogh, Bruegel the Elder, and others.

"I have to say, it's a spectacular museum and a wonderful collection of diverse art," Sprayregen recalled. "The curator's flavor of the history of various pieces was fascinating."

Gargaro thanked Sprayregen and LeBlanc for relinquishing their battle and striking a settlement that made Syncora an investor in Detroit's future.

"While during the heat of the bankruptcy battle we rarely, if ever, had moments like this to meet and get to know our opposition like we did that night at the DIA, it was obvious that both Jamie and Claude were very impressed with what they saw and clearly understood why we were fighting as hard as we could to preserve our great museum for our and future generations," Gargaro said.

For Sprayregen, the trip was also a chance to clear the air with Rosen. The judge's doodle on the back of a legal pad—the first outline of the grand bargain—will be displayed somewhere in the DIA, a reminder of the clash that nearly destroyed the museum.

"Not withstanding the toughness of the negotiations and the mediation, and massive divergence in views of how the case should have been handled, I had come to have enormous respect for Judge Rosen's talents, and we found we had a shared passion for baseball and Winston Churchill," Sprayregen said.

Sprayregen even brought along a copy of *The Churchill Factor*, by Boris Johnson, the new book on their shared idol, to give to Rosen.

Of course, in the midst of World War II, Churchill once famously told the boys of Harrow School to "never yield to force" nor "to the apparently overwhelming might of the enemy."

"Never, never, never—in nothing great or small, large or petty, never give in except to convictions of honor and good sense," Churchill said.

Like any principled student of Churchill, Sprayregen did not abandon his core beliefs about the museum even after his trip through its halls. The visit, he said, "reinforced for me" that the city should have explored other alternatives for monetizing the art— such as financing deals or renting the art to other museums, options the city's experts had written off as implausible.

"It brought home to me the facileness, inapplicability, and cartoon quality of the allegedly competing alternatives as to the view that it would have been a tragedy to break up the collection and sell it off or it should have all been sold off immediately for cash," he explained. "That was never the argument."

The cartoonish nature of the spat between the financial creditors, the DIA, the retirees, and Detroit is, fittingly, crystallized in a framed piece that now hangs in Rosen's chambers. Drawn by a colleague of mediator Elizabeth Perris, the sketch depicts a pocket watch–sporting conductor gathering tickets from passengers at a train station.

The conductor's name badge says, "Jerry," and the train is emblazoned, "Grand Bargain Express." The travelers include a police officer, firefighter, and retiree.

Underneath is an inscription: "All Aboard the Detroit Train! Get Your Tickets Now for the Best Seats! Missing This Train Is Very Risky Business!"

Below the inscription are the signatures of Rosen's mediation team.

"As Churchill said, this is our finest hour," Driker signed.

WHETHER THE GRAND Bargain Express will stay on the tracks remains an open question.

Many of Detroit's challenges are intractable and cannot be addressed in a municipal bankruptcy. Detroit's unemployment crisis, which corresponds directly with the lack of an educated workforce, is a major obstacle to the city's revitalization. It seems altogether impossible to address this challenge without a holistic overhaul of federal, state, and local education policies, economic development strategies, worker retraining programs, and mass transportation options. But in a polarized political environment, it's also unrealistic to expect substantial progress on these issues.

You can turn the lights back on, tear down the abandoned homes, upgrade public safety equipment, hire more police officers and firefighters, and improve the dilapidated mass transit system, but Detroit's neighborhoods will remain mostly impoverished until policymakers identify realistic and affordable ways to help people find jobs.

That starts with good schools. But the appalling state of public education in Detroit remains a barrier to the city's resurgence. Without acceptable schools, families won't consider moving to Detroit, and many will continue to leave. In 2013, for example, 54 percent of Detroit eighth-graders scored below basic achievement levels in reading, according to the National Center for Education Statistics. That compared with 32 percent for large U.S. cities and 23 percent for schools nationwide.

About 102,000 students left Detroit Public Schools from 2003–04 to 2013–14, as many fled for charter schools and others left for suburban schools. The governor's attempts at rehabilitating public education in Detroit by appointing a series of emergency managers for the school district and assigning the worst schools to a new entity called the Education Achievement Authority have failed to erase deficits or markedly improve test scores. The city's numerous charter schools, a refuge for some students, vary tremendously in quality and accessibility.

But there are positive signs for the high percentage of Detroiters for whom the education system has failed. Snyder's Community Ventures program offers a feasible route into the workforce for the chronically unemployed in Detroit, providing practical help such as funds for daycare, a ride to work, or help building a resume.

There's a measure of certainty that downtown Detroit's revitalization will continue as investors pick strategic locations to expand their companies and hire local workers—with hopes that the recovery will gradually spread into the neighborhoods. Downtown apartment vacancy rates are low, and real estate developers are planning new units. That will translate into income-tax dollars for public safety and transportation, which will improve the lives of people living in high-crime areas.

Billionaire Dan Gilbert has purchased or controls more than seventy buildings in downtown Detroit and brought many businesses to the area, including the headquarters of his mortgage giant, Quicken Loans. His investments have included substantial renovation projects and a private security apparatus that has improved public safety but also drawn scrutiny from concerned citizens. On the whole, Gilbert has breathed new life into streets that were mostly abandoned a decade ago.

Billionaire Mike Ilitch and his family are investing in a new downtown hockey arena for the Detroit Red Wings, with hopes of attracting new apartments and nightlife in the surrounding area. Renderings look promising, though critics are upset that the city and state authorized the use of future taxpayer dollars to support the project.

There's also reason for optimism about Midtown Detroit, which is anchored by the DIA, several other museums, Wayne State University, and major medical campuses. The Midtown area has experienced a highly publicized influx of young professionals with artistic sensibilities—urban pioneers attracted to the city's gritty quality—who are often derided as disconnected white hipsters with no grasp of the plight of Detroit's neighborhoods. They may be somewhat naive about the severity of Detroit's challenges, but they too have a role to play in the city's comeback.

Nonetheless, the legacy of racial tension in Detroit continues to exert a corrosive effect. Community leaders from all walks of life, including leaders from the city's wealthy suburbs, must work to counteract racial inequality for Detroit to have any hope of an inclusive recovery. Without substantial progress on racial issues, the path to a brighter future will be jagged.

Meanwhile, fears are never far off in Detroit that political gridlock between the mayor and City Council will resurface and stall the city's recovery. A failure on behalf of the city's elected leaders to effectively implement Orr's investment plan would retroactively render the largest municipal bankruptcy in U.S. history a missed opportunity.

But the empowering compromise that ended Detroit's bankruptcy fuels a hope that the city can move beyond its dysfunctional political past. In the end, all major creditors supported the city's bankruptcy plan—which was unthinkable when the case began.

It was "a watershed moment in modern urban history," said Rip Rapson, CEO of the Kresge Foundation. "I think from a perspective of municipal finance, from a perspective of civic-coalition building, from the perspective of philanthropic roles, from virtually any perspective you can construct, this was one of the most remarkable moments we've seen in the modern history of American cities."

In a city known worldwide for its industrial ruins, the bankruptcy provided a palpable spirit of renewal and a clear route to fiscal sustainability.

"I am radically optimistic about Detroit's future," said Darren Walker, CEO of the Ford Foundation. "I have never been so inspired and gratified by anything I've done professionally. Detroit, for me, is so much about the opportunity for this country. While the bankruptcy—the grand bargain—was certainly not perfect, it put Detroit back in the starting block."

Walker pointed back to the initial meeting with foundation leaders and bankruptcy mediators about the grand bargain.

"It was a moment of depression in the city because there seemed to be no way out. At every turn all I heard was negativity and a sense of hopelessness about the future," he said. "Today we are in a very different place in the city. Does that mean that the inequality issues there are settled—the fundamental issues of race and class, the real sense on the part of incumbent, low-income residents out in the neighborhoods that they may be marginalized or forsaken for the new creative class?"

Those issues remain. "That is the challenge—and the opportunity—for Detroit going forward," Walker said.

The clash in the courtroom and in mediation during the bankruptcy was a natural outgrowth of years of flawed civic leadership amid a macroeconomic implosion.

"The good news is there's a real roadmap to drive Detroit into a ditch. It's been clearly articulated," Walker said. "All we need to do is look back over the past two or three decades. So there's got to be a different roadmap to make Detroit great, to make Detroit hum, to make Detroit soar. That's what the leadership in Detroit has to do. That's what we in philanthropy have to do."

That's what we as citizens must do.

"At the beginning of the Detroit case, we fought and we objected and we litigated," Judge Rhodes said. "But in the end, the only thing to do was to help the City of Detroit and its people. It is who we are.

"It is us."

Epilogue

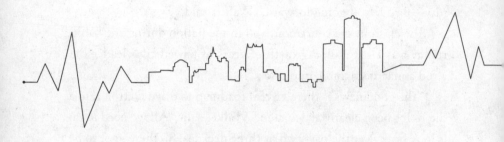

At the dawn of 2017—which marks the fiftieth anniversary of the 1967 Detroit riots, an explosion of racial inequality, political rebellion, and police brutality that accelerated the city's descent—Detroit remains at the visceral intersection of despair and hope. Bankruptcy, though, turned the city toward hope.

More than two years after exiting Chapter 9, Detroit's finances are stable, fueling a steady improvement in services that is making the lives of ordinary Detroiters better and attracting investment to core business areas. "I remain confident, if not more confident now, about the city's future than I was when I confirmed the plan" of adjustment, Judge Steven Rhodes said.

"At its heart the bankruptcy was an exercise in stabilization," said Rip Rapson, CEO of the Kresge Foundation, a key funder of the grand bargain. "What the last two years have demonstrated is it has been possible to use that platform to accelerate and to begin constructing a suite of quality-of-life activities that move into the realm that Detroiters have talked about for quite a long time, which is re-imagining their future."

With a lighter debt load and responsible spending, Detroit is headed toward a third consecutive surplus for the fiscal year ending in June 2017, estimated at $30 million. "That's a great trajectory from where the city was just a few short years ago," said Kevyn Orr, who returned to Jones Day to lead the law firm's Washington, D.C., office several months after his tenure as emergency manager ended. "So that's positive and gratifying."

Judge Gerald Rosen, the bankruptcy's lead mediator, said the financial performance has "exceeded the expectations of even the most optimistic."

"If you had told people that they would hit their marks two years in a row, people would have said, 'Wow, really? I don't think so,'" said Rosen, who was set to retire in early 2017 and form a private mediation practice with Rhodes.

In another unexpected turn of events, Detroit's population loss is slowing down rapidly. After six decades of contraction, the city lost only 3,107 residents from July 2015 to July 2016. And from July 2016 to July 2017, Detroit may gain a few thousand residents, said local demographer Kurt Metzger.

"I'm very confident that the city of Detroit is growing now and that will be reflected in the next report," Mayor Mike Duggan told the *Detroit Free Press*. "We're at a historic tipping point."

Fueling the trend are investments in the downtown and midtown areas, where young professionals and empty nesters are renting renovated apartments and businesses are expanding. Apartment occupancy rates in those areas were 98 percent in 2016 as monthly rent averaged $1.99 per square foot, up from $1.41 in 2010. Developers have credible plans for 4,804 new housing units throughout the city, including 790 affordable dwellings, as of September 2016.

If the city returns to population growth—or even just stability—Detroit's financial recovery may exceed the bankruptcy team's revenue projections. That's because consultants designed the plan based on a projection that Detroit's population would fall from 688,000 in 2013 to 625,152 in 2023, decline further through 2029, and not return to growth until 2034. With more people, state revenue sharing could be higher than projected, and taxes may top expectations. The city receives about $136,000 in annual revenue from an average 100-unit development.

"I am enthusiastic about what Detroit is achieving," said James Doak, a Miller Buckfire investment banker who advised the city on settlements aimed at spurring investments. "I am completely realistic about its challenges, but money and talent are coming. It can't be fixed—it shouldn't be fixed—in a day. This is a massive home renovation project. You don't renovate it all at once because if you renovate it all at once you're going to get it wrong."

The lingering challenge remains desolate neighborhoods not experiencing the growth of downtown and midtown. Sonya Mays— who advised Orr during the bankruptcy, now serves as CEO of real estate firm Develop Detroit, and was elected to the school board in November 2016—said the key is to nurture development benefiting all Detroiters, not just the privileged class. Develop Detroit's vision is for "mixed-income development," said Mays, who is pursuing "zero-displacement" development in neighborhoods such as North End and Woodbridge.

"There still is a large difference between the energy and investment of what's going on in the central business district versus what is filtering out to the rest of Detroit," Mays said. "We know it's going to be a process to figure out how to do equitable development. There are very few places in the country that have figured out how to honestly balance the competing forces in gentrification and further redevelopment."

There are some encouraging signs: About 14,247 Detroiters who were not employed during the bankruptcy had jobs as of September 2016, a 3 percent growth rate that outstripped the national rate of 1.4 percent and Michigan's 1.8 percent. The Ilitch family's new downtown hockey arena is set to open in fall 2017, and the Detroit Pistons struck a deal in late 2016 to move from suburban Detroit to share the Red Wings' venue. Dan Gilbert has continued his acquisition spree of downtown real estate. By fall 2016, he owned or controlled more than eighty Detroit properties totaling 10 million square feet. And at least two Fortune 500 companies, auto supplier Adient and financing firm Ally, have selected downtown Detroit for their headquarters since the bankruptcy.

Still, income Inequality, dysfunctional schools, insufficient economic opportunity, and a rampant adult illitcracy crisis remain significant impediments. Only 49 percent of Detroiters aged sixteen to sixty-four are employed, compared to a national average of 68 percent. And nonresidents hold three-fourths of the jobs in the city. "A lot of nuts-and-bolts basic things needed to be fixed" during the bankruptcy, Rapson said. "Now you pivot to the much more complex and nuanced challenges," such as "economic mobility" and education. "Those are issues that have defied almost every community in America. The solution was more apparent to how you get the lights back on than how it is you get underprepared workers ready to take the next generation of high-tech jobs."

Job growth is critical because it improves the lives of Detroit's residents but also because it bolsters the city government's bottom line. For every 1,000 previously unemployed residents who enter the workforce at an average salary of $30,000, the city reaps about $720,000 annually in income taxes.

The bankruptcy plan projected $483 million in new revenue over ten years, based on expectations of additional cash flow tied to investments in services, improved tax collection, and other restructuring. But outside economists and city officials projected in September 2016 that revenue would increase only 4.2 percent to $1.05 billion from fiscal 2017 through 2021. It's vital for the city to exceed those projections so it can continue investing in services such as police, fire, buses, and blight demolition.

John Hill, chief financial officer for Detroit, said those projections reflect the city's new "conservative" budgeting. "What we've chosen to do is to not budget any of the surpluses until they show up," Hill said. "We're very conservative with projecting our revenues, and we're conservative as well in making sure all of the reoccurring expenses are there."

One route to more revenue is to convince the state legislature to force all employers of Detroit residents working outside the city to withhold Detroit income taxes from worker paychecks. Forcing them to do so would increase Detroit's annual revenue by $10 million to $25 million.

Meanwhile, investments in new software that were made possible by the bankruptcy, as well as the restructuring team's actions and the Duggan administration's efforts, have increased property-tax collection rates. The city collected 70 percent of property taxes due in fiscal 2016, up from 50 percent a year earlier. This occurred in part because reappraisals lowered assessments to realistic levels. That contributed to a $27 million increase in property taxes over the originally budgeted amount in fiscal 2016. If those collection rates continue to increase, the city's finances could improve significantly in the years to come.

"People who believe their bills are fairer are more likely to pay them. That's what we're actually seeing happen," Hill said. "Also, our collections capability and communications with our residents about the bills have improved substantially." Accordingly, the city is finding enough wiggle room to invest in services, as envisioned by the bankruptcy team. City-funded investments have included new police and fire vehicles and communications equipment, pay raises, software to manage finances and human resources, parks improvements, graffiti removal, and buses. As envisioned by Orr's team, the city forced all finance employees to reapply for their jobs, hired new talent, and installed new recordkeeping systems.

Demolition crews have razed about 10,000 of an estimated 40,000 blighted homes that are too damaged to be rehabilitated. Another 40,000 blighted residential structures have been identified as candidates for renovation by Duggan's Detroit Land Bank Authority.

The blight removal process, though, has raised concerns about the demolition process. The FBI confirmed in 2016 that it had launched an investigation into the Land Bank's handling of U.S. Department of the Treasury funding for blight demolition after costs rose sharply under Duggan's administration. After previously ranging from about $8,500 to $10,000 per home under former Mayor Dave Bing, costs escalated to an average of $16,400 at one point in 2015 under Duggan. The Treasury Department, which has allocated more than $250 million to Detroit's demolition effort, halted the federally funded process for a few months in 2016 until new administrative controls could be put in place. Although the outcome of the investigation was unclear at the time of this writing, the FBI probe serves as a reminder that Detroit must continually guard against a reversion to the kleptocratic ways that plunged the city into chaos under the Kwame Kilpatrick regime.

In other areas, however, progress is evident. Bolstered by cash freed up through the bankruptcy and federal funds to acquire new buses and add new routes, the Duggan administration is overhauling the city's dilapidated transit system. The Department of Transportation had nearly 200 buses running on time in fall 2016, an increase of more than 40 percent from winter 2014. That's an example of how Detroit's bankruptcy has directly improved the lives of the city's residents.

In perhaps the city's greatest success since bankruptcy, crews have replaced the entire street-lighting system with new infrastructure and light-emitting diodes. In a city that had 40 percent of its streetlights out by 2013, it's a tangible improvement for residents living far from the bustling central business district.

"When you look at the bankruptcy itself, it worked. Fundamentally it was about improving services for citizens. That's the point of Chapter 9," said Governor Rick Snyder, who authorized the bankruptcy. "I made the right decision. And I think history has proven that."

ONE POST-BANKRUPTCY DEVELOPMENT that concerned city officials was the revelation in late 2015 that Detroit's projected pension gap could be larger than previously anticipated. Orr's restructuring team had designed the bankruptcy to give Detroit ten years of breathing room in which it would not have to make any pension contributions. Unions successfully beat back Orr's attempt, later endorsed by Judge Rhodes, to switch active workers to less-costly 401(k)-style plans. Consequently, advisers projected that beginning in the 2024 fiscal year, Detroit would owe about $111 million to its pension funds. But in late 2015, actuarial firm Gabriel Roeder Smith switched to newly formulated mortality assumptions to calculate projected liabilities. Accordingly, the city's estimated payment in 2024 was updated to about $200 million.

After the increased payment was publicized, Duggan threatened to sue Orr's team of bankruptcy advisers for allegedly using outdated actuarial tables to calculate the pension gap. Duggan's communications director did not make the mayor available for comment for this epilogue. Orr, whose firm could be a target of a city lawsuit, declined to comment on the situation.

Orr "would be understandably disgruntled if anybody thinks that he was managing numerical outcomes in a way that was not appropriate because that was just not the case," said Rich Baird, Snyder's close adviser. "Kevyn Orr is one of the most sophisticated and intelligent guys that I've ever worked with, and I can tell you that actuarial projections are still as much art as they are science. I'm not going to [ignore] the fact that the pension cliff is a very big deal, and it's close to double what was originally projected. But the cliff is 2024. We've got time, and Mike's got time to stabilize and manage revenue streams."

During the case, Orr regularly shared information with Duggan regarding the plan of adjustment. "Every Thursday at 10 a.m., he and Kevyn and I and Stacy Fox would meet behind closed doors and we would hash out whatever conflicts there might be privately so that publicly we could present a united front, or we would agree to be silent when there was stress in the family," Baird said.

An examination of the pension funding gap suggests the outlook may improve. For starters, the city's primary general retirement pension plan posted an increase of only 2.6 percent on its investments in the year ended June 2015. That poor performance, coupled with what was likely another disappointing year ended June 2016, exacerbated the pension system's expected shortfall. But a strong stock market rally after Donald Trump's election in November 2016 offered hope that the pension investments will quickly regain lost ground.

What's more, Detroit's bankruptcy team fought to set a low expected rate of return on the city's pension investments: 6.75 percent, far below the average nationwide rate of 7.62 percent among government funds, according to the National Association of State Retirement Administrators. The conservative approach was prudent because it leaves room for market gains to exceed expectations and for Detroit's new fund leaders to improve their performance following years of poor investments by past trustees. "The portfolio is not the most efficient, let's put it that way," said Nick Khouri, Michigan's treasurer and chairman of the Financial Review Commission that oversees Detroit's finances.

Of course, if the market tanks through 2024, all government pension plans are in trouble— not just Detroit's. Actuarial projections are, by their very nature, educated guesses, including mortality predictions, which determine how much money must be budgeted to cover pension obligations. Gabriel Roeder Smith adjusted the city's projected pension gap after adopting the Society of Actuaries' mortality table projections for private-sector plans, released in October 2014. But Detroit's bankruptcy settlement was already teed up for the judge's approval by then.

In addition, private-sector mortality rates can differ from public-sector rates—which is underscored by the fact that the Society of Actuaries is developing mortality tables for public plans that will better fit Detroit's situation. Detroit's projected pension payment will be updated again when those figures are released.

"I know the mayor is concerned that there was some improper judgment about all of this during the bankruptcy case," Judge Rhodes said. "I don't see it myself. Not at all." Hill, Duggan's chief financial officer, said it's critical for the city to prepare for the worst. "I don't think it's too early to sound the alarm," he said.

To be sure, if Detroit should be condemned for using older mortality tables, so should most other government plans. A 2015 study by the Boston College Center for Retirement Research found that 73 percent of public-sector pension plans relied on the Society of Actuaries' 2000 mortality tables as of 2013.

Accusing the bankruptcy team of impropriety is "just emotional rhetoric and just doesn't hold any water," said Baird, who continues to meet regularly with Duggan. "I know and I love our Detroit mayor, I really do—but Mike is not a guy who stays quiet, reflects a few days, and then decides what he's gonna say. He shoots first and he asks questions later. From my conversations with him, I think he's settled way down. I don't think you're going to see this thing headed back to the courts."

Duggan's threat serves a political purpose, though. It reminds angry voters that he opposed the appointment of an emergency manager, even though he later cooperated with Orr and now reaps the political benefits of a leaner balance sheet. "It is just politics," Miller Buckfire investment banker Ken Buckfire said. "Everyone involved knew at the time of the potential for underfunding."

The reality, Buckfire said, is the future remains uncertain. "A lot can happen in ten years," he said. "We provided Detroit with a ten-year period of financial stability in which to restore livability—and they've got exactly that. That is being validated by the fact that so much private capital is now coming into Detroit to invest in new businesses and real estate development. The market is voting with its capital that the plan will succeed."

Financial details aside, a Duggan lawsuit may fare poorly because the plan of adjustment, as ordered by the judge, allows no "liability to any person or entity for any act or omission in connection with, relating to or arising out of" the bankruptcy, unless the advisers displayed gross negligence. Using the same generally accepted actuarial tables as everyone else would hardly seem to constitute "gross negligence."

Even if the pension gap remains a significant issue, the city can map out a plan to address it proactively. To the mayor's credit, this is already occurring. In fiscal 2016, the city set aside $20 million from its surplus to help close the pension gap. This is a responsible step that would have been unthinkable in years gone by in Detroit. "Our biggest asset we have right now is the time to strategize and change those numbers," Hill said.

While criticizing the bankruptcy team for ignoring "warning signs" in favor of "self-congratulatory media tours" and "inflated fees," Police and Fire Retirement System pension spokesman Bruce Babiarz praised the city's steps to address the crisis. "The important point is that this complex pension funding issue, a matter impacting cities across the nation, is being professionally and proactively addressed. All parties are taking a serious and hard look at viable options to solve this matter."

LESS THAN A YEAR after Detroit emerged from bankruptcy, Michigan's governance model of emergency management came under fire when the world learned of the water crisis in the city of Flint.

While Detroit's emergency manager gave the city a second chance at life, Flint's emergency managers took a divergent path. They severed Flint's purchasing deal with Detroit in pursuit of cheaper water and plowed ahead with a plan to temporarily use the Flint River while awaiting pipeline construction that would allow them to eventually draw water from the cleaner Lake Huron. After a series of monumental bureaucratic blunders, Flint residents were poisoned with lead, causing irreparable physical harm in a community already tormented by industrial disinvestment, racial inequality, and rampant poverty. Two of Flint's emergency managers, Darnell Earley and Gerald Ambrose, were hit with felony charges by Michigan attorney general Bill Schuette in December 2016 for allegedly embracing the switch to save money despite the dangers. Several other officials, including state and city bureaucrats, have also been charged for their roles in the crisis.

Flint's humanitarian crisis called into question Snyder's reliance on emergency management. In Detroit, the model worked because Orr understood that he had to build a political consensus for major decisions, resembling the typical democratic process. After a contentious beginning to his tenure, he struck working relationships with the mayor and City Council, eventually winning their votes for the regional water deal, grand bargain, and entire bankruptcy restructuring plan. He also voluntarily relinquished control of the fire department, finances, blight removal, and lighting to Duggan shortly after the mayor took office.

In Flint, however, the City Council never endorsed the emergency managers' plan to use the Flint River water. Flint's crisis illustrates the danger of suspending democracy and giving unelected emergency managers control of everything. Even when there's no nefarious intent, few, if any, singular leaders have the financial, operational, and political skills to oversee all aspects of a major city.

Meanwhile, emergency management has also failed the schoolchildren of Detroit. After a series of several emergency managers failed to permanently balance the Detroit Public Schools budget, bolster educational outcomes, or stem enrollment declines, the governor appointed the briefly retired Judge Rhodes as the district's final de facto emergency manager in early 2016. In that role, officially titled transition manager, Rhodes was tasked with convincing the state legislature to pay off the district's debts and transfer schools to a new, separate district without the residual financial baggage. He succeeded. After the district neared payless paydays in spring 2016, the legislature authorized a $617 million bailout and restructuring plan allowing Detroit voters to elect a school board that would take over January 1, 2017. The move ended emergency management, subjecting the school board to oversight from the same Financial Review Commission that oversees the city's finances.

While Detroiters have been clamoring for control of their schools for years, the district continues to face profound challenges, including dilapidated buildings, a ring of corrupt principals recently exposed by federal prosecutors, poverty, broken families, and competition from charter schools.

His stint leading the district left Rhodes with "mixed" reviews of emergency management. "On the one hand, the city of Detroit bankruptcy case would have been a nightmare without an emergency manager. On the other hand, it's clear to me that DPS was under emergency management for way too long," Rhodes said. "The fundamental problem with emergency management is this: When any organization is insolvent—and by insolvent I mean unable to pay its debts, as opposed to balance-sheet insolvency—in most cases it is unrealistic to expect that a change in management by itself will solve that problem. And that's what emergency management is—it's a change in management. There almost always has to be, in addition to a change in management, an infusion of new capital, new resources."

After Flint's disaster and the Detroit schools quagmire, a bipartisan state panel recommended that Snyder adopt three-person panels of emergency managers, instead of single appointees. This would allow for the appointment of specialized talent and would spread out the pressure. Snyder said he would consider changes. "I'm open to having a dialogue," he said. "You can always improve things. And we did learn some lessons from Flint."

SINCE THIS BOOK WAS RELEASED, I've often been asked for my perspective on the lessons of Detroit's bankruptcy. Here's one that resonates: Someday the bill will come due. Promises mean nothing unless you can back them up. This applies to all walks of life, but especially to government. In Detroit, the bill came due in 2013, when the city filed for Chapter 9 bankruptcy. Detroit illuminates the harsh reality of democracy. We, as Americans, elect politicians who tell us what we want to hear. We elect politicians who make promises to us that they can't keep. And we reward them for perpetuating the status quo, even when the status quo is leading us down a path toward destruction.

Detroit, in that small way, is simply a reflection of the broader American political system. Coleman Young understood this.

"Detroit's special place in urban American history has been as its great indicator, a condensed, microcosmic, accelerated version of Everycity, USA," the longest-serving Detroit mayor wrote in his autobiography in 1994. "In the evolutionary urban order, Detroit today has always been your town tomorrow. . . . Troubled and forsaken as the times have conspired to leave it, Detroit . . . is as important to the nation right now as it has ever been—maybe more so, because right now it is telling us that the cities are in trouble. Detroit is the advance warning—the flashing red light and siren—for what could be a catastrophic urban meltdown, and the country had damn well better pay attention."

In Detroit, retirees paid the bill for promises that were issued many years ago by politicians who understood they would never be held accountable. Pensioners sacrificed to give the city a hope for a better future.

More than two years later, the pain still resonates. "I don't think the retirees have been properly thanked," said Ryan Plecha, attorney for Lippitt O'Keefe Gornbein, who represented the retiree associations during the bankruptcy. "Unfortunately they're becoming an afterthought to the development that's going on. If the retirees wouldn't have voted yes, we'd still be in court and none of this would be happening. I don't think that can be stressed enough."

Their sacrifices, not to mention those of bondholders and other creditors that suffered, should linger as a warning sign to other cities that manage their finances irresponsibly. "What the bankruptcy did for other cities was to show them to stop and look at where they are," said Shirley Lightsey, president of the Detroit Retired City Employees Association. "They should never allow themselves to get to the point the city of Detroit was at. That's the only legacy we can leave to other cities."

ACKNOWLEDGMENTS

I owe a debt of gratitude—excuse the unfortunate pun—to innumerable people for their support in writing this book.

As a reporter for the *Detroit Free Press*, I had a front-row seat to a remarkable story with no shortage of compelling characters, historic implications, profound moments, and intense battles. Covering Detroit's bankruptcy for the *Free Press* was an enormous but rewarding challenge, and it would have been impossible without visionary leaders and teammates who played crucial roles in explaining this story to the masses.

I am grateful for the incredibly talented and dedicated team of past and present *Free Press* editors and reporters for supporting me as I covered the case. They reported the bankruptcy with me and endured my unnatural interest in prolonged conversations about the courtroom drama, backroom intrigue, and considerable personal consequences of the bankruptcy. They included Nancy Andrews, Paul Anger, Tresa Baldas, Steve Byrne, John Gallagher, Greg Gardner, Joe Guillen, Matt Helms, Stephen Henderson, Robert Huschka, Nancy Kaffer, Christopher Kirkpatrick, Nancy Laughlin, Eric Millikin, Stefanie Murray, Amalie Nash, Alisa Priddle, Brent Snavely, Steve Spalding, Mark Stryker, Martha Thierry, Susan Tompor, Tom Walsh, Carlton Winfrey, Ashley Woods, and many others.

I am thankful to my agent, Karen Gantz, for taking a chance on me. I'm especially obliged to my publisher, W. W. Norton & Company, and book editor Brendan Curry for believing that I could do this and for shaping this book into a compelling read. I'm also enormously appreciative of Mary Babcock for outstanding copyediting.

In addition to those listed above, I'm blessed to have had numerous other journalism mentors, including Mike Hill, Frank

Weir, Tom Kirvan, Brian Cox, Renee Lapham Collins, Andy Chapelle, Carol Schlagheck, Art Brooks, Kevin Devine, Tony Dearing, Paula Gardner, David Callaway, Laura Petrecca, and many others I wish I could list here. I am also privileged to work with the outstanding newsroom at *USA Today*, which generates world-class journalism every day, and am thankful for the organization's wonderful support. Thank you to my friend Jason Idalski, whose copyediting skills were invaluable. And thank you to my friend Caleb Cohen and his company, Mockingbird-Productions.com, for directing his relentless energy and talents to help build a website for me, NathanBomey.com.

I'm very grateful to my parents, Randy and Deanna, my brother Dan, and my in-laws Lynn and Ben, for their love and support.

It's hard to put into words how much I'm thankful to my wife and best friend, Kathryn, for her love, encouragement, and editing skills!

To all the sources I interviewed for this book, including those I could not name, I want to express my sincere appreciation for your cooperation. This would not have been possible without you.

Lastly, to the people of Detroit, thank you for exemplifying a relentless spirit of hope and endurance. As Father Gabriel Richard put it, let us together hope for better things.

NOTE ABOUT SOURCES

I conducted original interviews with numerous people involved in Detroit's bankruptcy specifically for this book. I spoke to many of them several times, virtually all on the record. A few sources could not be quoted on the record because of the sensitivity of their positions in the case, and they are not cited in the notes section. The amount of records pertaining to Detroit's bankruptcy was staggering. Parties filed more than ten thousand documents with the court, many of which were hundreds of pages long. Court filings can be found in the U.S. Bankruptcy Court, Eastern District of Michigan (Case No. 13-53846), and many are available for free online at kccllc.net/Detroit. In addition to sifting through those records, I also reviewed and cited hearing transcripts and depositions; obtained numerous emails, corporate records, union documents, and historical materials; cited published news reports, including some of my own; and consulted with industry experts. This book is an amalgamation of that research. My goal was to distill an incredibly complex bankruptcy case into a readable narrative faithful to the events on the ground and helpful to anyone who wants to learn from Detroit—-the good and the bad. Without compromising confidentiality agreements with key interviewees, I've listed specific sources and interviews below. In some cases, information that is readily available publicly is not referenced.

NOTES

Prologue: 4:06 p.m.

ix   July 18, 2013, was a bad day: Author interview with Bill Wertheimer, October 23, 2014.

ix   "We pay you enough": Ibid.

x   requested the governor's permission: Author interview with Kevyn Orr, January 26, 2015.

x   "Not uncommonly": Author interview with David Heiman, January 6, 2015.

xi   When Nowling discovered: Details of the race to the courthouse were constructed based on court transcripts, depositions, and personal interviews with several people involved in the bankruptcy who requested anonymity because of the sensitivity of this episode.

xi   "We were very nervous": Author interview with Heiman, January 6, 2015.

xi   "I'm committed to my process": The governor's remarks and actions on the day of the bankruptcy are based on interviews with sources who requested anonymity because they were not authorized to speak publicly.

xii   "Mike, do you think": This exchange is based on a transcript of Mike Nicholson's court testimony during Detroit's bankruptcy eligibility trial in the U.S. Bankruptcy Court, Eastern District of Michigan, November 5, 2013.

xii   "We knew damn well": Author interview with Wertheimer, October 23, 2014

xiii "Their view was": Nathan Bomey, John Gallagher, and Mark Stryker, "How Detroit Was Reborn," *Detroit Free Press*, November 9, 2014. http://on.freep.com/10QofVG.

xiii "As your legal counsel": These events are based on sources who agreed to discuss the matter on condition of anonymity.

xiv   "I'm standing right by": Ibid.

xiv   "They were concerned". Ibid.

xiv   "Let's file": Author interview with Orr, January 26, 2015.

xiv   "We only filed sixteen pages": Author interview with Heiman, January 6, 2015.

xv   "Excuse me, your honor": This exchange derives from an Ingham County Circuit Court transcript, July 18, 2013.

xv   "Aquilina, of course, was pissed": Author interview with Robert Gordon, October 30, 2014.

xv   "It was my intention": Ingham County Circuit Court transcript, July 18, 2013.

xv   "I think our heart skipped a beat": Author interview with Heiman, January 6, 2015.

Introduction

1   four out of every ten dollars: *City of Detroit Proposal for Creditors*, June 14, 2013. http://www.detroitmi.gov/Portals/0/docs/EM/Reports/City%20 of%20Detroit%20Proposal%20for%20Creditors1.pdf.

1   Without drastic action: Ibid.

2   enacted an income tax: Nathan Bomey and John Gallagher, "How Detroit Went Broke," *Detroit Free Press*, September 15, 2013. http://on.freep. com/1btfzDr.

2   Young . . . slashed spending: Ibid.

2   Kilpatrick . . . cut several thousand jobs: Ibid.

3   "To have lived through the vibrant Detroit": Author interview with Shirley Lightsey, January 21, 2015.

3   city had more murders: These 2012 statistics were drawn from the FBI's Uniform Crime Reporting Statistics database. Full figures: Detroit (386), St. Louis (113), Milwaukee (91), Cleveland (84), Pittsburgh (41). Accessed October 6, 2015. http://www.ucrdatatool.gov/.

3   By 2013, about 40 percent: Detroit Public Lighting Authority, *2014: A New Era in Street Lighting in Detroit: An Annual Progress Report of the Public Lighting Authority*, 2014. http://www.pladetroit.org/wp-content/ uploads/2015/09/2014-Annual-Report-FINAL.pdf.

3   workers would hit "send": Deposition of Beth Niblock for the bankruptcy plan confirmation hearing, July 31, 2014.

3   About half of the city's residents: Testimony of Caroline Sallee from a court transcript of the bankruptcy plan confirmation hearing in the U.S. Bankruptcy Court, Eastern District of Michigan, September 8, 2014.

4   "Every case is about people": Author interview with Steven Rhodes, February 19, 2015.

4   "We Americans believe": Steven Rhodes, transcript of Commencement Address, Walsh College, Troy, Michigan, January 24, 2015.

4   "Relatively speaking": Author interview with Ron Bloom, February 3, 2015.

4   "Detroit had the misfortune": Ibid.

5   "one tough nerd": Nathan Bomey. "Rick Snyder, in Super Bowl Ad, Asks Voters to Embrace 'One Tough Nerd,'" AnnArbor.com, February 8, 2010. http://bit.ly/1KKPpOl.

5   "yellow-dog Democrat": Author interview with Kevyn Orr, January 26, 2015.

6   "As I look at the landscape": Author interview with Darren Walker, December 19, 2014.

Chapter 1: The Nerd

7   Born in 1958: Nathan Bomey, "Profile: Rick Snyder Brings Successful Private-Sector Experience to Gubernatorial Race," AnnArbor.com, July

4, 2010. http://www.mlive.com/politics/index.ssf/2010/07/rick_snyder_
governor_gateway.html.

7   At age sixteen: Carol Cain, "Carol Cain: Politicians Should Learn from Milliken, Buck Party Politics," *Detroit Free Press*, August 11, 2014. http://bit
.ly/18iEf7r.

7   But academics were his passion: Bomey, "Profile: Rick Snyder."

8   "The vast majority of people": Author interview with Rich Baird, January 15,
2015.

9   "Frankly, I believe": Ibid.

9   "He came into the Detroit office": Author interview with Chris Rizik,
November 17, 2014.

9   population had already plummeted: Kofi Myler, "Detroit's Population from
1840 to 2012 Shows High Points, Decades of Decline," *Detroit Free Press*,
July 23, 2014. http://bit.ly/1w9zPER.

9–10 Michigan's unemployment rate: U.S. Bureau of Labor Statistics, "Current
Unemployment Rates for States and Historical Highs/Lows." http://www.bls
.gov/web/laus/lauhsthl.htm. Accessed February 24, 2015.

10   "When I moved to Detroit": Author interview with Governor Rick Snyder,
January 16, 2015.

10   Rick and Sue Snyder moved to Chicago: Bomey, "Profile: Rick Snyder."

10   "Ted Waitt was a visionary": Author interview with Baird, January 15, 2015.

10   In 1991, the Snyders moved: Bomey, "Profile: Rick Snyder."

11   "Ted was really a marketing genius": Author interview with Rizik, November
17, 2014.

11   grow from 700 employees: Bomey, "Did Rick Snyder Ship Jobs Overseas
While at Gateway?" AnnArbor.com, June 24, 2010. http://www.annarbor
.com/business-review/did-rick-snyder-ship-jobs-overseas-at-gateway.

11   "He was kind of the adult supervision": Vickie Elmer, "Rick Snyder's Run:
From Gateway to the Governor's Race," *Ann Arbor Observer*, May 2010.
http://annarborobserver.com/articles/rick_snyder_s_run_full_article.html.

11   Snyder cut personal checks: Bomey, "Profile: Rick Snyder."

11   $200 million to Johnson & Johnson: Nathan Bomey, "Johnson & Johnson
Renames HealthMedia Unit after Mix of Ann Arbor Layoffs, Hiring,"
AnnArbor.com, January 27, 2012. http://www.annarbor.com/business
-review/johnson-johnson-renames-healthmedia-unit-after-mix-of-ann-arbor
-layoffs-hiring/.

11   Rick and Sue were on a dinner date: Susan Demas, "The Nerd Shall Inherit
the State?" *Dome Magazine*, June 16, 2010. http://domemagazine.com/
features/f20610.

12   "The moment that happened": Interview with Rizik, November 17, 2014.

13   flow of cash from Lansing: Joan Hunault, Jim Stansell, Mary Ann Cleary,
Bethany Wicksall, and Ben Gielczyk, "Legislative Analysis: Local Government and School District Fiscal Accountability Act," House Fiscal Agency,
February 24, 2011. http://www.legislature.mi.gov/documents/2011-2012/
billanalysis/House/pdf/2011-HLA-4214-6.pdf.

13   handshake deal: David Ashenfelter, "Handshake Deal with State

Haunts Detroit," *Bridge*, March 15, 2013. http://bridgemi.com/2013/03/handshake-deal-with-state-haunts-detroit/.

13   Ken Buckfire lived on Frisbee Street: Author interview with Ken Buckfire, October 9, 2014.

14   "the turnaround king": Interview with Ken Buckfire, "The Turnaround King," *Power Lunch*, CNBC, June 29, 2010. http://nbcnews.to/1EOrpHV.

14   "When the city had problems": Author interview with Buckfire, October 9, 2014.

14   "to provide our insights": Quotations are from a copy of the letter from Ken Buckfire to Andy Dillon, December 9, 2010.

15   "deficit elimination bonds": Suzette Hackney and Naomi R. Patton, "Bing to Seek Council's OK to Sell $250M Bond," *Detroit Free Press*, November 20, 2009. http://archive.freep.com/article/20091120/NEWS01/911200474/Bing-seek-council-s-OK-sell-250M-bond.

16   "That's good business": Author interview with Buckfire, December 16, 2014.

16   In April 2012, the City Council signed: Details of the consent agreement between Detroit and the State of Michigan are found in the city's "Financial Stability Agreement." http://www.michigan.gov/documents/treasury/Detroit_Fiscal_Stability_Agreement_382287_7.pdf.

16   "It could have worked": Author interview with Andy Dillon, February 2, 2015.

16   "It became clear Detroit": Author interview with Buckfire, October 9, 2014.

16   "The condition of the city": Author interview with Buckfire, December 16, 2014.

17   On Election Day in November 2012: Details of the election can be found on the Michigan Department of State website. http://miboecfr.nictusa.com/election/results/12GEN/90000001.html. Accessed October 6, 2015.

17   But on the day after Christmas 2012: Enrolled Senate Bill No. 865, State of Michigan, 96th Legislature, regular session of 2012, December 26, 2012. http://1.usa.gov/1PnpbI6.

Chapter 2: Deal of the Year

18   "How did you go bankrupt?" Ernest Hemingway, *The Sun Also Rises* (New York: Simon & Schuster, 1954), 141.

18   total value . . . of private property: Nathan Bomey and John Gallagher, "How Detroit Went Broke," *Detroit Free Press*, September 15, 2013. http://on.freep.com/1btfzDr.

19   "pushers": Steven Gray, "Coleman Young, Revisited," *Time*, December 2, 2009. http://ti.me/1WpGxoy.

19   city enjoyed a period of relative stability: An analysis of the *City of Detroit Comprehensive Annual Financial Report for the Fiscal Year Ended June 30, 2002*, shows a city government in remarkably good health compared to what would happen just a few years later. Debt, pensions, and retiree health care costs represented

only 13 percent of the budget, and the pension funds had a collective surplus. http://www.detroitmi.gov/Portals/0/docs/finance/cafr/2002_CAFR.pdf.

19   city's pension funds: *City of Detroit Comprehensive Annual Financial Report for the Fiscal Year Ended June 30, 2002.*

20   "hip-hop mayor": Steven Yaccino, "Kwame M. Kilpatrick, Former Detroit Mayor, Sentenced to 28 Years in Corruption Case," *New York Times*, October 10, 2013. http://nyti.ms/1AqDcMT.

20   Kilpatrick had lied under oath: Jim Schaefer, M. L. Elrick, Joe Swickard, and Ben Schmitt, "Kilpatrick Admits Guilt, Resigns Office," *Detroit Free Press*, September 5, 2008. http://archive.freep.com/article/20080905/NEWS01/809050375/Kilpatrick-admits-guilt-resigns-office.

20   "I want to tell you, Detroit": Mike Wilkinson, "Detroit 'Set Me Up for a Comeback,'" *Detroit News*, September 5, 2008. http://bit.ly/1sFkxck.

20   FBI discovered that Kilpatrick: Details on the FBI's bust of the criminal activity of Kilpatrick, Jeffrey Beasley, Bobby Ferguson, and Ronald Zajac are available in three FBI press releases: U.S. Attorney's Office, Eastern District of Michigan, "Jury Convicts Former City Treasurer, Pension Officials of Conspiring to Defraud Pensioners through Bribery," December 8, 2014, http://1.usa.gov/1AB0JZt; "Former City of Detroit Treasurer Jeff Beasley Indicted for Taking Bribes and Kickbacks in Return for Approving Investments by the Two City Pension Funds," February 28, 2012, http://1.usa.gov/17wz2b2; and "Former Detroit Mayor Kwame Kilpatrick, Contractor Bobby Ferguson, and Bernard Kilpatrick Sentenced on Racketeering, Extortion, Bribery, Fraud, and Tax Charges," October 17, 2013, http://1.usa.gov/1IaYQIIL.

21   On December 6, 2005: Details of the award Kilpatrick received are documented in the *City of Detroit Comprehensive Annual Financial Report for Fiscal Year Ended June 30, 2005.* http://www.detroitmi.gov/Portals/0/docs/finance/cafr/CAFR2005.pdf.

21   "fiscal stabilization bonds": Bomey and Gallagher, "How Detroit Went Broke."

22   shortfall of $1.7 billion: *City of Detroit Comprehensive Annual Financial Report for Fiscal Year Ended June 30, 2005.*

22   He threatened to lay off: Bomey and Gallagher, "How Detroit Went Broke."

22   "I remember Council members saying": Author interview with Joseph Harris, November 14, 2014.

23   complex borrowing scheme: Details on the pension obligation certificates-of-participation (COPs) deal and the structure of the deal are found in numerous city documents, including the *City of Detroit Comprehensive Annual Financial Report for Fiscal Year Ended June 30, 2005.*

23   cities cannot carry: Ibid.

24   In a rare moment of political lucidity: An account of the City Council's ruminations, statements, and votes regarding the COPs and swaps deal is found in the Council's minutes: City of Detroit, *Journal of the City Council*, January 5, 2005. http://www.detroitmi.gov/Portals/0/docs/City%20Clerk/2005%20Council.pdf.

24   "Throughout all my research": Ibid.

25   "have decided to gamble the city's future": Ibid.

26   "made no financial sense": Author interview with Ken Buckfire, October 9, 2014.

26   Lewis & Munday wrote: The law firm's letter supporting Detroit's COPs deal was included on pages G-1 and G-2 of the "$1,440,000,000 Taxable Certificates of Participation Series 2005 Issued by the Detroit Retirement Systems Funding Trust 2005" circular distributed to investors, 2005. http://bit .ly/1Ozn7N3.

26   "The obligation of the city": This quote is taken directly from Lewis & Munday's letter cited in the previous note.

26   initial ratings on the insured COPs at a pristine AAA: These ratings were included in the offering circular, "$1,440,000,000 Taxable Certificates of Participation Series 2005 Issued by the Detroit Retirement Systems Funding Trust 2005."

26   "The challenge for Baird": Marianne Foster, "Robert W. Baird & Co.: Baird Public Finance Deal Recognized as the Bond Buyer's Midwest Regional Deal of the Year," Wisconsin's Business News Service, December 8, 2005. http://www.wisbusiness.com/printerfriendly.iml?Article=50551.

27   city's eroding finances: Karen Pierog, "S&P Downgrades Detroit Bonds to Junk Status," Reuters, January 6, 2009. http://www.reuters.com/ article/2009/01/07/us-detroit-sp-idUSTRE50608720090107.

27   "What we told UBS was": Author interview with Harris, November 14, 2014.

28   "I remember the discussions": Ibid.

28   banks could cancel the swaps contracts: Author interview with Buckfire, October 9, 2014.

29   "This is what really got the city": Ibid.

Chapter 3: Kevyn Orr

30   Kevyn Orr's path: Kevyn Orr's biographical details are based on an author interview with Kevyn Orr on January 26, 2015, and the State of Michigan's biography of the emergency manager. http://www.michigan.gov/detroitcantw ait/0,4839,7-293--297207--,00.html. Accessed October 6, 2015.

30   "My dad came and picked me up": These recollections are based on author interview with Orr, January 26, 2015.

31   "Some white surfer boys": Ibid.

31   first black member of the local yacht club: Brian Dickerson, Matt Helms, and Todd Spangler, "New Detroit Emergency Financial Manager Kevyn Orr Takes on Challenge of a Lifetime," Detroit Free Press, March 24, 2013. http://bit.ly/1LjEPl7.

32   helped lead the agency's role in the Whitewater investigation: Michael A. Fletcher, "The Man Who Is Trying to Save Detroit," Washington Post, July 20, 2013. http://wapo.st/1wmpRFS.

33   Jones Day's competitors for the job: Author interview with Ken Buckfire, December 16, 2014.

33   Jones Day attorneys conducted extensive research: Details about the firm's background research on Detroit are contained within an internal document titled "Presentation to the City of Detroit," January 29, 2013.

33   "We couldn't find anybody": Author interview with Buckfire, December 16, 2014.

34   "I think I used the term": Author interview with Rich Baird, January 15, 2015.

34   "burn down the city of Detroit": Charlie Langton, "Shabazz Discusses Why He Said Burn the City Down," CBS Detroit, March 30, 2012. http://cbsloc.al/1DQ JoAo.

34   "And I just went off": Discussions between Orr, Baird, and Jones Day managing partner Steve Brogan, at the January meeting and later concerning Orr becoming the emergency manager, are based on author interviews with Orr on January 26, 2015, and Baird on January 15, 2015.

35   "Baird's eyes lit up": Author interview with Buckfire, December 16, 2014.

37   "Here's your call to action": Author interview with Orr, January 26, 2015.

37   "He saw this almost as a calling": Author interview with Baird, January 15, 2015.

37   Despite their political differences: The conversation between Governor Rick Snyder, Orr, and Baird about the emergency manager job is based on independent author interviews on January 16, 2015, January 26, 2015, and January 15, 2015, respectively.

38   "The governor is sending an emergency manager": Joe Guillen and Kathleen Gray, "Detroit City Council Appeals Financial Manager Decision, Requests Modified Plan," Detroit Free Press, March 12, 2013. http://bit.ly/1A4BuvZ.

38   "I don't want to pull that cudgel": Kirk Pinho, "Detroit's Emergency Manager Says He's 'All In' for the 'Olympics of Restructuring,'" Crain's Detroit Business, March 14, 2013. http://bit.ly/1VGgcFO.

38   "one of the greatest turnarounds": Ibid.

39   brought Oreo cookies: Matt Helms, "Protesters Demand to Speak with Bing, Orr, Pray outside Office," Detroit Free Press, April 1, 2013. http://bit.ly/1hY2Tig.

39   "As opposed to having a city council": Joe Guillen, "Jesse Jackson Calls for Mass Protest against Detroit's Emergency Financial Manager," Detroit Free Press, March 22, 2013. http://bit.ly/1JR45tp.

40   "I didn't realize people": Author interview with Orr, January 26, 2015.

40   "What do people think about this?": Ibid.

40   "Oh, they think you're an Uncle Tom": Ibid.

41   "Bill, I need your help": Author interview with Bill Nowling, February 12, 2015.

41   "You're a politician": Ibid.

41   "My great-granddaddy": Author interview with Orr, January 26, 2015.

41   "Everyone was terrified": Author interview with Buckfire, October 9, 2014.

42   "Look, if all you're going to do": Author interview via email with Steve Spencer, February 9, 2015, and author interview with Orr, February 25, 2015.
42   "Steve, let me be real clear on this": Ibid.

Chapter 4: Project Debtwa

43   some 85 percent of the city's computers: This statistic comes from Detroit chief information officer Beth Niblock's expert report for Detroit's bankruptcy confirmation hearing, titled "Report of Beth Niblock, Chief Information Officer for the City of Detroit," May 5, 2014. http://www.detroitmi .gov/Portals/0/docs/EM/Bankruptcy%20Information/9%20Detroit%20 -%20Expert%20Report%20-%20Niblock%20Report.pdf.

43   About 70 percent of the city's accounting entries: This estimate comes from the *City of Detroit Proposal for Creditors*, June 14, 2013. http://www.detroitmi .gov/Portals/0/docs/EM/Reports/City%20of%20Detroit%20Proposal%20 for%20Creditors1.pdf.

43   "catastrophic": Ibid.

44   "Project Debtwa": This phrase is found on Miller Buckfire documents from before the bankruptcy. The nickname "Debtwa" was also discussed in open court as documented in the transcript of an eligibility trial hearing in the U.S. Bankruptcy Court, Eastern District of Michigan, November 4, 2013.

44   "The lack of reinvestment": Author interview with Chuck Moore, January 29, 2015.

45   five times greater than the national average: This comparison is based on statistics cited in the *City of Detroit Proposal for Creditors*, June 14, 2013.

45   In 2012, the crimes reported: These statistics were drawn from the FBI's Uniform Crime Reporting Statistics database. http://www.ucrdatatool.gov. Accessed October 6, 2015.

45   Many incidents languished: Ibid.

45   city government had slashed: *City of Detroit Proposal for Creditors*, June 14, 2013.

46   about 40 percent of the city's streetlights were not working: Ibid.

46   groundbreaking study: The Detroit Blight Removal Task Force delivered this incredible report based on a comprehensive effort to map the city's blighted properties, resulting in an online database and report. *Detroit Blight Removal Task Force Plan*, May 27, 2014. http://report.timetoendblight.org/intro/.

46   About 60 percent of fires: This is from the *City of Detroit Proposal for Creditors*, June 14, 2013.

46   "If you think your neighbor painting": Free Press Editorial Board, "Q&A with Kevyn Orr: Detroit's Emergency Manager Talks about City's Future," *Detroit Free Press*, June 16, 2013. http://bit.ly/1GrkGVs.

46   "Certainly we qualify": Author interview with Kevyn Orr, January 26, 2015.

46   about 13 percent of the applications: This statistic is based on the Detroit

inspector general's investigation documenting unemployment compensation abuses, in a report titled *Emergency Manager Order No. 8, Initial 60 Day Report, July 2011–March 2013*, August 20, 2013. http://www.detroitmi.gov/Portals/0/docs/Inspector%20General/EMO8_FINAL_REPORT_Sept_26_2013_202.24.06_PM_1.pdf.

47   In the Department of Transportation: The absenteeism statistic was reported in Detroit's "Fourth Amended Disclosure Statement with Respect to Fourth Amended Plan for the Adjustment of Debts of the City of Detroit" accompanying its "Fourth Amended Plan for the Adjustment of Debts of the City of Detroit," May 5, 2014. The disclosure statement is available at http://bit.ly/1ZJgzyU. The fourth version of the plan of adjustment listed here is available at http://1.usa.gov/1Ga3Ejf.

47   "We all looked at each other": Author interview with Heather Lennox, February 9, 2015.

47   "Kevyn was a great battlefield general": Author interview with Ken Buckfire, October 9, 2014.

47   Chuck Moore and Ernst & Young advisor Gaurav Malhotra concluded: *City of Detroit Proposal for Creditors*, June 14, 2013.

47   "If you simply assume": Author interview with Buckfire, December 16, 2014.

48   In a two-hour closed-door meeting: The financial conditions of the city revealed in Orr's meeting at the Westin hotel are all taken directly from the *City of Detroit Proposal for Creditors*, June 14, 2013.

48   "People didn't like it": Author interview with Buckfire, October 9, 2014.

49   "Who gets up in the morning": Author interview with Bill Nowling, February 12, 2015.

49   "We were the constituency": Author interview with Steve Spencer, October 24, 2014.

49   "I have never, ever": This quote comes from a transcript of Mike Nicholson's court testimony during Detroit's bankruptcy eligibility trial in the U.S. Bankruptcy Court, Eastern District of Michigan, November 5, 2013.

50   "There was no sharing": Author interview with Moore, January 29, 2015.

50   emergency alert system had malfunctioned: Tresa Baldas, "Detroit Fire Department Has Alert System Made of Pop Cans, Doorbells," *Detroit Free Press*, September 6, 2014. http://bit.ly/1wHyzcn.

50   "The city has to continue": Author interview with David Heiman, January 6, 2015.

51   bill for those pension promises: *City of Detroit Proposal for Creditors*, June 14, 2013.

51   Altogether, 32,427 people: These retiree numbers and average pension figures come from "Expert Report of Martha E.M. Kopacz regarding the Feasibility of the City of Detroit Plan of Adjustment" prepared for Judge Steven Rhodes, July 18, 2014. http://bit.ly/1LSROpU.

51   Four people were still receiving: Data provided by the Detroit Retirement Systems.

51   Corruption dogged the pension boards: Details on the FBI's bust of the crim-

inal activity of Kilpatrick, Jeffrey Beasley, and Ronald Zajac are available in two FBI press releases: U.S. Attorney's Office, Eastern District of Michigan, "Jury Convicts Former City Treasurer, Pension Officials of Conspiring to Defraud Pensioners through Bribery," December 8, 2014, http://1.usa .gov/1AB0JZf; and "Former City of Detroit Treasurer Jeff Beasley Indicted for Taking Bribes and Kickbacks in Return for Approving Investments by the Two City Pension Funds," February 28, 2012, http://1.usa.gov/17wz2b2.

52   long-running practices: Details on the inner workings of the 13th check and annuity savings diversion were discussed in "Declaration of Charles M. Moore in Support of City of Detroit, Michigan's Statement of Qualifications Pursuant to Section 109(c) of the Bankruptcy Code" filed in the U.S. Bankruptcy Court, Eastern District of Michigan, July 18, 2013. http://bit.ly/1jsUeFx.

53   city's pension funds lost: Financial details of the impact of the 13th check and annuity savings diversion can be found in Detroit's "Fourth Amended Disclosure Statement," May 5, 2014.

53   One pensioner, for example, had contributed: Author interview with Moore, January 29, 2015.

53   "There were many, many hundreds": Ibid.

54   "It's always been a bug": Nathan Bomey and John Gallagher, "Nearly $1 billion in Bonuses Paid from Ailing Detroit Pension Fund," *Detroit Free Press*, September 8, 2013. http://bit.ly/1waH2Vj.

54   If those funds had been reinvested: Nathan Bomey and John Gallagher, "How Detroit Went Broke," *Detroit Free Press*, September 15, 2013. http://on.freep.com/1btfzDr.

54   that figure would have almost certainly topped $2 billion: Detroit's "Fourth Amended Disclosure Statement," May 5, 2014.

54   "It would have been a much, much": Author interview with Moore, January 29, 2015.

54   Orr ordered an internal probe: Joe Guillen, Matt Helms, and Alisa Priddle, "Kevyn Orr Orders Corruption Probe of Pensions, Benefits; Unions Vow Fight against Cuts," *Detroit Free Press*, June 20, 2013. http://bit.ly/1DXfYAK.

54   threatened to use his powers: Joe Guillen, "Hawaii-Bound Pension Trustees May Face Removal by Emergency Manager," *Detroit Free Press*, May 17, 2013. http://bit.ly/1Lqcsn8.

55   "I was begging": Author interview with Robert Gordon, October 30, 2014.

55   "The problem is government pensions": Author interview with Lennox, February 9, 2015.

56   top 100 publicly traded U.S. companies: Milliman, *Corporate Pension Funding Study*, 2014. http://us.milliman.com/PFS.

56   Orr's team concluded that: The city's proposed assumed rate of return is documented in "Declaration of Charles M. Moore," July 18, 2013.

56   Government pension plans projected: *NASRA Issue Brief: Public Pension Plan Investment Return Assumptions*, May 2015. http://bit.ly/1hY7JvX.

57   "They had grossly underestimated": Author interview with Buckfire, October 9, 2014.

Chapter 5: Chapter 9

59   rates of approximately $1,000 per hour: Nathan Bomey, "Judge Appoints $600-an-Hour Attorney to Keep Tabs on Detroit Bankruptcy Legal Fees," *Detroit Free Press*, August 19, 2013. http://bit.ly/1Gx4kuL.

59   Heiman had a breadth of bankruptcy experience: See David Heiman's biography at http://www.jonesday.com/dgheiman/. Accessed October 8, 2015.

59   Bennett, a denizen of southern California: See Bruce Bennett's biography at http://www.jonesday.com/bbennett/. Accessed October 8, 2015.

59   He had joined Jones Day in 2012: Mike Spector and Jennifer Smith, "Bruce Bennett to Leave Dewey for Jones Day," *Wall Street Journal*, May 13, 2012. http://on.wsj.com/1zJiqEs.

59   Lennox was fresh off: Jacqueline Palank, "Detroit Bankruptcy Lawyers Break a Glass Ceiling," *Wall Street Journal*, August 4, 2013. http://on.wsj.com/1DrLq7v.

59–60 Ball had spent considerable time: Chelsea Emery, "Chrysler Bankruptcy Lawyer Oversees Juggling Act," Reuters, April 29, 2009. http://reut.rs/1BwBqMO.

60   After graduating from high school: Author interview with Stephen Hackney, November 21, 2014.

60   Syncora insured or owned: Ibid.

61   "He's a very smart": Author interview with James H. M. Sprayregen, November 21, 2014.

61   Syncora was believed to be facing: Nathan Bomey, "Meet Detroit's Leading Bankruptcy Opponent (and It's Not Pensioners)," *Detroit Free Press*, April 28, 2014. http://bit.ly/17ZysCK.

61   city was quietly negotiating: Author interview with Ken Buckfire, October 9, 2014.

62   "No one is talking to us": Author interview with Hackney, November 21, 2014.

62   "We offered an olive branch": Author interview with Kevyn Orr, January 26, 2015.

62   "I'm hanging out all day": Hackney's entire reaction comes from the author interview with Hackney, November 21, 2014.

63   "a good friend of mine": Author interview with Orr, January 26, 2015.

63   "This really set the tone": Author interview with Hackney, November 21, 2014.

63   "It basically said": Ibid.

63   "nastygram": Author interview with Orr, January 26, 2015.

64   "We don't care how you got cancer": Author interview with Bill Nowling, February 12, 2015.

66   "A lot of the other Chapter 9 cases": Author interview with Bruce Bennett, December 30, 2014.

67   successfully collecting only about 53 percent of the property taxes: *City of Detroit Proposal for Creditors*, June 14, 2013, p. 81. http://www.detroitmi.gov/

Portals/0/docs/EM/Reports/City%20of%20Detroit%20Proposal%20for%20
Creditors1.pdf.

67   In 2013, about 34 percent: Income data from U.S. Census Bureau, *American FactFinder*, 2013 American Community Survey 1-year estimates. http://factfinder.census.gov/faces/nav/jsf/pages/index.xhtml. Accessed February 25, 2015.

67   "This level of debt": This quote is taken from a letter from Orr to Governor Rick Snyder requesting authorization to file for bankruptcy, July 16, 2014.

68   governor's trusted advisor: The recommendations by Richard Baird and Mike Gadola were revealed in Snyder's court testimony and are documented in the court transcript of the eligibility trial in the U.S. Bankruptcy Court, Eastern District of Michigan, October 28, 2013.

68   "The thing you've got to understand": Author interview with Rich Baird, January 15, 2015.

69   Michigan is one of at least thirty-five states: Alicia H. Munnell and Laura Quinby, *Legal Constraints on Changes in State and Local Pensions*, Center for Retirement Research at Boston College, August 2012. http://crr.bc.edu/wp-content/uploads/2012/08/slp_25.pdf.

69   "The constitution does not say": Author interview with Governor Rick Snyder, January 16, 2015.

69   "I shouldn't be imposing": Ibid.

70   "We had exhausted all the other options": Ibid.

Chapter 6: Sacrosanct?

71   Born in Levintown, Pennsylvania: Biographical details based on author interview with former judge Steven Rhodes, February 19, 2015.

71   "I loved engineering": Author interview with Rhodes, February 19, 2015.

71   "the greatest insolvency rock-and-roll band": The Indubitable Equivalents web site. http://abiband.com/. Accessed September 26, 2015.

71   After graduating from Purdue: Author interview with Rhodes, February 19, 2015.

72   "If you have a choice": Author interview with Doug Bernstein, October 29, 2014.

73   Rosen called the judges in the Eastern District: Author interview with Judge Victoria Roberts, February 11, 2015.

73   "I was pleased and delighted": Author interview with Rhodes, February 19, 2015.

73   Rhodes told Rosen he would accept: Ibid.

73   "I was convinced of the importance": Ibid.

74   Rosen grew up in Oak Park: David Ashenfelter, "Meet Gerald Rosen, the Judge Who Is Trying to Save Detroit," DeadlineDetroit.com, December 6, 2013. http://bit.ly/1ERYrqJ.

74 Some colleagues expressed apprehension: Author interview with Roberts, February 11, 2015.

74 "What do you think Churchill": Nathan Bomey, John Gallagher, and Mark Stryker, "How Detroit Was Reborn," *Detroit Free Press*, November 9, 2014. http://on.freep.com/10QofVG.

75 Rhodes agreed to keep: Author interview with Rhodes, February 19, 2015.

75 "Judge Rosen is a political animal": Nathan Bomey, "Q&A: Detroit Bankruptcy Judge on Pensions, DIA, Fees," *Detroit Free Press*, February 20, 2015. http://on.freep.com/1ARC1Zd.

76 privately proposed pension benefit cuts of more than 50 percent: This figure is based on consultation with numerous sources and review of retiree committee documents prepared by the investment bank Lazard.

78 "We weren't actually 100 percent sure": Author interview with Sharon Levine, October 10, 2014.

78 "forbids": "Objection of the Detroit Retirement Systems to the Eligibility of the City of Detroit, Michigan to Be a Debtor under Chapter 9 of the Bankruptcy Code," court document filed in the U.S. Bankruptcy Court, Eastern District of Michigan, August 19, 2013. http://bit.ly/1hJpWfV.

79 "Everyone gets two minutes": Author interview with John Pottow, December 10, 2014.

79 "We would be thrown directly": This remark comes from a transcript of a hearing before Judge Rhodes in the U.S. Bankruptcy Court, Eastern District of Michigan, in which individual pensioners were given a chance to speak in open court, September 13, 2013.

79 "Many of my coworkers": Ibid.

80 "We said we don't want an emergency manager": Ibid.

80 "A hundred people came": Ibid.

80 "I heard many gut-wrenching": Author interview with Rhodes, February 19, 2015.

80 "Would we be kicked out of bankruptcy": Author interview with David Heiman, January 6, 2015.

81 He recognized that the law prevented creditors: Leslie Wayne, "Orange County's Artful Dodger; the Creative Bankruptcy Tactics of Bruce Bennett," *New York Times*, August 4, 1995. http://nyti.ms/1AMjQkj.

81 "You won't find this": Interview with Bruce Bennett, December 30, 2014.

81 "If you had asked me": Ibid.

82 "Negotiations didn't have to": Ibid.

82 "Meaning the city wasn't in good faith": This remark comes from a court transcript of the eligibility trial hearing in the U.S. Bankruptcy Court, Eastern District of Michigan, October 23, 2013.

83 "I believe I'm following": Court transcript of the eligibility trial hearing in the U.S. Bankruptcy Court, Eastern District of Michigan, October 28, 2013.

83 "absolute" contract: Court transcript of the eligibility hearing in the U.S. Bankruptcy Court, Eastern District of Michigan, October 15, 2013.

83 "We have laws": Ibid.

83   "If the City of Detroit were to cease": Court transcript of the eligibility hearing in the U.S. Bankruptcy Court, Eastern District of Michigan, October 21, 2013.

83   "sacrosanct": Brent Snavely and Nathan Bomey, "Detroit EM Orr Forced to Defend Comment That Pensions Are 'Sacrosanct,'" *Detroit Free Press*, November 5, 2013. http://bit.ly/1PvQJHW.

83   "What I was trying to say": Author interview with Kevyn Orr, January 26, 2015.

84   "Were you attempting to mislead": The courtroom exchange presented in the next few paragraphs involving Greg Shumaker, Orr, Rhodes, Claude Montgomery, and Bruce Bennett is drawn from the court transcript of eligibility trial hearing in the U.S. Bankruptcy Court, Eastern District of Michigan, November 4, 2013.

84   "I was speechless": Author interview with Shirley Lightsey, January 21, 2015.

85   "I think his view was": Author interview with Orr, January 26, 2015.

85   "One of the things that doesn't": Court transcript of eligibility trial hearing in the U.S. Bankruptcy Court, Eastern District of Michigan, October 28, 2013.

86   "Everything is broken": This remark and the succeeding account, in which police chief James Craig discusses the conditions of the police department, come from the court transcript of eligibility trial hearing in the U.S. Bankruptcy Court, Eastern District of Michigan, October 25, 2013, and the *City of Detroit Proposal for Creditors*, June 14, 2013.

87   "state of service delivery insolvency": This remark and others on Detroit's eligibility for bankruptcy in this chapter come from Rhodes's oral opinion delivered in the U.S. Bankruptcy Court, Eastern District of Michigan, December 3, 2013.

87   "I think Steve Rhodes thought": Author interview with Pottow, December 10, 2014.

88   "He was pretty harsh": Ibid.

88   "I thought I could win": Author interview with Bruce Bennett, December 30, 2014.

89   "We in bankruptcy impair contracts": Bomey, "Q&A."

89   "We ran them over": Author interview with Orr, January 26, 2015.

89   "He basically said to the creditors": Author interview with Ken Buckfire, October 9, 2014.

90   "We were ready to go": Author interview with Lightsey, January 21, 2015.

Chapter 7: Swaps Saga

91   pension obligation certificates-of-participation: Details on the pension obligation certificates-of-participation (COPs) deal and the structure of the deal are found in numerous city documents, including the City of Detroit's *Compre-*

hensive Annual Financial Reports starting in 2005. http://www.detroitmi.gov/
How-Do-I/City-of-Detroit-CAFR-Find-How-Do-I-City-of-Detroit-MI.

91   "complex and confusing": This remark comes from Rhodes's oral opinion
in the bankruptcy eligibility trial, delivered in the U.S. Bankruptcy Court,
Eastern District of Michigan, December 3, 2013.

91   "nothing more than a common bet": Ibid.

92   "The city was starting to bounce checks": Author interview with Ken Buckfire, December 16, 2014.

92   Orr had asked the U.S. Securities and Exchange Commission: Orr recounts
details of his communications with the Securities and Exchange Commission
in his deposition on the second swaps deal, December 31, 2013.

93   Buckfire set up talks: This episode, including Curland's reaction, is documented in Buckfire's deposition on the first swaps settlement, August 29,
2013.

93   "They had financial leverage": Author interview with Buckfire, December 16,
2014.

94   He directed the Kirkland lawyers: Author interview with Stephen Hackney,
November 21, 2014.

94   "Early on I saw": Author interview with James H. M. Sprayregen, November
21, 2014.

95   "Esprit de corps starts": Author interview with Hackney, November 21, 2014.

95   infrastructure was 120 years old: JC Reindl, "Why Detroit's Lights Went
Out, and How the City Plans to Get Them Back On," *Detroit Free Press*,
November 17, 2013. http://bit.ly/1Nyb0Pz.

95    $185 million overhaul: Detroit Public Lighting Authority, *2014: A New
Era of Street Lighting in Detroit: An Annual Progress Report of the Public Lighting Authority*, 2014. http://www.pladetroit.org/wp-content/
uploads/2015/09/2014-Annual-Report-FINAL.pdf.

96   "The lighting plan seems to exist": This comes from Syncora's court objection
to Detroit's Public Lighting Authority funding plan, November 6, 2013.

96   "They got dealt a shitty hand": Author interview with John Pottow, December 10, 2014.

96   "We're going to be the junkyard": Ibid.

96   "There is no dispute": The exchange in open court between Robert Hamilton,
Bill Arnault, and Judge Rhodes comes from the court transcript of a hearing
in the U.S. Bankruptcy Court, Eastern District of Michigan, over the legality of Detroit's spending plan to rehabilitate streetlights, November 27, 2013.

97   "It was always used": Author interview with Hackney, November 21, 2013.

98   *Detroit Future City*: John Gallagher, "Detroit Works Unveils 'Future City'
Concept, Suggests Uses for Vacant Land," *Detroit Free Press*, January 8,
2013. http://bit.ly/1R92ZiZ. An executive summary of the organization's
recent report can be found at http://detroitfuturecity.com/wp-content/
uploads/2014/12/DFC_ExecutiveSummary_2nd.pdf.

98   "The speed of the process": Author interview with Hackney, November 21,
2013.

99   "Without it the city cannot operate": This quote and the succeeding remarks from Orr and Rhodes are based on a transcript of the first swaps trial hearing in the U.S. Bankruptcy Court, Eastern District of Michigan, December 18, 2013.

99   Attorneys had prepared legal memos: Ibid.

100   so-called safe-harbor law: A good explanation of the impact of safe-harbor laws on swaps in bankruptcy can be found in Mary Williams Walsh, "'Safe Harbor' in Bankruptcy Is Upended in Detroit Case," New York Times, December 23, 2013. http://nyti.ms/1FqF4dv.

100   "I believe we got the best deal": Court transcript of the first swaps trial hearing in the U.S. Bankruptcy Court, Eastern District of Michigan, December 18, 2013.

100   "You could feel that Rhodes": Author interview with Hackney, November 21, 2013.

100   "I don't get it": The entire exchange between Rhodes, Greg Shumaker, and Tim Cullen comes from the court transcript of the first swaps trial hearing in the U.S. Bankruptcy Court, Eastern District of Michigan, December 18, 2013.

101   "It starts to go sideways": Author interview with Orr, January 26, 2015.

101   "I don't care, OK?": Ibid.

102   "I've always thought the COPs were illegal": The exchange in Rhodes's chambers is based on several confidential interviews.

102   "Why did you settle": Author interview with Buckfire, December 16, 2014.

102   "Your honor, I had no leverage": Ibid.

103   "They were all German banks": Author interview with Carole Neville, October 23, 2014.

103   Privately, Rhodes told the city: Several sources confirmed this figure on condition of anonymity.

103   "Oh, Jerry": Author interview with Orr, January 26, 2015.

103   Rosen reserved an extra dose: This account of the mediation, including Rosen's statements, is based on Orr's deposition on the swaps settlement, December 31, 2013.

104   "I said, 'Well if you think'": Author interview with Orr, January 26, 2015.

104   "He explained the deal": Interview with Robert Gordon, October 30, 2014.

105   "We were all completely stunned": Ibid.

105   emergency manager acknowledged: Orr's testimony and questioning by Caroline English is based on the court transcript of the second swaps trial hearing in the U.S. Bankruptcy Court, Eastern District of Michigan, January 3, 2014.

107   "We were all emailing each other": Author interview with Hackney, November 21, 2014. "The 50-50 testimony was actually bad because there were eight chain-linked issues," Hackney explained. "And the swap counterparties had to win all of them. So if they're all 50-50, it suggests that the actual settlement should have been, like, one-sixty-fourth of the potential value—because it was one over two to the eighth."

107 "That was a knock-the-ball": Author interview with Neville, October 23, 2014.

108 "The banks didn't even bother": Court transcript of the second swaps trial hearing in the U.S. Bankruptcy Court, Eastern District of Michigan, January 13, 2014.

108 "Jerry would get up and say": Author interview with Hackney, November 21, 2014.

109 "At a time when the people": Court transcript of the second swaps trial hearing in the U.S. Bankruptcy Court, Eastern District of Michigan, January 13, 2014.

109 "He didn't ask questions": Author interview with Hackney, November 21, 2014.

109 "I'll never forget him": Ibid.

110 "I thought, 'OK, hopefully'": Author interview with Orr, January 26, 2014.

110 "The court stated earlier": Quotes from Rhodes's rejection of the second swaps settlement are from a court transcript of his oral ruling in the U.S. Bankruptcy Court, Eastern District of Michigan, January 16, 2014.

111 "I take my daughters to preschool": Author interview with Hackney, November 21, 2014.

111 "There was a flurry": Ibid.

111 "That shocked everybody": Author interview with David Heiman, January 6, 2015.

111 "What's your number": This exchange with Rhodes is based on confidential interviews.

111 "Rhodes shocked everyone": Author interview with Buckfire, December 16, 2014.

112 "It was very hard": Nathan Bomey, "Q&A: Detroit Bankruptcy Judge on Pensions, DIA, Fees," *Detroit Free Press*, February 20, 2015. http://on.freep.com/1ARC1Zd.

112 "It turned out": Ibid.

112 "He was in a position": Author interview with Heiman, January 6, 2015.

Chapter 8: Pills Over Picasso

113 Detroit Museum of Art: Mark Stryker, "DIA in Peril: A Look at the Museum's Long, Tangled Relationship with Detroit Politics and Finances," *Detroit Free Press*, September 8, 2013. http://bit.ly/18nn8kW.

113 Michigan Supreme Court ruled: Information about this 1915 ruling is based on the "Pretrial Brief of the Detroit Institute of Arts in Support of Confirmation of the Sixth Amended Plan for the Adjustment of Debts of the City of Detroit," May 27, 2014. http://bit.ly/1RfQFgl.

114   "if the city should at any time": Clyde Burroughs, Detroit Museum of Art trustees report, January 27, 1920.

114   "In no sense should we appear": Ralph Booth, *Detroit Museum of Art Annual Report for the Year 1918*. http://bit.ly/1VXpoWv.

114   "All of the councilmen": Clyde Burroughs, Detroit Museum of Art trustees report, January 27, 1920.

115   "They really, truly believed": Author interview with Annmarie Erickson, December 15, 2014.

115   "This change marks the beginning": Quote is from the DIA's court brief supporting the plan of adjustment, May 27, 2014.

115   In the 1920s: Information on the DIA in this paragraph is from Stryker, "DIA in Peril."

116   "The beauty of art and the spiritual": "Monument to Detroit, Speakers Call New Art Institute," *Detroit News*, October 8, 1927, as cited in "Response of the Detroit Institute of Arts to Objections to the City's Amended Plan of Confirmation," May 27, 2014. http://bit.ly/1RN7LD4.

116   "Ken, I've got good news": Ken Buckfire recounts this exchange in an author interview, October 9, 2014.

117   "We didn't want to sell it": Ibid.

117   "We knew creditors": Author interview with Bruce Bennett, December 30, 2014.

118   "Philosophically, my view": Author interview with Kevyn Orr, January 26, 2015.

118   "To send a message": Author interview with Bennett, December 30, 2014.

118   "This is a lose-lose for the governor": Author interview with Andy Dillon, February 2, 2015.

119   "We parted from that meeting": Author interview with Gene Gargaro, January 29, 2015.

119   "stiffened our spines": Author interview with Erickson, December 15, 2014.

120   "We said, 'The DIA Corporation trustees'": Author interview with Buckfire, October 9, 2014.

120   "The next day it's in the news": Author interview with Orr, January 26, 2015.

120   "I think I used the F-word": Author interview with Bill Nowling, January 26, 2015.

121   "And I figure he's gonna": Nowling recounted this exchange with the French reporter in an author interview, February 12, 2015.

121   "The day he did that": Author interview with Erickson, December 15, 2014.

122   "We gave that very little weight": Author interview with David Heiman, January 6, 2015.

122   "It was a difficult moment": Author interview with Governor Rick Snyder, January 16, 2015.

122   "It would be a crime": Mark Stryker and John Gallagher, "DIA's Art Collection Could Face Sell-Off to Satisfy Detroit's Creditors," *Detroit Free Press*, May 24, 2013. http://bit.ly/1wgxKXS.

122   "Our job is not to protect art": Email from Nowling to Orr, May 28, 2013.

123   "Pills over Picasso": Author interview with Ryan Plecha, January 21, 2015.

124   "It's not even a question": Author interview with Buckfire, October 9, 2014.

124   "As I sit here today": Author interview with Erickson, December 15, 2014.

124   "It really was a false premise": Ibid.

125   "They feel a little whipsawed": Email from Nowling to Orr, June 3, 2013.

125   "Things change": Email from Orr to Nowling, June 4, 2013.

125   "'Asked' is a more polite way": Email from Buckfire to city officials and Christie's, July 25, 2013.

125   "quick and dirty": Ibid.

125   They had perused the museum in plainclothes: Christie's executive Vanessa Fusco discussed this trip in an email to Erin McAndrew, July 26, 2013.

125   "All I can think of": Judith H. Dobrzynski, "Appalled by Christie's 'Vulture' Behavior," *Real Clear Arts* (blog), July 23, 2013. http://www.artsjournal.com/realcleararts/2013/07/appalled-by-christies-vulture-behavior.html.

125   "Our name/brand is being": Email from Christie's Americas president Doug Woodham to fellow Christie's executives, July 30, 2013.

126   "These were people": Author interview with Erickson, December 15, 2014.

126   "You will facilitate": Ibid.

126   "We didn't want to provide": Ibid.

126   "Are you hiding it?" Ibid.

127   But Christie's estimated that 2,773: Woodham outlines Christie's findings in a letter to the city, December 17, 2013.

127   "We told Gargaro": Author interview with Buckfire, October 30, 2014.

Chapter 9: You Can't Eat Principles

130   back of the Ampad legal pad: Details of the sketch are taken from a photo of the document.

131   "I said, 'God bless'": Author interview with David Heiman, January 6, 2015.

131   "I don't generally [take] cell phone calls": Author interview with Eugene Driker, February 9, 2015.

133   "You guys could use some help": Author interview with Governor Rick Snyder, January 16, 2015.

133   "I was his data analysis person": Ibid.

133   "I told him [I was] happy to have him": Ibid.

134   "Our question was, could we": Author interview with Steve Spencer, October 24, 2014.

134   Under Spencer's proposal: The proposal, which had several variations, is contained within private documents prepared by the investment bank Lazard for the retiree committee, November 2013 and December 2013.

135   "If you had unanimous": Author interview with Ron Bloom, February 3, 2015.

135   "Unless you provided": Ibid.

135   "We had never come out and said": Ibid.

136 "wide support from creditors": This assessment is contained within a private PowerPoint presentation delivered by Lazard bankers to the Official Committee of Retirees on December 13, 2013, and obtained for this book from a confidential source.

136 "We could speak to each other": Author interview with Spencer, October 24, 2014.

137 "I was always scared to death": Author interview with Mariam Noland, December 17, 2014.

137 "Geez, it's really nice": Noland shared her full exchange with Rosen in ibid.

138 "Foundations don't move fast": Author interview with Noland, December 17, 2014.

139 "When someone calls": Author interview with Darren Walker, December 19, 2014.

139 "He was extraordinarily articulate": Author interview with Alberto Ibargüen, January 20, 2014.

140 "I'm looking at him thinking": Author interview with Kevyn Orr, January 26, 2015.

140 "I think people thought": Author interview with Heather Lennox, February 9, 2015.

141 "Judge, that's a huge amount": Rip Rapson recounted his exchange with Rosen in an author interview, February 27, 2015.

142 "I was convinced that you could": Author interview with Driker, February 9, 2015.

142 "was pretty depressing": Author interview with Walker, December 19, 2014.

143 "But you can solve this": Ibid.

143 "Boy": Author interview with Ibargüen, January 20, 2015.

143 "What you're asking us to do": Author interview with Walker, December 19, 2014.

143 "Foundations don't often get engaged": Ibid.

143 "You keep the cultural treasure": Author interview with Ibargüen, January 20, 2014.

143 "At the outset, we thought": Author interview with Driker, February 9, 2015.

144 "If people are going to give": Author interview with Noland, December 17, 2014.

144 "In my world": Author interview with Ibargüen, January 20, 2015.

144 Walker's presence: The endowment numbers were accessed in February 2014 from the Ford Foundation, Kresge Foundation, Knight Foundation, and Foundation Center websites.

145 "This isn't going to happen": The cab ride conversation is based on author interviews with Ibargüen, January 20, 2015, and Walker, December 19, 2014.

145 "Darren had been president": Author interview with Ibargüen, January 20, 2015.

145 "I ignored the fifty": Ibid.

146 "I had gotten calls": Author interview with Rapson, February 27, 2015.

147   "You know, Nelson Mandela said": The conversation between Rosen and
      Walker is based on a confidential source.

147   "She usually is not a fan": Author interview with Ibargüen, January 20, 2015.

147   "I think this is wonderful": Ibid.

148   "Listen, you piker": Ibid.

148   "I'm inspired": Ibid.

148   "Darren, when the history": This conversation is based on a confidential source.

148   "It was creative": Author interview with Walker, December 19, 2014.

149   "It gave the judge the leverage": Author interview with Noland, December 17,
      2014.

149   "grand bargain": John Gallagher and Mark Stryker, "Can—and Should—
      Charitable Foundations Help Rescue Detroit Pensions, DIA Artwork?"
      Detroit Free Press, November 19, 2013. http://bit.ly/1OZ2c4Z.

149   "It's time to go back to the governor": This conversation is based on a confi-
      dential source.

149   "Really?!": Ibid.

150   "I could see that being potentially": Author interview with Snyder, January
      16, 2015.

150   "In a lot of ways": Ibid.

150   "It's completely unfeasible": Mark Stryker, Matt Helms, and John Gallagher,
      "DIA May Be Asked to Ante Up $100M to Break Free from City," *Detroit
      Free Press*, January 17, 2014. http://bit.ly/1MTvAIg.

151   "We're putting up": Author interview with Noland, December 17, 2014.

151   "I went through the DIA's financials": The conversation between Snyder and
      Rosen is based on a confidential source.

151   "All this business": Gene Gargaro recounted his negotiation with the gover-
      nor in an author interview, January 29, 2015.

152   "I can't tell you": Author interview with Gargaro, January 29, 2015.

152   "I felt like, damn": Author interview with Annmarie Erickson, December 15,
      2014.

154   Orr proposed monthly pension check cuts: All details of Orr's proposal are
      contained within the city's first "Plan for the Adjustment of Debts of the City
      of Detroit," filed in the U.S. Bankruptcy Court, Eastern District of Michi-
      gan, February 21, 2014. http://bit.ly/1X9JIRK.

154   "We weren't sure whether": Author interview with Robert Gordon, October
      30, 2014.

155   "Some people were so upset": Author interview with Shirley Lightsey, Janu-
      ary 21, 2015.

155   "shut the city down": Bill Laitner, "Detroit Pension Protesters Offer Own
      Bankruptcy Plan, Vow to Shut City Down," *Detroit Free Press*, February 24,
      2014. http://bit.ly/1LKi9sq.

155   "We're calling on 20,000": Ibid.

155   "If it's a choice": Author interview with Lightsey, January 21, 2015.

156   "the building, the land": Author interview with Don Taylor, January 21, 2015.

156   "Profound change": Rhodes's words come from a court transcript of a hearing in the U.S. Bankruptcy Court, Eastern District of Michigan, January 22, 2014.

157   "The art was a great promise": Author interview with Ron Bloom, February 3, 2015.

157   "Ron was the most dangerous person": Author interview with Spencer, October 24, 2014.

158   In a groundbreaking accord: Nathan Bomey, "Detroit Pensioners Back Grand Bargain in Bankruptcy Vote, Creditors Object: What Pensioners Voted to Accept," *Detroit Free Press*, July 22, 2014. http://bit.ly/1JzQx7N.

159   negotiators came to believe that a combination: The retiree committee's strategy in negotiation is based on interviews with several confidential sources.

159   "I don't think the pensioners": Author interview with Orr, January 26, 2015.

160   "It is my belief": Gerald Galazka is quoted from the court transcript of a hearing in the U.S. Bankruptcy Court, Eastern District of Michigan, giving individuals a chance to protest the plan of adjustment, July 14, 2014.

161   "What's wrong with these people?": Author interview with Lightsey, January 21, 2015.

161   "And uncertainty doesn't pay the bills": Author interview with Plecha, January 21, 2015.

161   "You can't eat principles": Author interview with Lightsey, January 21, 2015.

Chapter 10: Haircuts

163   "That mediation": Author interview with David Heiman, January 6, 2015.

163   city's UTGO bondholders: Nathan Bomey, "What to Expect in Detroit's $18-Billion Bankruptcy Vote Due Today," *Detroit Free Press*, July 11, 2014. http://bit.ly/1PvY8qB.

163   Coleman and Heiman tagged along: Author interview with Heiman, January 6, 2015.

163   They warned Frankie the barber: The barber's presence at the session is based on an anonymous source. Heiman and Blackstone's Tim Coleman also discussed it here: Jacqueline Palank, "Detroit Bond Insurer Reached Haircut Deal over Haircuts," *Wall Street Journal*, November 7, 2014. http://on.wsj.com/1sfNyGV.

163   "You know": Author interview with Heiman, January 6, 2015.

163   "Guess where I am?": This conversation is based on a confidential source.

164   "The decision here": Nathan Bomey, "Detroit, Bondholders Urged to Settle Debt Dispute or Risk Losing in Court," *Detroit Free Press*, February 19, 2014. http://on.freep.com/1DWrieX.

164   bondholders agreed to accept: The settlement is documented in Rhodes's oral opinion confirming Detroit's plan of adjustment in the U.S. Bankruptcy Court, Eastern District of Michigan, November 7, 2014. http://1.usa.gov/1MuIV7y.

164 "That was a very pivotal moment": Author interview with Heiman, January 6, 2015.

165 Orr had threatened to sue the banks: Author interview with Kevyn Orr, January 26, 2015.

165 "She came to see her son": Author interview with Stephen Hackney, November 21, 2014.

166 "Guys, if you want": Ibid.

166 "Your son's a nice guy": Ibid.

166 "Always meet a boy's mom": Author interview with Orr, February 25, 2015.

166 "It was an example": Author interview with Hackney, November 21, 2014.

166 first time in about three decades: Moody's Investors Service, "U.S. Public Finance Weekly Credit Outlook," February 13, 2014.

166 virtually unprecedented move: Details of this move come from the city's lawsuit filed January 31, 2014, against the service corporations that issued the COPs and swaps. http://bit.ly/1ajkUT6.

167 "You took my money": Author interview with Orr, January 26, 2015.

167 "We weren't going to roll over": Author interview with Steve Spencer, October 24, 2014.

168 Spencer compiled a 259-page pitch book: The pitch book contains extensive material on the DIA collection.

168 Four investors delivered tentative bids: These bids are documented in several locations, including FGIC's opening statement in Detroit's bankruptcy confirmation trial in September 2014.

168 "Spencer's plan": Author interview with Hackney, November 21, 2014.

168 "I knew they were going": Author interview with Orr, January 26, 2015.

169 "It's like . . . Apocalypse Now": Author interview with Orr, February 25, 2015.

169 "There are a lot of issues": Author interview with Heiman, January 6, 2015.

169 "This institution lifts the city": Author interview with Annmarie Erickson, December 15, 2014.

170 Hackney popped a gigantic subpoena: This subpoena, filed in the bankruptcy docket, is dated March 28, 2014. http://bit.ly/1GKNkAb.

170 "We were literally going": Author interview with Erickson, December 15, 2014.

170 Detroit accused Syncora: Nathan Bomey, "Meet Detroit's Leading Bankruptcy Opponent (and It's Not Pensioners)," Detroit Free Press, April 28, 2014. http://bit.ly/17ZysCK.

170 "Let's keep the war analogies": Ibid.

171 Orr hired Michael Plummer: All details of Michael Plummer's assessment come from "Expert Witness Report of Michael Plummer," submitted July 8, 2014. http://bit.ly/1VXq66d.

172 "Anything can be sold": Author interview with James H. M. Sprayregen, November 21, 2014.

172 FGIC retained an art expert: All details of Victor Wiener's assessment, including the quotation, are found in "Expert Report Prepared by Victor Wiener, Director of Victor Wiener Associates, LLC," July 25, 2014. http://1.usa.gov/1NgqSUg.

172 "It was pretty awful": Author interview with Erickson, December 15, 2014.

173   "When the expenses of an enterprise": Rhodes made this comment in his eligibility opinion, December 3, 2013.

174   "All of my friends called here": Author interview with Mariam Noland, December 17, 2014.

174   "I can imagine": This remark comes from the court transcript of a hearing before Rhodes in the U.S. Bankruptcy Court, Eastern District of Michigan, June 26, 2014.

174   "The foundations believe": Ibid.

174   "It's not fair": Ibid.

175   "My attitude was always": Author interview with Alberto Ibargüen, January 20, 2015.

175   "He shook my hand": Author interview with Erickson, December 15, 2014.

Chapter 11: Fixing the City

176   "No one was there": Author interview with Bill Nowling, February 12, 2015.

177   buildings on the island needed basic repairs: The conditions of Belle Isle before the state took over and after it made repairs are discussed at length in *Belle Isle Park*, a report on upgrades, September 18, 2014. http://1.usa.gov/1AxuZqn.

177   sinking into the Detroit River: Stephen Henderson, "A Bit of History Can Show the Way to a Better Belle Isle," *Detroit Free Press*, July 26, 2012. http://bit.ly/1FzZMlX.

177   "I walked into one": Author interview with Kevyn Orr, February 25, 2015.

177   "It's a thousand acres": Ibid.

178   one of the only major cities in the United States: Author interview with Chuck Moore, January 29, 2015.

178   "The state of solid-waste pickup": Ibid.

178   Orr privatized the system: Matt Helms, Joe Guillen, John Gallagher, and JC Reindl, "9 Ways Detroit Is Changing after Bankruptcy," *Detroit Free Press*, November 9, 2014. http://on.freep.com/1xcjTX7.

178   "People were thrilled": Author interview with Stacy Fox, February 3, 2015.

179   "Do we really need to go there?": Ibid.

179   "bad blind date": Author interview with Orr, February 25, 2015.

180   "I knew Mike": Author interview with Fox, February 3, 2015.

180   "Our objectives were": Ibid.

181   "Kevyn wouldn't let him": Author interview with Rich Baird, January 15, 2015.

181   Within months, the lighting overhaul: Christine Ferretti, "Detroit Relights Neighborhoods at Blazing Pace," *Detroit News*, June 15, 2015. http://bit.ly/1TnRdn8.

181   Over a three-year stretch: This statistic derives from "Summary of GLWA Regional Partnership," distributed by the Oakland County Board of Com-

missioners Water Alternatives Study Committee, September 10, 2014. http://
bit.ly/1PxqzqB.

182 DWSD operated under federal oversight: A summary of the water department's history of federal oversight is contained within Judge Sean Cox's order
terminating the case, March 27, 2013.

182 Mayor Kwame Kilpatrick leveraged: U.S. Attorney's Office, Eastern District of
Michigan, "Former Detroit Water Director Sentenced in Kilpatrick Corruption Case," FBI, Detroit Division, May 22, 2014. http://1.usa.gov/1LLZpqI.

182 Miller Buckfire, which had already: Miller Buckfire's assessment of the Cox
committee proposal was revealed in an email exchange with the Treasury
Department, March 26, 2013.

183 "Why would they do anything": Email from Bob Daddow to Ken Buckfire,
October 15, 2013.

184 Detroit water rates were exceptionally low: Details of Lazard's approach to
the water deal come from a private assessment delivered to members of the
retiree committee in January 2014.

184 "Anytime I talk about Detroit": Paige Williams, "Drop Dead Detroit," New
Yorker, January 27, 2014. http://nyr.kr/1CGisA0.

184 "came in and dealt with us": Tom Walsh, "Crunch Time Looms in Detroit
Bankruptcy," Detroit Free Press, March 27, 2014. http://bit.ly/1DXOOIm.

185 "He said I was treating him": Author interview with Buckfire, October 9,
2014.

185 "I'm a Detroiter by birth": Author interview with L. Brooks Patterson, February 25, 2015.

186 "It would have been": Author interview with Buckfire, October 9, 2014.

186 "I have no idea": Author interview with Patterson, February 25, 2015.

186 "Of course not": Author interview with Buckfire, October 9, 2014.

186 "desperate": This line comes from a letter from Gerald Poisson to Orr, April
7, 2014.

187 "This was in the beginning": Author interview with Orr, February 25, 2015.

187 "If there is any exposure": This remark is from an email from Daddow to
Dennis Muchmore, December 12, 2013.

187 "sense": Rhodes's remarks come from the court transcript of a bankruptcy
hearing in the U.S. Bankruptcy Court, Eastern District of Michigan, April
17, 2014.

188 "Rich was the governor's advisor": Author interview with Buckfire, October
30, 2014.

188 "We were dramatically underinvested": This comment comes from a transcript of Mike Duggan's bankruptcy deposition for the plan confirmation
hearing, August 1, 2014.

188 "Sean Cox was instrumental": Author interview with Orr, February 25,
2015.

188 "It's just me and Brooks": Ibid.

189 "We got along really well": Author interview with Patterson, February 25,
2015.

189 "If there's any failing": Author interview with Orr, January 26, 2015.

189 Nearly half of Detroit water accounts: *Detroit Free Press* staff, "Detroit Water by the Numbers: Almost $80M Owed by Residential Customers," *Detroit Free Press*, July 18, 2014. http://bit.ly/18rN8eW.

189 $118 million: Joe Guillen, "Detroit to Resume Water Shutoffs for Delinquent Customers," *Detroit Free Press*, March 22, 2014. http://bit.ly/1E1LWvM.

189 "human right": The United Nations Human Rights Office of the High Commissioner for Human Rights issued its statement, "Detroit: Disconnecting Water from People Who Cannot Pay—An Affront to Human Rights, Say UN Experts," on June 25, 2014. http://bit.ly/1arSTda.

189 "This is literally a jungle": The Detroit Water Brigade posted this Fox 2 Detroit broadcast on July 11, 2014. http://youtu.be/3KOzc6Syndg.

190 "Okay, you go deal": This is from a transcript of Duggan's bankruptcy deposition for the plan confirmation hearing, August 1, 2014.

190 "I was trying": Ibid.

191 "I'd never even heard": Author interview with Amanda Van Dusen, January 16, 2015.

191 deal saved the water department more than $100 million: "Market Response to Detroit Water and Sewerage Department Bonds Exceeds Expectations," City of Detroit press release, August 27, 2014. http://bit.ly/1UalYJR.

191 In a historic breakthrough: Nathan Bomey and Matt Helms, "Detroit, Suburbs OK Regional Water Deal; $50M Yearly to Upgrade System," *Detroit Free Press*, September 9, 2014. http://bit.ly/1LOSkYm.

Chapter 12: "Get the Damn Buttons"

193 "I personally started": Author interview with Jase Bolger, January 26, 2015.

194 "There were legislators": Author interview with Kevyn Orr, January 26, 2015.

195 "By having this grand-bargain pool": Author interview with Governor Rick Snyder, January 16, 2015.

196 "In a very conservative caucus": Author interview with Randy Richardville, February 9, 2015.

196 "Every single zip code": Author interview with Don Taylor, January 21, 2015.

196 "This is no small concession": This quote comes from Shirley Lightsey's prepared testimony before the House Committee on Detroit's Recovery and Michigan's Future in Lansing, Michigan, May 15, 2014. http://1.usa.gov/1LeKxn4.

197 "I'm one that believes": This is from a transcript of Brenda Jones's bankruptcy deposition for the plan confirmation hearing, August 4, 2014.

197 "Nobody on Wall Street": Author interview with Ken Buckfire, October 9, 2014.

198 "I understand that he wanted": Author interview with Richardville, February 9, 2015.

199   "We had to be convinced": Author interview with Bolger, January 26, 2015.
199   "I hail from southwest Michigan": Kathleen Gray, "Michigan House Over-
      whelmingly Approves $195 Million in State Aid for Detroit," *Detroit Free
      Press*, May 22, 2014. http://bit.ly/1DfSBNn.
199   "I think he saw this as a call": Author interview with Bill Nowling, February
      12, 2015.
200   "He's talked to five people": Nowling recounted this entire exchange with
      Judge Rosen in an author interview, February 12, 2015.
200   "My normal inclination": Ibid.
201   Rosen pressured Orr to do something: Author interview with Orr, February
      25, 2015.
201   "So I said, 'OK, we'll order the buttons'": Orr recounted the buttons purchase
      in an author interview, February 25, 2015.
201   "I did twelve different scenarios": Author interview with Nowling, February
      12, 2015.
202   pensioners had voted overwhelmingly: Nathan Bomey, "How Creditors Voted
      on Detroit's $18 Billion Bankruptcy Plan," *Detroit Free Press*, July 22, 2014.
      http://bit.ly/1DfW0Mj.

Chapter 13: The Empty Cabin

203   newspaper advertisement screamed: Jerry Vile's ad is discussed in Bryan
      Gottlieb, "Jerry Vile's Sale of the Century," *Detroit Metro Times*, August 13,
      2013. http://bit.ly/1Ae7Jc3. It is visible at http://i.imgur.com/vpBO2AC.jpg.
203   In another stunt: Photos of the DIA plastic vulture protest posted on May 8,
      2014, can be viewed on Vile's Facebook page. http://on.fb.me/1FZW0WS.
      Accessed October 8, 2015.
204   "You know where you're going": This statement is based on a confidential
      source.
204   "You never understood": Author interview with Stephen Hackney, November
      21, 2014.
205   "I guess an interesting question": Ibid.
206   "There was this idea": Author interview with Carole Neville, October 23,
      2014.
206   "Judges": Sandra Svoboda, "Judge Rosen Full Remarks," WDET 101.9 FM,
      June 9, 2014. http://bit.ly/1wnjwnZ.
207   "The debtor—the city": Author interview with James H. M. Sprayregen,
      November 21, 2014.
208   "agenda-driven, conflicted": These accusations and the ones that follow were
      contained within Syncora's "Second Supplemental Objection to the Debtor's
      Plan of Adjustment," August 12, 2014. It was later stricken from the court
      record.

209   "We got lots of calls": Author interview with Sprayregen, November 21, 2014.
209   "Wait until you hear this": Author interview with Eugene Driker, February 9, 2015.
209   "There's a good reason": Ibid.
209   "We believed that was": Author interview with Sprayregen, November 21, 2014.
210   "The minute I got home": Author interview with Driker, February 9, 2015.
210   "Desperation is seldom pretty": "City of Detroit's Motion to Strike in Part Syncora Guarantee Inc. and Syncora Capital Assurance Inc.'s Second Supplemental Objection to the Debtor's Plan of Adjustment," filed in the U.S. Bankruptcy Court, Eastern District of Michigan, August 18, 2014. http://bit.ly/1jIAiht.
210   "They really stepped in it": Author interview with David Heiman, January 6, 2015.
210   "I love Steve Hackney": Author interview with Neville, October 23, 2014.
210   "It is important for all": This entire exchange between Hackney and Rhodes comes from a court transcript of a pre-trial conference for the plan confirmation hearing in the U.S. Bankruptcy Court, Eastern District of Michigan, August 25, 2014.
212   Allegations that Rosen and Driker "colluded": Rhodes's rebuke of Syncora's arguments are contained within his "Order Granting in Part Motion to Strike and Order to Show Cause Why Sanctions Should Not Be Imposed," U.S. Bankruptcy Court, Eastern District of Michigan, August 28, 2014. http://bit.ly/1LeLCLq.
212   "In virtually all respects": Author interview with Steven Rhodes, February 19, 2015.
212   "They were in no position to 'collude'": Rhode's rebuke of Syncora's arguments, August 28, 2014.
213   "Rhodes put a lot": Author interview with Stephen Hackney, November 21, 2014.

Chapter 14: One Bullet, Two Creditors

215   "I think FGIC took": Author interview with Carole Neville, October 23, 2014.
216   "is the one that you think is appropriate?": This exchange between Stephen Hackney and Steven Rhodes is taken from the court transcript of a pre-trial conference for the plan confirmation hearing in the U.S. Bankruptcy Court, Eastern District of Michigan, August 21, 2014.
216   By slashing more than $7 billion: The figures in this paragraph are based on an untitled presentation to the Milken Institute delivered by Kevyn Orr on April 27, 2015. http://bit.ly/1MurnaE.
216   With the debt reductions: Ibid.

216 Over approximately a year: Ibid.
217 "We wanted a defined contribution plan": Author interview with Heather Lennox, February 9, 2015.
217 "I think we got Detroit as much": Author interview with Bruce Bennett, December 30, 2014.
217 "The money could only be used": Author interview with Alberto Ibargüen, January 20, 2015.
218 called for compensating pensioners: These figures illustrating the proposed disparity in treatment between pensions and financial creditors are found in the "Fourth Amended Plan for the Adjustment of Debts of the City of Detroit," May 5, 2014. http://1.usa.gov/1Ga3Ejf.
218 "We don't have to resolve": Author interview with Bennett, December 30, 2014.
219 worth only about $455 million: This is documented in a court transcript of the confirmation trial hearing in the U.S. Bankruptcy Court, Eastern District of Michigan, September 3, 2014.
220 "extremely well maintained": Ibid.
220 "Let me ask you this": This entire exchange between Alfredo Perez and Rhodes is from the court transcript of the confirmation trial hearing in the U.S. Bankruptcy Court, Eastern District of Michigan, September 3, 2014.
221 "We are not in a house": Marc Kieselstein's argument and his exchange with Rosen are from the court transcript of the confirmation trial hearing in the U.S. Bankruptcy Court, Eastern District of Michigan, September 3, 2014.
223 "They've got a billion-five": The exchange between Perez and Rosen is from the court transcript of confirmation trial hearing in the U.S. Bankruptcy Court, Eastern District of Michigan, September 3, 2014.
225 "I assumed and believed": Nathan Bomey, "Q&A: Detroit Bankruptcy Judge on Pensions, DIA, Fees," Detroit Free Press, February 20, 2015. http://on.freep.com/1ARC1Zd.
225 "To me, it was quite wasteful": Author interview with David Heiman, January 6, 2015.
225 "Only in Detroit": Author interview with Ken Buckfire, October 9, 2014.
226 "The premise was": Author interview with Ryan Bennett, February 10, 2015.
226 They reached tentative terms: Chad Livengood and Robert Snell, "Syncora Reaches Comprehensive Deal in Detroit Bankruptcy," Detroit News, September 30, 2014. http://bit.ly/1Jt0m5C.
226 Technically, the deal equaled: The 13 percent figure is based on Orr's presentation to Milken Institute, April 27, 2015.
227 "The way our deal is structured": Author interview with James H. M. Sprayregen, November 21, 2014.
227 "We are deeply sorry": Syncora's apology is contained within its "Corrected Syncora Guarantee Inc. and Syncora Capital Assurance Inc.'s Notice of Settlement in Principle," filed in the U.S. Bankruptcy Court, Eastern District of Michigan, September 15, 2014. http://1.usa.gov/1ndanPB.

227 "He was very apologetic": Author interview with Eugene Driker, February 9, 2015.

227 "Kirkland made a lot of money": Author interview with Sprayregen, November 21, 2015.

228 "The concept of a mediator": Author interview with Rhodes, February 19, 2015.

228 "I know Jamie isn't": Author interview with Kevyn Orr, January 26, 2015.

229 "We had one bullet": Author interview with Buckfire, October 9, 2014.

229 "I love Alfredo": Author interview with Hackney, November 21, 2014.

229 "We were cognizant": Author interview with Sprayregen, November 21, 2014.

229 "major tactical error": Author interview with Steve Spencer, October 24, 2014.

229 "The pensions would have screamed": Ibid.

230 FGIC agreed to procure a deal: Matt Helms, "Detroit Deal with Creditor Includes Joe Louis Site," *Detroit Free Press*, October 16, 2014. http://on.freep .com/1DieWw1.

230 Like Syncora, FGIC technically: The 13 percent figure is based on Orr's presentation to Milken Institute, April 27, 2015.

230 "At 6:15 in the morning": Author interview with Steve Spencer, October 24, 2014.

231 "You guys fought": Ibid.

231 "As much as I disagree": Ibid.

232 About 51 percent: Orr's presentation to Milken Institute, April 27, 2015.

233 "There are people out there": Author interview with Bruce Bennett, December 30, 2014.

Chapter 15: The Rhodes Test

234 "In Chapter 9 of the bankruptcy code": Rhodes's remarks approving the bankruptcy plan, quoted throughout this chapter, are found in his prepared oral opinion approving the plan of adjustment, November 7, 2014. http://1 .usa.gov/1MulV7y.

235 "I'd been practicing law": Author interview with Eugene Driker, February 9, 2015.

235–36 At least two polls suggested: Two polls showed voters supported the governor's strategy in Detroit. One Glengariff Group poll commissioned by the Detroit News and WDIV-TV (documented in the following note) showed that 49 percent of voters supported the governor's handling of the matter, while 35 percent disapproved. A separate poll conducted by EPIC-MRA for the *Detroit Free Press* and WXYZ-TV showed that 54 percent of Michigan voters approved of Snyder's handling of urban issues, compared to 35 percent. See Matt Helms, "Poll: Most Approve of Snyder's Handling of Urban Issues," *Detroit Free Press*, October 6, 2014. http://on.freep.com/1vKtRMe.

236 And a separate poll commissioned: Chad Livengood, "Poll: Snyder Keeps Lead in Governor's Race," *Detroit News*, October 28, 2014. http://detne.ws/1JNywke.

236 "I just took it as doing my job": Author interview with Governor Rick Snyder, January 16, 2015.

236 "People don't appreciate": Author interview with Kevyn Orr, February 25, 2015.

237 collected more than $170 million: Nathan Bomey, Joe Guillen, and Brent Snavely, "Detroit Paid Advisers $170 Million in Bankruptcy," *Detroit Free Press*, December 31, 2014. http://on.freep.com/1B2WmrP.

237 "What happened in Detroit": Rhodes's remarks approving the bankruptcy plan, November 7, 2014.

238 "Our litigator came up to me": Author interview with Annmarie Erickson, December 15, 2014.

240 "I hope his legacy": Nathan Bomey, "Q&A: Detroit Bankruptcy Judge," *Detroit Free Press*, February 20, 2015. http://on.freep.com/1ARC17d.

240 "It's habit, it's expectations": Author interview with Orr, February 25, 2015.

241 "Hey": Ibid.

241 Syncora's bankruptcy strategists strolled through: This account of the visit by Syncora's representatives to the DIA after the bankruptcy is based on interviews and email correspondences in February 2015, including with James H. M. Sprayregen and DIA chairman Gene Gargaro.

241 "I have to say": Author interview via email with James H. M. Sprayregen, February 21, 2015.

242 "While during the heat": Author interview via email with Gene Gargaro, February 21, 2015.

242 "Not withstanding the toughness": Author interview via email with Sprayregen, February 21, 2015.

242 "never yield to force": Churchill's quotes are found at http://www.winstonchurchill.org/resources/speeches/1941-1945-war-leader/never-give-in. Accessed October 8, 2015.

242 "reinforced for me": Author interview via email with Sprayregen, February 21, 2015.

244 54 percent of Detroit eighth-graders: National Center for Education Statistics, "The Nation's Report Card, Reading: 2013 Trial Urban District Snapshot Report, Detroit Public Schools, Grade 8." http://1.usa.gov/1Lxid1L.

244 About 102,000 students left Detroit Public Schools: Detroit Public Schools, *Comprehensive Annual Financial Report (CAFR) for the Fiscal Year Ended June 30, 2014.* http://bit.ly/1JwA3jp.

244 Community Ventures program offers a feasible route: Nathan Bomey, "Finding Jobs in Detroit: Retraining Program That Works," *Detroit Free Press*, February 18, 2015. http://on.freep.com/1Jnr2dX.

245 Billionaire Dan Gilbert has purchased or controls: John Gallagher, "Five Years in, and Dan Gilbert's Just Beginning," *Detroit Free Press*, August 15, 2015. http://on.freep.com/1Ptescn.

245 new downtown hockey arena: Bill Shea, "On Cost, Financing of Wings

Arena: Here Are Answers," *Crain's Detroit Business*, September 21, 2014. http://bit.ly/1v6cNyP.

246 "a watershed moment": Author interview with Rip Rapson, February 27, 2015.

246 "I am radically optimistic": Author interview with Darren Walker, December 19, 2014.

247 "At the beginning of the Detroit case": Steven Rhodes, transcript of Commencement Address, Walsh College, Troy, Michigan, January 24, 2015.

Epilogue

248 "I remain confident": Author interview with Steven Rhodes, December 1, 2016.

248 "At its heart": Author interview with Rip Rapson, December 9, 2016.

249 Detroit is headed: Ronald Rose, "Detroit Financial Review Commission Biannual Report No. 4," State of Michigan Department of Treasury, November 29, 2016. http://bit.ly/2hwDbnq.

249 "That's a great trajectory": Author interview with Kevyn Orr, November 22, 2016.

249 "exceeded the expectations": Author interview with Gerald Rosen, December 12, 2016.

249 the city lost: John Wisely and Kristi Tanner, "Duggan Sees Positive in Detroit Population Loss," *Detroit Free Press*, May 20, 2016. http://on.freep.com/1XmKX1q.

249 "I'm very confident": Ibid.

249 Apartment occupancy rates: "City of Detroit Economic Development Overview," Financial Review Commission Presentation, October 31, 2016. http://bit.ly/2gJ70CB.

249 Developers have credible plans: Ibid.

250 population would fall: U.S. Bankruptcy Court, Eastern District of Michigan, Southern Division, "Report of Caroline Sallee," July 8, 2014. http://bit.ly/2gLzQk.

250 The city receives: "City of Detroit," Financial Review Commission.

250 "I am enthusiastic": Author interview with James Doak, December 16, 2016.

250 "mixed-income development": Author interview with Sonya Mays, December 21, 2016.

250 About 14,247 Detroiters: "City of Detroit," Financial Review Commission.

251 more than eighty: Ibid.

251 two Fortune 500: Michael Wayland, "Adient Moving to Downtown Detroit's Marquette Building," *Detroit News*, November 30, 2016. http://detne.ws/2gK8gVt.

251 Only 49 percent: "City of Detroit," Financial Review Commission.

251 "A lot of nuts-and-bolts": Author interview with Rapson, December 9, 2016.

251 For every 1,000: "City of Detroit," Financial Review Commission.

251 revenue would increase only 4.2 percent: George A. Fulton, John Hill, and Jay Wortley, "Consensus Revenue Estimating Conference," September 22, 2016. http://bit.ly/2gJ70CB.

252 "What we've chosen": Author interview with John Hill, December 27, 2016.

252 $10 million to $25 million: Fulton, Hill, and Wortley, "Consensus."

252 The city collected 70 percent: Ibid.

252 $27 million increase: Ibid.

252 "People who believe": Author interview with Hill, December 27, 2016.

252 City-funded investments: Ann Storberg, "Financial Review Commission's Biannual Report on Detroit," State of Michigan Department of Treasury, November 24, 2015. http://bit.ly/2hFsssg.

253 Demolition crews have razed: "City of Detroit," Financial Review Commission.

253 The FBI confirmed: Joe Guillen, "Early Legal Bills for Detroit Demolition Probe Top $81,000," Detroit Free Press, October 10, 2016. http://on.freep. com/2h59TsS.

253 ranging from about $8,500 to $10,000: Ibid.

253 costs escalated to an average of $16,400: City of Detroit Meeting Video Archives, "Mayor Duggan Demo Presentation to City Council," October 15, 2015. http://bit.ly/2k0HbLw

253 nearly 200 buses: "City of Detroit," Financial Review Commission.

254 "When you look at": Author interview with Rick Snyder, December 6, 2016.

254 owe about $111 million: Rose, "Detroit Financial Review."

254 updated to about $200 million: Ibid.

254 Duggan threatened to sue: Robert Snell, "$491 Million Pension Shortfall May Be Result of Using Outdated Actuarial Tables," Crain's Detroit Business, February 28, 2016. http://bit.ly/2hwCPLQ.

254 "would be understandably": Author interview with Rich Baird, December 7, 2016.

255 increase of only 2.6 percent: "Legacy Pension Plan (Component II) of the General Retirement System of the City of Detroit," June 30, 2015. http://bit. ly/2hRyBxP.

255 average nationwide rate of 7.62 percent: National Association of State Retirement Administrators, "NASRA Issue Brief: Public Pension Plan Investment Return Assumptions," February 2016. http://bit.ly/1hY7JvX.

255 "The portfolio": Author interview with Nick Khouri, December 9, 2016.

256 private-sector mortality rates: Society of Actuaries, "RP-2014 Mortality Tables Report," October 2014. http://bit.ly/2hRwOZQ.

256 is developing mortality tables: Author interview via email with Michael Nowak, December 14, 2016.

256 "I know the mayor": Author interview with Rhodes, December 1, 2016.

256 "I don't think": Author interview with Hill, December 27, 2016.

256 A 2015 study: Alicia H. Munnell, Jean-Pierre Aubry, and Mark Cafarelli,

"How Will Longer Lifespans Affect State and Local Pension Funding?" Center for Retirement Research at Boston College, April 2015. http://bit. ly/2iJOcDQ.

256   "just emotional rhetoric": Author interview with Baird, December 7, 2016.

257   "It is just politics": Author interview with Ken Buckfire, December 1, 2016.

257   "liability to any person": U.S. Bankruptcy Court, Eastern District of Michigan, "Eighth Amended Plan for the Adjustment of Debts of the City of Detroit," October 22, 2014. http://bit.ly/2iiA7tS.

257   set aside $20 million: Rose, "Detroit Financial Review."

257   "Our biggest asset": Author interview with Hill, December 27, 2016.

257   "warning signs": Author interview via email with Bruce Babiarz, December 22, 2016.

258   hit with felony charges: Paul Egan and Elisha Anderson, "Emergency Managers, City Officials Charged in Flint Water Crisis," *Detroit Free Press*, December 20, 2016. http://on.freep.com/2hPXNFK.

259   City Council never endorsed: Paul Egan, "Flint Council Video Shows Path Away from Detroit Water," Detroit Free Press, February 4, 2016. http://usat. ly/2hzUMJT.

259   $617 million bailout: David Eggert, "Michigan Governor Rick Snyder Signs $617M Detroit Schools Bailout," *Associated Press*, June 21, 2016. http:// on.freep.com/28X0jHe.

259   "On the one hand": Author interview with Rhodes, December 1, 2016.

260   bipartisan state panel: Ron Fonger, "Flint Water Crisis Proposals Could Overhaul Michigan Emergency Manager System," MLive.com, October 19, 2016. http://bit.ly/2imDPW3.

260   "I'm open": Author interview with Snyder, December 6, 2016.

261   "Detroit's special place": Coleman Young and Lonnie Wheeler, *Hard Stuff: The Autobiography of Mayor Coleman Young* (New York: Viking, 1994).

261   "I don't think": Author interview with Ryan Plecha, December 3, 2016.

261   "What the bankruptcy did": Author interview with Shirley Lightsey, December 3, 2016.

INDEX